Public sector management in Europe

Public sector management in Europe

Edited by
Norman Flynn and Franz Strehl

PRENTICE HALL
HARVESTER WHEATSHEAF

LONDON   NEW YORK   TORONTO   SYDNEY   TOKYO
SINGAPORE   MADRID   MEXICO CITY   MUNICH

First published 1996 by
Prentice Hall Europe
Campus 400, Maylands Avenue
Hemel Hempstead
Hertfordshire, HP2 7EZ
A division of
Simon & Schuster International Group

Typeset in 10/12pt Palatino
by Dorwyn Ltd, Rowlands Castle, Hants

Printed and bound in Great Britain by
T.J. Press Ltd, Padstow

Library of Congress Cataloging-in-Publication Data

Public sector management in Europe / edited by Norman Flynn and Franz
Strehl.
       p.   cm.
    Includes bibliographical references and index.
    ISBN 0–13–241159–8
    1. Administrative agencies–Europe–Management.   2. Europe–
–Politics and government–1989–   I. Flynn, Norman.   II. Strehl,
Franz, 1948–   .
JN94.A5P82 1996
354.4–dc20
                                                                              95–47476
                                                                                    CIP

British Library Cataloguing in Publication Data

A catalogue record for this book is available
from the British Library

ISBN 0–13–241159–8

1 2 3 4 5   00 99 98 97 96

Contents

1

Introduction

Norman Flynn and Franz Strehl

This is a book for managers and students of management who are interested in management of the public sector in a selection of European countries. The work is based on interviews, secondary sources and specially commissioned work from people in the countries studied. The authors have not used exactly the same research template in each country, since changes in the management process have different origins and themes in the countries studied.

We have tried to maintain a critical stance about the countries we investigated. In many cases, the governments at national and subnational level and certain international agencies have an interest in promoting their reforms as successful. The language of management, including performance orientation, a focus on outputs and customers, lean management, increased efficiency, economy and effectiveness, and so on are all part of the everyday jargon of management consultants and the promoters of reforms. In some reports we found that the language had not even been translated from the American to the local language. We hope that we have been able to see through enough of the rhetoric to allow people to compare their own experience with that of people in other countries.

The countries represent a range of structural arrangements, cultural attitudes to the state and management traditions. Sweden and the Netherlands are included as social democratic states which have traditions of relatively autonomous subnational governments and a liberal attitude to the state and the relationship between workers, the employers and the public sector. Germany and Austria are federal systems, underpinned by strong constitutions and a tradition of *Rechtsstaat* (a state based on a written constitution and statutes). Managerial reforms are likely to be different in states where there is constitutional protection both for tiers of government and for state employees. The dimension of management within a framework of law and legal norms as constraints on managerial action was also important. Switzerland is the most federal of European states, operating with principles of subsidiarity for its tiers of government, a relatively low level of public expenditure and fewer problems of fiscal stress caused by unemployment. We chose France because it has a tradition of a unified civil service, competitive entry to public service and a traditionally centralized system of administration. The United Kingdom has claimed to be a leader in the field of privatization and the move towards market-type mechanisms for the control of public services. Sixteen years of single-party rule have allowed a fairly consistent reform programme which has not been possible in countries with less extreme electoral systems and more power-sharing in government.

Of course it would have been interesting to include more countries and we hope that our efforts will encourage more scholars to make comparisons between a larger group of countries.

All books about change are by definition out of date by the time they are printed. In this case we stopped the investigations in April 1995.

RESPONDING TO PRESSURES

There is an argument that there are economic and social pressures on the institutions of the states in Europe which make reform of the management methods used in the public sector essential. These pressures either produce material changes in the production and distribution of public services, or a rhetorical and ideological response from governments and public servants which creates the impression of change.

There are cyclical budgetary pressures: periods of recession depress the tax base and generate increased demands on public spending because of higher unemployment. The economic cycle changes the proportions of gross domestic product (GDP) devoted to public expenditure, sometimes national budgets go into deficit and there is a call to reduce expenditure.

Since 1989, all the countries in our sample saw public expenditure increase as a proportion of GDP. While pressures on spending do not automatically generate a response in changed management methods, these increases in the ratio of public spending to GDP make politicians and managers look for more efficient ways of doing things. If this is the case, then it might be expected that the biggest changes are sought in those countries with the highest proportions of public spending to GDP, such as the Netherlands, Sweden and France, and less pressure in those countries where the proportions are lower, such as Switzerland, Germany and the United Kingdom. This is broadly correct, with two exceptions: the United Kingdom's sustained reform programme despite a spending ratio of about 40 percent; and the failure of early attempts at reforms in the Netherlands despite a ratio of 55 percent. The explanation for the different weight given to reform programmes probably lies in the strength of the government in power, its length of tenure and unity of ideas within the ruling party. Coalition governments and frequent changes of control are not the conditions for a sustained reform programme.

Since reductions in service cause dissatisfaction and political unpopularity, attempts are made to maintain service levels while reducing expenditure, by increasing productivity and overall efficiency. This in turn has two implications. First, the organizations of the state have to be able to demonstrate their productivity levels and productivity improvement, which explains the great efforts made in most countries to develop performance measurement systems. Secondly, they have to reduce unit costs, which leads both to an interest in cost calculations and to staff reductions, new methods of working, leaner management structures, etc. Even if these efforts were unsuccessful or unnecessary managerially, they would be essential politically: budget constraints without at least appearing to make productivity improvements would be politically irresponsible.

There is also a broader argument. Western European economies are in competition with the other two main trading blocs, North America and Asia, and increasingly with the Eastern European countries, frequently hosting plants owned by West European companies In some industries, especially manufacturing, competition is based to a large degree on unit labour costs. Western European countries, especially those in the north, have high social wage costs, which impair international cost competitiveness. This may be exacerbated in some cases by an ageing population, creating demands for social expenditures. While this lack of competitiveness can be cushioned by tariffs, in the long term the General Agreement on Tariffs and Trade (GATT) will reduce the effectiveness of this option. Hence, improved productivity together with a reduction in the role and scope of tax-funded state activities are said to be essential for the long-term competitiveness of Europe as a whole. In other words, globalization of business generates pressures on the public sector both for efficiency improvements and reductions in scope.[1]

Global competition has had another impact. Companies which were facing competitors from lower-cost countries and retained capacity in Europe have been forced radically to examine their costs and working practices. Very often this involved reducing the size of the workforce, including management and supervision. Once companies had shown that it could be done, governments also demanded reductions in the size of public sector workforces. Frequently, governments appointed managers and management consultants to transfer experience from the private to the public sector.

There is also an argument that people have demanded higher quality services. In the early 1980s, service industries in Europe became more competitive. Relaxation of restrictive practices in industries such as banking and airlines forced companies to compete for customers, not just through price but also through customer service. This had two impacts on the public sector. First, it started to raise the expectation of citizens about how well services could be provided. If the bank can reduce its queues and waiting times, why should the tax collector keep me waiting? If I can buy my airline ticket instantly through a computer terminal, why should my pension generate a mountain of paper correspondence? Secondly, it showed that there were better ways of providing services than simply having bureaucracies working for their own convenience. Customer surveys, finding out how people like to deal with their affairs with the state, listening to complaints, redesigning access to services all became part of the progressive public sector manager's repertoire.

In some countries there was also political or ideological pressure for change. Privatization, reduction of the role of the state, the use of markets became objectives in their own right, as neo-liberalism became an alternative to the post-war social democratic consensus.

When we started this work, we assumed that there would be a convergence of ideas about how public services are managed and a common response to these pressures. Or perhaps similar constitutions may lead to similar administrative and management arrangements. Perhaps long Napoleonic or Prussian traditions might leave identifiable traces despite periods of modernization and constitutional change. Or perhaps long periods of rule by social democratic or Christian democratic parties might have produced an identifiable approach to administration. We quickly found that there were reasons to doubt the idea of convergence.

The pressures on the public sector do not produce a reflex response from politicians and managers. There are many variables which affect how reforms are designed and implemented, including the constitutional arrangements in place, political opinions at national and subnational level, public attitudes towards the state and its employees, and the skills and knowledge of public sector managers.

First, there are different constitutional arrangements. In countries where there is a strong central government with powers over the whole of the administration, centrally driven reforms are easier to implement than in countries where subnational government is both relatively large and constitutionally protected.

Secondly, the neo-liberal arguments are clearly political: the use of market mechanisms as administrative instruments is not an idea free from ideological belief, which is stronger among Christian democrats and conservatives than among social democrats and socialists. Of course there are exceptions to this general rule: it is difficult to find strong ideological bases for policy in the Netherlands; socialist parties in the United Kingdom and elsewhere seem to be as market-minded as many Christian democrat parties. However, it would seem that convergence towards markets, both for service delivery and in respect of the labour market for civil and other public servants, would require an ideological commitment.

Thirdly, there are different cultural attitudes towards the role and nature of the state. The acceptability of relatively high taxation and a high level of state involvement in economic and social life has developed unevenly in Europe since the war. Responses to fiscal deficits which demand a significant reduction in state activity therefore meet different levels of resistance in different countries. A call for a 25 percent increase in efficiency in public services in Austria, for example, has produced little result despite successive recent election swings to the right.

If there was no convergence between countries, perhaps we would be able to find general tendencies within countries, or perhaps tendencies among groups of countries with similar characteristics.

There are two respects in which such neat classifications are not appropriate. First, many countries have a diversity of approaches to management in different sectors or even in different ministries. This is more the case in countries where local authorities are autonomous. In Sweden, for example, the Conservative administration which was in control of Stockholm County Council until 1994 adopted a version of market-type mechanisms in health-care and even attempted to privatize Stockholm's major hospital, while other local administrations had different policies. Secondly, even where organizations are apparently under unified control, there can be great differences in approach. In the United Kingdom for example, the Foreign and Commonwealth Office has managed to resist almost entirely the move towards the establishment of Executive Agencies in central government as did the Foreign Office in Sweden. In Austria different ministries have different approaches to performance measurement and management.

Klages and Löffler[2] hypothesize that differences in national administrative cultures and traditions are diminishing and that researching differences in modernization strategies at the macro level (nation state level) will be less useful than looking for local differences in approach from which to learn: 'this implies that comparative country studies done with binoculars will become irrelevant. Instead it will be more profitable to limit the analysis of micro-level strategies to one (part) of a political system which allows the use of the microscope.'

In many cases the reforms echo the list of 'new public management' features identified by Hood in 1991,[3] such as improved accountability, the creation of more autonomous units with performance measures and targets, the introduction of competition and cost reduction. While the OECD PUMA group[4] reports the results of its survey, the authors favour the direction in which change is progressing and identify a convergence of views and actions towards a 'managerial' approach. The survey consists mainly of a search for elements of managerialism in the countries surveyed. It mostly ignores changes which are outside the 'managerial' paradigm.

The second reason to be slightly sceptical of the convergence thesis is that there may be a gap between the official reports and rhetoric and the degree to which reforms are really implemented. For example the *déconcentration* in France is reported by the OECD group as if there were a genuine devolution of managerial power to units. Other commentators suggest that the existence of new mechanisms for control does not necessarily change the power relationships. For example, Champaigne *et al.*[5] are of the opinion that the contractual relationship between ministries and accountability centres in France is still blurred for two reasons: nobody knows what would be the result of either side failing to meet its part of the contract; and the lack of proper methods of evaluation. Their conclusion was that the new arrangements simply reinforced the old technocratic, hierarchical relationships.

Kickert[6] regards the 'new public management' collection of managerial features as an Anglo-American phenomenon. An approach to management which takes account of democracy and the existence of the legal state will be different from a top-down, instrumentalist approach to management and administration. He argues that governance is concerned with managing policy networks rather than steering employees. In the specific case of the Netherlands, there is not an identifiable, strong central government which is susceptible to reforms in the way in which the US federal government or the UK central government might be. Responses to fiscal and other pressures are therefore unlikely to produce a formulaic response, picking and mixing from performance management, decentralized budgeting and the rest of the kit of managerial reforms.

These arguments present problems for methodology and presentation. If Klages and Löffler's hypothesis that there is both convergence between countries and diversity within them holds true, then the nation state may not be a relevant unit or object of analysis. However, we have taken the view that, in some countries at least, there is a degree of consistency in approach which makes the country a relevant unit of analysis. For example, the widespread use of competition imposed by central government on ministries and local authorities which has occurred in the United Kingdom could not have happened in a decentralized system such as that of the Netherlands. The continued central government control over budgets and personnel which persists in France could not have been sustained in a state in which there is constitutional protection of the autonomy of subnational units of government.

Nation states still have defined legal and structural arrangements which give some coherence to the process of public sector reform within countries. While we have seen similarities in some aspects of managerial change among the countries we looked at, the nature of the states themselves has had a strong influence on the direction of change. Constitutional arrangements and the legal basis of the state are clearly an important influence both on the nature of managerial work and the extent and direction of reforms. In a *Rechtsstaat*, managerial reforms have to be preceded by a lengthy parliamentary process. In a federal structure, the influence of central government may be small. But there is probably a deeper level at which the promotion or resistance to managerial change can be explained. If the culture of a country is extremely individualistic, citizens with incomes resist paying tax and resent state intervention, and public servants would be able to generate little support if they tried to resist managerial changes, either resulting in higher productivity or lower pay. In places where the role of the state is accepted, public officials and professionals are respected, and even an ideologically driven government with neo-liberal tendencies would find it hard to make deep cultural changes to the public services. Of course, countries may no more have unified cultures than they have homogeneous state apparatus: regional variations are large.

The second issue, trying to separate the rhetoric from the action, implies that it should be possible to evaluate reforms. The PUMA group recognizes that there has not been extensive evaluation:

> *Given the emphasis on performance and result assessment under the new managerialism, it remains disappointing that, even while there recognising the difficulties associated with evaluation, many member countries continue to report no formal or systematic monitoring or evaluation of their public sector management reform exercises.*[7]

RELATIONSHIPS BETWEEN TIERS OF GOVERNMENT

There is a variety of arrangements between the different levels of state activity in the countries studied. In the cases of Austria and Germany the subnational governments have constitutional protection from interference in their affairs by federal government. In practice there is collaboration among the levels of government and normally a high degree of consensus. In the United Kingdom, all local government activities are subject to legislation in the national parliament. Local authorities are not allowed to carry out functions unless explicitly allowed to do so by legislation. In Switzerland, the principle of subsidiarity applies: federal government cannot take on functions which can be performed at canton level, nor can cantons take on responsibilities which can be performed at municipal level. In Sweden, local authorities can take on any responsibilities unless they are forbidden to by law.

These differences are partly a result of the historical development of the particular states. The Dutch state is based on a corporatist alliance of interest groups which relies on relatively autonomous subnational government and non-governmental organizations to hold its structure together. Germany and Austria are still strongly influenced by the Basic Laws enacted after the Second World War to prevent the central state from becoming too powerful. France has a complicated set of relationships between its 36,000 communes, 96 departments and 22 regions with a set of interdependencies between the localities and the centre. In the United Kingdom, many services were originally developed by municipalities during the nineteenth century. Public health, urban planning and slum clearance, water and drainage services have their origins in municipal enterprise. Gradually these matters were adopted in national legislation and many of the services were taken over by national government.

These differences have an impact on the management of the public sector. Different constitutional and financial arrangements among tiers of government produce a different locus for the main activities of management and produce a different set of constraints on managerial behaviour.

The first impact is on the degree to which services can be citizen or customer oriented. If the local administration is simply delivering a national service, with centrally defined standards, the local managers have little reason to help organize the local democratic decision-making process to take account of citizens' views of the services. Any changes the local population might want cannot be delivered without changing national laws, legal norms, resource allocation and standard setting. Similarly, the organization of local consumer feedback can lead only to those changes which are permitted under central controls. If, however, there is a high degree of local autonomy, then the use of such processes can be an important part of the management process. Hence, there has been a strong development of citizen- and customer-oriented activity in Germany at municipal and city-state levels, in the Netherlands and in the Swiss cantons. While municipalities in the United Kingdom have also made efforts in this direction, the initiative has been taken away by central government in Citizen's Charters and in the publication of national league tables for municipal services.

The second impact is on the degree to which the local level managers can engage in real strategic management and planning. If there is no possibility of adjusting the range and the nature of services provided because these matters are subject to national decrees and control, there is no need for local strategic planning. The same is true for fundamental local decision-making by politicians. Strong federal laws, legal norms and programmes strengthen the hands of local administrators in relation to their local politicians. In Austria and Germany the subnational governments carry out a mixture of tasks for which they are directly responsible and others which they carry out either jointly with or on behalf of the federal government.

Conversely, strong local autonomy makes it difficult for federal governments to initiate large policy changes or major reform programmes. Hence the Netherlands' Great Efficiency Operation was confined to the central government level. The German federal government has found it difficult to reform public services on the same lines as some other countries because of the constitutional autonomy of the subnational governments. France and the United Kingdom have used the relatively centralized powers of the national governments to pursue reforms such as performance budgeting and accountability for outputs. The United Kingdom has been able to force a range of changes at municipal level, such as competitive tendering for services and increased autonomy for schools which would have been difficult to achieve in a less unitary state.

The same argument applies to personnel systems. Where bargaining is decentralized, as in the Netherlands, it is difficult for central government to institute changes in the way in which people are paid. However, the argument is slightly more complicated than a simple centralized–decentralized difference. In centralized systems, such as the civil service recruitment and pay systems in Austria and Germany, the constitutional protection of the civil service and individual civil servants also make changes in personnel management difficult, requiring changes in the constitutional law.

In times of fiscal difficulty, it is sometimes convenient for central governments to decentralize responsibility for some services. If the responsibility for delivery can be transferred from central to provincial or municipal level, so can the political difficulties of either raising taxes or cutting funding for services. Hence in the Netherlands, some municipal leaders greet increased local tax-collecting powers as a mixed blessing. The autonomy of the former East German *Länder* is not matched by their practical capacity to raise sufficient local taxes to carry out their functions.

STRUCTURAL ARRANGEMENTS

There is a wide variety of structural arrangements for public services. An important dimension is the relationship between the units which deliver services and the governmental policy structures. Such a division can occur within services which are provided at national and local levels. There are three possible ideal types of relationship.

A unified hierarchy, with budgets and instructions flowing down from the top of the hierarchy to employees who deliver services

Germany, Austria and Switzerland have not moved away from the idea of the classical bureaucracy at central government level, with civil servants occupying positions and carrying out functions defined by law and legal norms. The services are managed by the same people as those who make the policies about what should be provided. This model does not apply entirely at municipal level in Germany where there is an increasing use of external contractors to provide services.

This arrangement is epitomized by the bureaucratic characteristics defined by Max Weber. Activities are defined by laws, legal norms and rules. Positions are occupied by people who are qualified to occupy them and their positions are continuous as long as they abide by the rules which apply. The limitations of such an approach are said to be that public sector workers concentrate on complying with legal norms and the rules of their jobs, rather than on either producing results or satisfying service users. Defenders of such arrangements argue that they protect public sector workers against favouritism and nepotism in promotion and from the arbitrary use of power by politicians and managers in the hierarchy. Since performance is difficult to define and even more difficult to measure, then a bureaucratic hierarchy in which people know what their jobs are and what behaviours are expected of them is the best way to manage services.

An alternative view is that unless results, expressed either as outputs (the volume of services delivered) or outcomes (the results of services being provided) can be expressed, then management will necessarily be ineffective. People may occupy their positions to the satisfaction of the legal norms and administrative requirements but produce a low volume of services, or services that are ineffective.

Contractual arrangements

One proposed solution to this problem is a contractual arrangement between governments and units which defines services to be provided in exchange for funds made available. Here, instead of there being a budget for a unit, there is an agreement about what is to be produced and how much money will be made available to produce it. In the extreme there could be sanctions which apply if the defined levels of production are not met. In practice the sanctions in place in Europe for non-compliance are not severe.

The other argument for the separation of policy from service delivery is that they are different sorts of functions and require different sorts of people to carry them out. The process of analyzing a policy problem and advising ministers and others on the solutions is different from the process of managing service delivery. Traditionally people who rise to the top of public bureaucracies are those who gained the best marks in the entrance and promotion examinations and those who are closest to the top politicians. These people are unlikely to be the most skilled at service delivery and the management of people and systems which will produce a satisfied set of customers. Hence it is better to separate the functions, allowing policy makers to define policy and work on the specifications of the services required and the arrangements necessary to deliver them. Someone else can carry out the task of management.

Sweden has a long tradition of the separation of policy making from service delivery. Ministries in Sweden are small, with around 100 employees each (apart from the Foreign Ministry which is not organized on agency lines) whose responsibility is to make policy and negotiate performance contracts and budgets with a range of agencies. The autonomy of the agencies is defined and protected by law. There is an annual negotiation about what is expected of each agency and what funds are to be available to meet those targets. The small ministries do not manage anything expect the policy process (except in the Foreign Ministry which also contains diplomats).

France has been moving towards a form of agency arrangement, through accountability centres (*centres de responsabilité*) which negotiate performance agreements with their relevant ministry. It was intended that these agreements should create more managerial autonomy and less central control over the details of resource management.

The United Kingdom has established executive agencies which have agreements on running cost budgets and performance targets. The Netherlands is in the process of establishing agencies. In both France and the United Kingdom there is a tension between the three parties involved in the agreements: the agencies, the ministry (the parent ministry) and the Ministry of Finance. There are two problems with the simple separation of policy and service delivery: the first is that the boundary between the two is not always clear. In the case of France and the United Kingdom, it is argued that good policy can be developed only by people who know how services and policy can be practically administered: lack of experience in the field can result in impractical policies.

The second difficulty is that those in charge of policy often do not wish to relinquish control over service delivery. Ministers and senior policy-making civil servants enjoy the power of being able to intervene in the day to-day running of the agencies for which they are ultimately responsible. This applies also to central departments such as ministries of finance. Their power derives partly from being able to intervene in the management and financial control of ministries and other agencies. If there were simply an agreement between departments and their ministries and their running costs, the power of the finance ministry would be curtailed.

Managerial autonomy for agencies is limited by the finance ministries' desire and requirement to exercise control over public expenditure, sometimes in detail. Hence, managerial reforms which promise global budgets, local autonomy, performance targets rather than input controls, looser central controls over payment to workers, and looser regulations about investment in plant and equipment are often thwarted by the overriding need to keep spending under control, which is interpreted by some as the need to have detailed central control over the details of spending. If at the same time there is a need for overall financial stringency (as there often is), then there is a tendency towards the reduction of the autonomy of the apparently independent service delivery units. The chapter on the executive agencies in the United Kingdom shows an example of this.

Independent units which receive funding from taxation

The Netherlands has a rather different arrangement. There is a widespread use of para-governmental organizations (over 700 at national government level). Their size and influence vary, as does their legal status. Around two-thirds of them are independent corporate entities. The independence of most PGOs is fairly limited, since they are dependent on government money, and in many cases, the central government can appoint board members and veto decisions. So, since the government finances the non-profit sector from 50 to 100 percent, its grip on the PGOs is large, despite their independent status.

However, their status is different from that of the agencies, which are now being set up by the central government as independently operating executive organizations. The PGOs, unlike the agencies, are not a formal part of the government. Most PGOs can be found in social security, healthcare, education, agriculture and justice.

STRATEGIC MANAGEMENT, STEERING AND CONTROLLING[8]

In a hierarchical bureaucracy, work is performed according to calculable rules and general norms of behaviour.[9] In a *Rechtsstaat*, the rules and norms are based on laws. The main purpose of management structures and instruments of control is to ensure conformity with those rules and norms. In such a system, if the management process requires improved efficiency or a change in the mixture of products or services, there would need to be a change in the law.

In all the states we examined there have been attempts to redirect managerial effort from conformance to performance. This necessitates several changes in the way in which organizations work. There needs to be a process in which the purposes of the organizations are agreed and their activities and products are defined and measured. Once this has been achieved, there have to be ways of ensuring that they achieve an agreed level of output. This implies that people managing units of the organization are able to organize themselves to make an efficient use of resources, will be committed to the targets and will have a reason for achieving results. This is a different managerial task from complying with laws, legal norms and calculable rules.

The first requirement is a process by which the expected performances can be defined and agreed. All the sample countries are now attempting to do this. The Netherlands government and parliament agreed an approach in 1992, called 'towards more result oriented management', which set out ways in which the expected results of activities could be formulated into a type of internal contract, similar to a real contract with an external supplier of services. Austria now has a formal system in which political goals are made explicit and then translated into tasks, objectives and projects for officials. In Sweden, the agency objectives and targets are agreed as part of the planning and budgeting process between agencies and ministries. At *Land* and city level in Germany, there have been developments of a 'new steering model', which involves, among other things, agreement on outputs and performance. Switzerland has a new 'controlling' system which sets goals, makes priorities explicit, allocates resources and sets up evaluation criteria for performance. In the United Kingdom, departments agree goals and targets with agencies and set the resource and management framework to achieve the targets.

As is clear from the detailed descriptions of these processes, they are not without problems. It is often difficult to define objectives sufficiently tightly for the measurement of their achievement. Sanctions and rewards for performance sometimes make the targets less than effective. Targets can be set without reference to the citizens or the customers of the services. Whatever the difficulties, real efforts are being made to guide or steer public sector organizations, rather than simply make them conform to legal norms and rules of behaviour.

PLANNING AND BUDGETING SYSTEMS

There is a variety of approaches to planning and budgeting. Most countries have made attempts to design planning and budgeting processes which produce flexibility. Budgetary pressures have meant that new developments or changed priorities have to be financed either out of increased efficiencies or the abandonment of lower priority programmes. Hence, unless the whole process is to be incremental and static, rolling over previous years' budgets will be inadequate.

The elements of changes in the planning and budgeting processes are as follows:

1. Extending the planning period. Sweden, the United Kingdom, Austria and Switzerland have all made attempts at three-year financial forecasts. The more accurate the forecasts, the more sustainable is this process. In Sweden the budgeting period varies according to the predictability of the item. Those which are subject to large fluctuations, such as unemployment benefits, have a shorter budget period than those which do not vary so much. However, even in those countries which have extended the financial planning period, changes in tax revenues or demands tend to blow three-year forecasts and agreements off course.

2. Some countries are trying to move budgets from an input focus to an output focus, especially the Netherlands, Sweden and the United Kingdom. However, financial restraint has a tendency to focus the mind on the scale of the inputs, rather than the need for the outputs. This is an area where the rhetoric of output orientation becomes uncoupled from the reality of financial constraint.

3. Many countries are trying to move from detailed central control over the inputs (staffing levels, distribution of employment grades, expenditure on materials) towards 'global' or 'lump-sum' budgets. The argument is that local managers are better able to judge the most effective mixture of inputs than centrally based ministry of finance officials. These global budgets may be combined with output definitions in budgets. This too is an area where the appearance of radical change can deceive. For example, global budgets

are often overridden by rules or laws affecting personnel matters and staffing levels, thus reducing the apparent budgetary discretion of managers.

4. Some countries include a fundamental examination of the need for the function to be performed at all as part of the resource allocation process. The Netherlands introduced a series of 'reconsiderations', in which whole policy areas were subjected to scrutiny, both as to the effectiveness of policy and the need for it to exist. The United Kingdom has had a similar process of questioning the need for particular activities to be carried out at all, and if so whether they should be carried out by the state. In neither case have major services been discontinued.

MANAGING PEOPLE

A further requirement is a way of managing people which encourages them to join in with the process of working for outputs and results. There are two 'ideal type' approaches to the management of people in the public sector. At one extreme there is a civil service staffed by people who achieve high marks in a competitive examination, enter the service in their early twenties, progress up a well-defined scale, perhaps with some accelerated promotions, and stay in post until a secure retirement. Progress is achieved mainly by avoiding mistakes and conforming to the norms and culture of the ministries or departments. There may be attempts at making the organizations output or performance oriented, but the overwhelming norm is that people occupy positions and have security of tenure which obviates the need to demonstrate anything more than ordinary contributions. However, there are well-planned training and development schemes, at special institutions, which produce a high-quality employee who requires little direct supervision. Public servants have a special status and there is little or no interchange between the public and private sectors.

An opposite ideal type consists of a flowing group of people, some employed on short-term contracts, some working for consultancy or service companies. Pay is based largely on performance to measurable standards. Careers are made in many different organizations and people manage their own development and training. There is nothing fundamentally different between working in the private and public sectors and people switch between the two.

In practice neither extreme exists. The second seems to have characteristics which 'reformers' find desirable to avoid the dangers of rigidity and self-serving implied by the first type. While we can see tendencies to move from the first to the second type of organization, there are different speeds of movement and different emphases.

In some countries, governments believe that lifetime employment with progression on seniority through preset salary scales is not the way to promote performance-oriented work. Others are still operating a traditional administrative approach to human resource management, with an emphasis on security of tenure for state employees. However, there is a variety of approaches in the major personnel management aspects of recruitment, promotion, pay, training and development.

Recruitment and tenure

France, Germany and Austria still have a tendency to recruit through competitive examinations and to offer employees in the professional grades a very secure career. In France, positions and pension rights are protected, even if people make career moves into the private sector. There are some changes to the traditional system in Austria, where top civil service positions are now offered on short-term, renewable contracts.

Sweden, the Netherlands and the United Kingdom have varying degrees of decentralized recruitment and reduced security of tenure. In all cases people are recruited to particular positions rather than to the civil or public service as a whole. While recruitment for individual positions in the Netherlands is generally done among existing employees first (because the number of public employees is falling), probation periods for people in new posts are being extended. Dismissal is possible but on favourable terms for employees unless they are extremely inefficient or criminal.

Promotion

France, Germany, Austria and Switzerland still have promotion based mainly on seniority. Sweden, the United Kingdom and the Netherlands have mainly moved to a system of promotion by application to particular vacancies, rather than automatic progression from scale to scale. The main reason for this is to give managers the opportunity to select people who might be suitable for particular jobs, rather than be allocated the next person who is eligible for promotion. This is an important element of the idea of an organization managed for results, rather than a system of positions whose occupants are interchangeable.

Pay

Some governments have expressed a desire for a more flexible system of public sector pay determination, for three reasons[10]:

1. The external labour market, especially for specialists such as computer experts and accountants, means that rigid pay scales do not provide

enough flexibility in pay to be able to attract the best people. If grades apply to all jobs at a certain level, then everyone's pay at that level would have to be raised to be able to attract a particular specialist. Similarly there may be shortages of staff of a particular kind in some parts of a country: capital cities tend to have a greater demand for specialist labour than more remote areas. Nationally applied scales mean that governments cannot pay people at different rates in different locations.

2. Managers may desire flexibility to increase efficiency, by using performance-based pay to increase motivation or output.

3. If there are financial problems for the public sector, then fixed pay, especially with annual increases, may produce a higher pay bill than flexible pay. In countries with high unemployment, it may be possible to reduce pay of the workers in the public sector because there is competition to find jobs.

Pay bargaining is sometimes a national matter and sometimes devolved and carried out locally. In Sweden there is a national bargain over the size of the overall pay fund but the details of the pay settlements are negotiated locally. In the United Kingdom there is a cash limit on the funds available for public sector pay which is imposed rather than negotiated and the details are increasingly left for local bargaining or independent review.

The Netherlands has centralized pay bargaining with different agreements for each of eight sectors. The other countries mostly rely on centralized national pay bargaining, or a system of pay determination which does not involve bargaining. In Germany the *Beamte* level of civil servants does not bargain over their pay but the government has a commitment to defend their standard of living. In the United Kingdom there is a system of pay review which applies linkages between public sector pay and agreed indices.

There is some movement towards a performance-related element to pay, although the Austrian scheme is more like a job-related pay scheme than a performance-related one. The United Kingdom government introduced a performance-related pay element in 1985 for senior people and has made a commitment to performance-related pay in its Citizen's Charter, although the details of schemes are left to individual departments and agencies. In Sweden, the Netherlands and France bonuses are used, but these are not always closely tied to individual performance.

Training and development

Only Germany, Austria and France have national systems of training institutions designed to produce administrators schooled especially in administrative law. The Netherlands has privatized its national administration school which now competes with other schools for students at all levels. Similarly the United Kingdom has made its Civil Service College a self-financing (from 1996) competitive institution.

A centrally organized training programme, with different institutions for different levels of personnel, as in France, is a concomitant of a centralized bureaucracy organized on hierarchical lines, with progression through grades. It does not fit well with a devolved human resource management, with people managing their own careers and personal development by choosing their training and applying for individual positions.

Market and customer orientation

A recurrent theme is the desire to orient the public services towards the consumers of public services. While market type reforms are based on the service user as a 'customer', there is also a concern for the role of citizenship and rights. In France, for example, there has been a discussion of the 'citizen-user' (*citoyen-usager*), a term which combines the rights of service users as customers (the right to have one's preferences listened to and to be treated politely) with their rights as citizens (to be able to influence policy and decision-making).

Some administrations have adopted an approach to 'customer service' that is essentially internally focused. The service providers define service standards, publicize them and then try to implement and deliver the standards. The customers are not involved in the choice of criteria or in setting the expected standards, but do have a right of redress or compensation if the published standards are not met.

One aspect of customer orientation is the attempt to make existing services more accessible, in many cases by making a single access point to a range of services. This 'one-stop shop' idea has been implemented in many places, including German municipalities, Italian federal level government, the Netherlands and UK local government. However, from the customer's point of view, the one-stop shop rarely includes services provided by more than one level of government: municipalities may organize access to all their services in one place but the customer still has to travel to find the access to services from regional or federal level.

Along with improved accessibility, many administrations are trying to simplify procedures to make them more comprehensible to the customers. Forms are redesigned and simplified, procedures are explained and staff are trained to make services more user-friendly.

A second way of reorienting organizations is the establishment of an internal market. The argument is that service providers are not in a market relationship with their end-users who have no choice of provider and are dependent on the state for the service. Hence, there is no need for the service provider to satisfy customer requirements and preferences. A surrogate for such market power is an intermediary 'purchaser' which represents the state as the provider of the money and represents the service user as a consumer. Service providers therefore have to satisfy the purchasers that they are giving quality and value for money – they have to become 'market-oriented'. The transaction between purchaser and provider is a surrogate for the development of real market transactions between service providers and customers. This approach has been used in the health systems of the Netherlands, parts of Sweden and the United Kingdom, and in many municipalities in Germany and the Netherlands.

Whether it produces better services depends partly on the nature of the transaction. From the citizen's or service user's viewpoint, it may make no difference at all. If the purchaser is simply another employee of the government, nothing has changed: he or she is still confronted by state employees, whether they are labelled purchaser or provider. Similarly, if there is a monopoly in service provision, the purchaser has to use methods other than the threat of purchasing elsewhere to gain control over the service providers. In practice, the contracts between purchaser and provider can be similar to a relationship of direct supervision. Where the service provider has more professional expertise and knowledge than the purchaser, the relationship is such that the provider may remain internally oriented.

If the purchasers wish to use the threat of purchasing elsewhere to control services and their costs, they organize competitions among providers. This has been traditional in France since the nineteenth century and has been common in most countries for some services. There has been an increased use of contracting and competition especially in the United Kingdom, the Netherlands and Germany. While this enables purchasers to exercise a different sort of power over the service providers, it offers the service users neither control over the services nor choice.

In order to empower service users in this way, some administrations have offered the service users a free choice of service provider. Examples include the Netherlands' education system and the Stockholm health experiment (until 1994). If the service user has a complete free choice of service provider and the finance for service provision follows the consumer, then service providers have to be oriented towards getting and keeping customers.

User orientation is an area in which it is difficult to generalize at national level. Independent local governments have been using a variety of experiments with customer orientation or user control over services in many countries. Not all the experiments involve the use of market mechanisms but include a variety of forms of consultation and participation in decision making.

The main characteristics of the systems of planning, budgeting and personnel management in the sample countries are summarized in Tables 1.1–1.3. In the following chapters there are more details about the management arrangements in each of the sample countries.

Table 1.1. Structure of the public sector

Feature Country	Unified or agency	Relationship between tiers and autonomy	Accountability	Role of legal norms
Sweden	Agencies	Relatively independent counties and minicipalities	Systematic reporting on performance. Contracts between agencies and centre	Agency autonomy by law
United Kingdom	Agencies	Local authorities and agencies subject to central government control	Agencies through performance targets	Ministerial action more important than legal norms
Netherlands	Agencies being developed, widespread use of paragovernmental organizations	Constitution guarantees competence of subnational government	No detailed systems: reporting systems for expenditure	Wide definitions of competencies
France	Increasing number of accountability centres	Varying degrees of central government control over budgets and personnel. Recent tendencies towards centralization	Detailed performance reporting for accountability centres	Law-based administration
Germany	Unified	Highly autonomous *Länder* and municipalities	Well-structured reporting systems in the *Länder* and municipalities. No detailed accountability to federal government	Law-based administration
Austria	Unified	Relatively autonomous states and municipalities	Two fold system according to the rules of federalism: well-structured on all levels and between state and federal level	Law-based administration
Switzerland	Unified	Highly autonomous cantons High degrees of control over budgets and personnel within federal government	Global reporting of cantons Detailed reporting within federal government	Law-based administration

Table 1.2. Management processes

Feature Country	Planning, goals and objectives	Budgeting	Evaluation	Cost information	Customer orientation
Sweden	Three-year negotiation based on rational cycle Annual plans Consistent and detailed in many agencies	Performance-oriented three-year cycle Formal systematic procedure	Increasing emphasis on efficiency and effectiveness Related to budget cycle Negotiation based	Emphasis on expenditure	Use of individual choice and internal markets (education, health and welfare)
United Kingdom	Annual plans Numerical targets for agencies	Annual input based with three-year projections Annual efficiency improvement targets	Performance against targets for agencies Very little policy evaluation	Some unit costs System of accruals accounting	Quality targets, redress, Citizens' Charter, some customer surveys
Netherlands	Weak planning system Fragmentation Indicative planning	Some function-based and output-oriented	'Reconsideration' attached to annual budget process (80 policy fields covered), ministries report on policy evaluation programs	'Financial accountability operation' has increased cost awareness	Free choice schools Fragmented administrative system
France	In responsibility centres systematic procedure; annual plan based on three-year goals	Tendency towards global budgets In many areas high degree of centralization	No high degree of systematization	Emphasis on expenditure	Public service charter
Germany	Result-oriented planning systems on community level; input orientation at the *Länder* and federal level	Federal and *Länder* level: input-oriented, annual, three-year incremental forecasting; local level: experiments with flexible and global budgets	Few systematic procedures Emphasis on legal and financial aspects (auditing)	Emphasis on expenditure Local level developments of accrual accounting.	Developments towards improvement (local level: one-stop agencies)
Austria	Annual plans based on budget increasing developments	Input-oriented, annual three-year incremental forecast	Formal evaluation based on conformity to legal norms and proper use of resources Increasing emphasis on efficiency and effectiveness	Formal obligation to be implemented at federal level Well-developed basic information system	Uneven development by various organizations at all tiers
Switzerland	Emphasis on strategic planning and goal setting	Input-oriented, annual, three-year incremental forecast	Control cycle uses elements of output orientation Increasing emphasis on efficiency and effectiveness	Emphasis on expenditure cost information in place in some organizations	Direct feedback through political processes

Table 1.3. Personnel management

Feature Country	Recruitment and dismissal	Promotion	Pay, performance and incentives	Training	Personnel development
Sweden	Decentralized recruitment Decreasing security of tenure	Promotion on application for advertised posts, no career management	Decentralized pay bargaining, agreements create pay funds rather than pay increases Some move towards individual performance pay	Decentralized No central institution	Managed at individual agency level
United Kingdom	Increasingly management at the agency level More emphasis on short-term contracts	Promotion to jobs more than progression through grades	Decentralized pay bargaining within Treasury cash limits Increasing use of performance-related pay	Managed on individual agency level open markets for training provision Targeted number of training days	Managed at individual agency level Fast stream for policy grades
Netherlands	No central recruitment Recruitment for open positions is internal Dismissal flexibility by law	No career development policy Application to internal vacancies	Pay bargaining decentralized Performance-related bonuses Annual pay raise based on scale	No special training Decentralized Free discretion at all levels	Movement from job to job encouraged
France	Recruitment by competitive examination Highly secure tenure	Mainly based on seniority	Minimum wage National system Extensive use of bonuses	Nationally organized schools of administration Pre-employment, promotion and personal development training	Systematic and planned approach
Germany	Decentralized recruitment, highly secure tenure	Mainly based on seniority	Centralized (bargaining) system, poor performance relations, special pension funds, biannual automatic raise	Internal pre-entry training on all levels at schools of administration (emphasis on legal matters) personal development training	Systematic measures only in cities; some experiences at the *Länder* level
Austria	Open recruitment testing Security of tenure for top positions Short-term contracts with possible extension	Mainly based on seniority	Centralized bargaining Similar federal and state systems Biannual pay raise on scale Development of perform-ance-related elements	Obligatory for new recruits central provision open markets for all tiers Centralized supply and measures on individual organizational level	Managed on individual federal ministry, state and community level Concepts increasingly systematized and development-oriented
Switzerland	Centralized at federal level	Mainly based on seniority	Centralized pay bargaining Federal and canton systems	Increasing emphasis on systematized training on and off the job	Increasing emphasis on systematized personal career development

NOTES

1. See Eric Hobsbawm, *The Age of Extremes*, Michael Joseph (1994).
2. Helmut Klages and Elke Löffler, 'Public Sector Modernisation in Germany – Recent Trends and Emerging Strategies', IIAS Working Group on Public Sector Productivity, Helsinki (July 1994).
3. C. Hood, 'Public Management for all Seasons?', *Public Administration* **69** (1991).
4. Organization for Economic Co-operation and Development, *Public Management Developments: Survey 1993*, Paris (1993).
5. P. Champaigne, Y. Cottereau, G. Dallemagne and T. Malan, 'Les Processus de Modernisation dans L'Administration de l'Education Nationale', *Politiques et Management Public*, **11** (1) (1993).
6. W.J.M. Kickert, 'Public Governance in the Netherlands: An Alternative to Anglo-American "Managerialism"' (1994), unpublished paper, Erasmus Univerity.
7. Ibid, footnote 4.
8. The term 'controlling' in German refers to the process of strategic planning and implementation and reflects a proactive management. 'Control' is retrospective and is concerned mainly with audit and conformity to rules and norms. The French use of 'stratégique' is similar to the English and American use of strategic management. 'Steering' in American usage denotes a hands-off style of public provision, services being delivered under contract by independent companies and agencies. 'Steuerung' in German or the 'new steering model' refers to a holistic process of community governance.
9. M. Weber, *Economy and Society*, Bedminster Press (1968).
10. D. Marsden, 'Reforming Public Sector Pay', in OECD, *Pay Flexibility in the Public Sector*, Paris (1993).

2

Sweden

Stuart Wilks

SCALE AND SCOPE OF THE PUBLIC SECTOR

Measured by any criterion, the Swedish public sector is one of the largest of any industrialized nation (see Table 2.1). Together with Denmark, Norway and the Netherlands, Sweden is one of the four European countries where both government revenues and expenditure exceed 50 percent of gross national product (GNP).

Table 2.1. Government employment in Sweden as a percentage of total employment

1960	1974	1980	1990
12.8	24.8	30.3	31.7

Source: Sorensen (1993, p. 228).

Of the 1.6 million currently employed in the public sector, 1.2 million (about three-quarters of the total) work in local government, and 400,000 (one-quarter) for central government and the remaining state-owned companies. The importance of local government in the Swedish public sector should not be underestimated. Local government expenditure accounted for 28 percent of GNP in 1989 and outspends central government by two to one (Jones, 1990).

STRUCTURE

When placed in comparative perspective, two aspects of the institutional structures of Swedish public administration stand out. First, there is a strong formal separation of central government between very small ministries (which are responsible for policy) and much larger administrative agencies (which are responsible for implementation). Although the agencies are responsible for carrying out government policy they have a considerable degree of independence and cannot be instructed or directed by the ministries. Secondly, a very large number of functions are carried out by regional and local government which also have a remarkable degree of autonomy and freedom from central interference. Hence, a key feature of Swedish intergovernmental relations is the extent of administrative autonomy at different levels.

Central government

The separation of Swedish central government into ministries and agencies dates back to the late 1600s. However, the original conception that agencies should be relatively small bodies serving the ministries has, in effect, been reversed. Today the ministries are, by international standards, remarkably small institutions employing 100 or so people (with the exception of the Ministry of Foreign Affairs which has around 1000 staff). In total, the thirteen ministries employ a total of just 2000 people. By contrast the 170 or so administrative agencies have some 400,000 staff.

The ministries are headed by a member of the cabinet (*Regering*) who appoints the three most senior ministerial staff: the under-secretary of state, the permanent under-secretary and the under-secretary for legal affairs. The maintenance of such a small level of staff is made possible by the strong separation of policy and implementation functions. This division enables the ministries to take responsibility for important policy and strategic managerial issues, while leaving the agencies responsibility for implementation and service delivery, reflecting a clearly made distinction between routine and non-routine decisions in Swedish government (Jones, 1990). It should be noted, however, that in reality the separation of policy-making and implementation is more blurred than the formal model suggests. There are in fact significant informal contacts between ministries and agencies which give the latter an influence over policy (Pierre, 1993b, pp. 7–8).

Each ministry has a number of administrative agencies below it. The agencies are run on a day-to-day basis by a director general who is appointed for a six-year period by the relevant ministry. Long-term planning, however, is determined by a board made up of representatives from trade unions, employers' organizations, political parties, civil servants and employees from the agency.

Local government

Although the administrative agencies may also have local and regional boards, the most important forms of local and regional government are the elected county councils and municipalities. There are 23 county councils, and following a process of amalgamation in the 1970s there are now 284 municipalities. The role of local government is particularly important in areas of social policy such as healthcare, education and social services. Around 60 percent of all local government expenditure is on these three policy areas.

County councils are primarily responsible for healthcare and hospitals which constitute 80 percent of county council expenditure. County councils also share certain tasks with the municipalities such as public transport and regional planning and infrastructure.

The municipalities carry out a much wider range of functions. Municipalities have a number of compulsory tasks, regulated by government but with considerable local freedom to determine the planning and organization of services. These tasks include responsibility for key social welfare functions such as education, social welfare, childcare and care of the elderly. Although all provision in these areas must comply with a national minimum, service provision does vary since some municipalities may choose to add to state requirements and target certain groups (Berg *et al.*, 1993). Municipalities are also responsible for tasks such as rubbish collection and street cleaning, the emergency services, amenities such as power and water supply, sewage and waste management, aspects of physical planning, roads and parks, and they also engage in cultural affairs and the provision of leisure facilities. This broad range of functions indicates why local government constitutes such a large part of government spending. Services such as water and power supply are often provided by municipally owned companies.

An important feature of Swedish local government is the ability to conduct its own affairs. Local government is allowed to engage in any activity, provided that it is not expressly forbidden and that it is not successfully challenged by a citizen's appeal. Traditionally, municipalities have been able to set their own local income tax rates (which provide some 50 percent of local government income) although a central government freeze on local taxes was in operation between 1991 and 1994. At the same time, however, local government has been encouraged to experiment with new forms of management and service delivery and has gained further autonomy from the centre in its operations. The 1991 Local Government Act gave the municipalities much greater freedom over the organization of their committee structure and budgetary arrangements.

While the institutional structures of the Swedish state have remained more or less the same, the roles of the different tiers of government and the relationships between them have changed quite considerably in the last 15–20 years. A process of decentralization has occurred since the 1970s, transferring responsibility from central to local government. Initially, municipalities were amalgamated, reducing the total number of units from 1000 to 284 in order that more functions could be carried out at the local level. This process of decentralizing responsibility continued throughout the 1980s. More recently, tasks which were previously shared between different tiers of government, such as care of the elderly, have been entirely devolved to the municipal levels. Decentralization, and a broader shift away from rule-based management, have also meant that the administrative agencies have changed their role. The agencies now play a much greater role evaluating, advising and researching rather than instructing local government.

Part I

MANAGEMENT PROCESSES 1

Considerable change has taken place in the management of the Swedish public sector over the past ten years. Management structures and systems are in an ongoing process of transition from the traditional social democratic model to forms more commonly associated with new public management. However, due to the extent of institutional autonomy and governmental decentralization in Sweden, reform has taken place in an 'uneven' fashion, with marked variations observable in the practice of different agencies, county councils and municipalities.

Goals and objectives setting

Prior to the recent programme of extensive public sector reform, goals and objectives were more commonly set by specialist committees, particularly in areas of social policy. The goals of public sector activity were then pursued through a traditional public administration model of detailed rule and resource control. Significant changes have occurred over the past decade as part of the extensive reform of the Swedish budget process. In Sweden today the establishment of goals and objectives takes place as an integral part of the budget process and through dialog between the government, the ministries and the agencies. Long-term goals are set by government and parliament, and these goals are relayed by the ministries, as part of their general responsibility for policy formulation, to the agencies for which they are responsible through specific planning directives. A more detailed set of objectives is then established by the administrative agencies, pending governmental approval, as part of their request for resources which feeds directly into the budgetary process.

Planning

Traditionally the management of the Swedish public sector was based on plans, and in most sectors the agencies played a large planning role.

26

However, in recent years this has changed considerably as Swedish public services have rejected the traditional model of rational planning in favour of management by objectives. This shift away from public sector planning has directly accompanied the extensive programme of administrative decentralization which has made agencies more autonomous from central government and seen local government take on more responsibility for the management of public services.

At the national level there has been a shift away from rule and resource control to management by results and objectives. This shift towards management by objectives is summarized in a recent OECD publication which stresses that in Sweden, 'Improved public management is to be achieved by setting targets, clearly specifying the required results and analysing and evaluating the results achieved' (OECD, 1992). It should be noted, however, that there have been some problems in ensuring that all agencies successfully introduce management by objectives as part of the reform of the budget process (Ministry of Finance, 1993b, p. 9) In most policy areas broad targets are set by government, but the decisions about how these goals are to be achieved are largely to be determined at the local level. In education, for example, while there are clearly stated governmental targets, there is also a considerable degree of choice at the local level as to the instruments which will be used to attain these goals (Weyler, 1993). Planning is thus decentralized, with each municipality and individual schools being required to show how government targets for education will be met. The National Agency for Education then plays the role of supervising, following-up and assessing, and every three years is required to present a report on schooling in Sweden to the government. This report then feeds into the national development plan for education (Weyler, 1993).

The rejection of the traditional systems of rational planning has been particularly striking in the provision of healthcare at both the national and local level (Garpenby, 1992). According to Saltman and Von Otter (1992, p. 39) this has resulted more from a concern that, as a process, planning did not allow for the inevitably rapid rate of change in the healthcare sector. The build up of waiting lists became seen as a particular problematic result of a planned system of healthcare (Saltman and Von Otter, 1992, p. 39) and, as a result, several county councils have turned to more market-based systems such as DRG systems and performance-related pay to hospitals (Garpenby, 1992, p. 25). A payment system in which prices are fixed by the definition of the condition, not the actual cost of treating each individual patient.

The introduction of management by objectives has also become more common in a number of municipalities, representing a clear growth of managerialism in local government (Wise and Amna, 1992). A survey carried out in 1991 found that 50 percent of municipalities had introduced management by objectives, and over a third had linked this to the budget. However, it was also found that management by objectives had only been *properly* established in a handful of municipalities (Montin, 1993, p. 61). In Montin's view this raises particular concerns about how effective management by objectives will prove to be in local government. In particular, he suggests that the objectives are often too vague, the methods of evaluation ill-developed and the suitability of management by objectives to the Swedish political culture is often questionable (Montin, 1993, pp. 61–2). These flaws could also be said to be evident at the level of the administrative agencies where there is still, in reality, a process of muddling through taking place in the formulation of objectives, the matching of performance against plans and the agreement of evaluation methods and criteria.

Budgeting

The rapid growth of the public sector in the 1960s has meant that for more than twenty-five years there has been a need to introduce a more rational budgetary process in Sweden. Programme budgeting (PPBS) was first introduced in 1968 but failed to slow the growth of public sector budgets, largely because of absence of mechanisms to control costs and the lack of political commitment to the system. PPBS was subsequently abolished in 1978 but the concern to move away from an incremental budget model remained a political priority as the public sector deficit grew from 1975 onwards.

Since the mid-1980s, there has been a more gradual introduction of a three-year budget cycle intended to provide for a longer-term perspective in the financing of the public sector. In reality, it has proved extremely difficult to develop this long-term view because of a continuous need for crisis management and political intervention in the budgetary process. However, the overall intention is to move from detailed input control to management by results which will enable administrative agencies to have greater flexibility in their control over resources. Under the new model, administrative costs are determined for a three-year period and agencies are required to report back annually on their performance. Although this system suggests a link between resource allocation and the achievement of specified goals, the absence of any defined sanctions or incentives makes this link a very weak one.

These recent changes to the budget process in Sweden have meant that managers in administrative agencies have a considerable degree of flexibility in budgetary control. In part, greater control over budgets has been the quid pro quo for overall grant reductions, but it is also a product of a genuine decentralization of decision-making power. For example, the agencies now have much greater control over the management of pay and personnel than they did previously.

Significant changes have also taken place to the system of grant allocations to municipalities. The 100 plus different forms of grants which were previously given for specific expenditures have, since January 1993, been merged into a general block grant or grant-in-aid, together with a limited number of purpose-specific allocations. Municipalities are therefore given much greater freedom to determine the allocation of these funds and are compensated for the loss of certain subsidies by an increased freedom to determine their own spending policies (Riberdahl, 1992, p. 7).

Since 1986, the majority of municipalities have decentralized their budgetary and accounting functions to the level of individual committees (Haggroth, 1993, p. 83). Many municipalities have gone further than this and decentralized to the level of individual institutions (e.g. schools, nurseries), and have set up cost centres with responsibility for particular activities and for their own budgets. Similar systems are developing in many county councils in the provision of healthcare. For example, in Stockholm county, nine district health authorities have been established, each with their own budget (Garpenby, 1992).

Costs and cost information

Public sector accounting in Sweden has traditionally been expenditure rather than cost oriented. However, there have been a number of attempts to improve cost consciousness, such as the introduction of programme budgeting in 1968. More generally, there has been considerable attention to cost containment at all levels of government for over fifteen years. Concern about costs has stemmed from two sources. First, the general growth of the public sector and the burgeoning public sector deficit has produced a general governmental concern to reduce costs in the public sector. Secondly, studies carried out to assess the unit costs of service provision in Sweden in relation to the other Scandinavian countries have revealed Swedish public services to be considerably more expensive, adding to the concern about cost control (Sorensen, 1993, p. 230).

Consistent concerns about the size of the budget deficit have meant that a programme of cost reduction known as the 2 percent standard, or 'the cheese-slicer' was applied from the late 1970s. This general 2 percent reduction in public sector budgets was justified as a way of taking into account productivity increases in the public sector. It was estimated that private sector productivity grew at an average of 4 percent per annum and that the public sector could do at least half as well (Brunsson, 1993). However, the 2 percent standard had limited impact since there were no sanctions built in for agencies which failed to comply (Sorensen, 1993, p. 223).

The new budget process is also importantly focused on containing costs in the public sector and was introduced together with a targeted 10 percent cut in administration costs applied across agencies between 1989 and 1991. As a result of the new budget process, the availability and importance of cost information have increased significantly. The annual reports produced by the administrative agencies are intended to focus attention on costs.

In local governments operating under tight fiscal constraints attention to costs has become particularly important. Where a purchaser–provider split has been introduced, as has happened in many municipalities, managers will have a clear knowledge of how much services cost. More generally, the decentralization of budgetary responsibility in municipalities has made cost consciousness a much more significant managerial concern.

Evaluation

Compared to other polities, concern with evaluation is relatively new in the Swedish public sector. Traditionally there has been little attention to ex-post evaluation as performance was usually measured against plans and against budgets. A number of reasons could be suggested for this lack of systematic evaluation, such as the general political consensus about the activities of the state, the extent of decentralization, and the limited amount of resources available for evaluation. Arguably, as elsewhere in Europe, the Swedish public sector was typified in the immediate post-war period by a belief that government was a general panacea for social ills, and, as such, the need for evaluation was not even conceived of.

However, since the beginning of the Social Democrats' 'Renewal' programme, evaluation has become more important. With the resources available to the public sector ceasing to grow, or in many cases contracting, evaluation has become a critical concern to the government and public sector managers alike. As a result, evaluation has become a key part of the comprehensive programme of public sector reform and particularly of the new budget cycle, with its intention of moving from detailed input control to management by results. The administrative agencies are now required to assess and report on their performance in an annual report of expenditure, performance and productivity, which is then used to determine objectives and activities for the coming years.

A number of bodies are important in the evaluation of the public sector, including the National Audit Bureau, the Expert Group on Public Finance and the Swedish Agency for Administrative Development. The National Audit Bureau (RRV) is concerned with the auditing of finance and performance. The RRV has been praised by MacDonald (1992, p. 20) for its approach to evaluation, which is carried out with the co-operation of the agencies concerned, for instance through consultation over the measures to be used. The Expert Group on Public Finance is based at the Ministry of Finance and was established in 1981 as an independent group working at the levels of central and local government. In particular, the Expert Group was set up to evaluate the main functions of the welfare state and to study productivity and effectiveness in the public sector (OECD, 1990a, p. 102). The Swedish Agency for Administrative Development also plays an important part in developing data-processing methods and techniques to measure improved efficiency and effectiveness.

Within local government, evaluation has also grown significantly in importance. Whereas municipal activities were usually followed up in relation to budgets and plans, there are new concerns with the results of activities, the quality of service provision and the efficiency of organizations (Haggroth, 1993, p. 85). Evaluation is becoming especially important where purchaser–provider splits have been introduced and work is contracted out. Where management by objectives has been introduced there are, however, problems regarding evaluation since it has proved difficult to find good methods (Montin, 1993, p. 61). Evaluation at the local level is usually carried out by universities and by research units jointly owned by municipalities in different areas of the country.

However, despite the growth in concern with evaluation there remains a general recognition that evaluation methods remain poorly developed in Sweden and that a great deal of work remains to be done (Haggroth, 1993, pp. 86–90). In areas such as education where an extensive evaluation exercise has begun, there has been considerable controversy over the process and the nature of the measures used.

Market and customer orientation

Concern with market orientation increased significantly in 1991–4 when the Conservative–Liberal coalition was in power, although the Social Democrats had begun to move in this direction in the late 1980s. The trend towards the use of market mechanisms is especially pronounced in local government, often as a response to economic difficulties and fiscal constraints (Haggroth, 1993, p. 62). A number of policy areas at the local level are now commonly seeing the introduction of systems designed to enable 'consumer choice' (Haggroth, 1993, p. 71). Voucher systems are increasingly common in education (Weyler, 1993) but also in childcare and care of the elderly (Fernow, 1992; Haggroth, 1993). One of the main principles guiding the reform of care for the elderly introduced in 1992 was that more choice should be offered in the types of care and housing available (Hedin, 1993).

However, the biggest steps to increase freedom of choice have been taken in medical care (Haggroth, 1993, p. 101). Regular surveys of patient views on healthcare are now carried out and there is a growing concern with patient satisfaction (Berleen *et al.*, 1993). Where major reforms of medical services have been carried out there has been a strong focus on increasing patient choice. Hence, under the 'Stockholm Model' of healthcare developed since 1992, patients are able to choose GPs and hospitals. In hospital care, a DRG system has been introduced with the intention that money will follow patient choice.

The introduction of market mechanisms has not proved uncontroversial. There is particular concern that a tension has arisen between market-based systems and the traditional values on which Swedish public services were based (Garpenby, 1992; Haggroth, 1993). In the case of school vouchers there is concern that schools operating in areas with a large proportion of immigrant families will see an exodus of Swedish children (Huber and Stephens, 1993).

MANAGEMENT PROCESSES 2

Since the mid 1980s both local government and administrative agencies have been granted greater degrees of autonomy, with the result that managers have much greater control over matters such as personnel policy, internal organization and decision-making. At a central level the National Agency for Government Employees oversees the implementation of new personnel policies and negotiates with the main public sector unions. Within the local government sector bargaining over personnel issues also retains a centralized collective bargaining aspect, but individual counties and municipalities have taken on a far greater responsibility for all aspects of personnel policy in institutions such as schools, hospitals and prisons as a result of decentralization. Because of this, it is very difficult to present a generalized account of many key management processes in the Swedish public sector, since these vary between the numerous different agencies and municipalities. The following presents some of the general directions of change, supplemented by specific examples of particular practice where appropriate.

Recruitment/dismissal

Public sector recruitment is not centralized. Each ministry, agency and municipality is responsible for its own scheme of recruitment. The only exceptions are the politically appointed under-secretaries at the ministries and the senior executives in the agencies. Agencies can otherwise appoint their own personnel up to mid-executive level (MacDonald, 1992, p. 3). The comparatively low level of pay in the public sector has long been identified as causing problems of recruitment, particularly of expert and senior staff who tend to be lost to the private sector (Holmgren, 1986, p. 152; OECD, 1990a, p. 101). However, the recent shift to more flexible personnel policies has enabled public sector managers to make more discretionary pay awards to recruit and keep valued personnel, particularly at a senior level (OECD, 1990a; Wise, 1993).

Traditionally, all government employees in Sweden enjoyed considerable job security. Civil servants, other than political appointees, have enjoyed considerable security of tenure and were usually dismissed only in cases of professional misconduct or criminal offence (MacDonald, 1992, p. 4). More generally, up until the early 1980s those employed in the public sector had the security that the general growth of government made their jobs secure.

In times of considerable readjustment and change there is no longer such security of employment. Recognizing this, the Swedish government has introduced, after negotiation with the main public sector unions, a 'Job Security System' for administrative agencies. This aims to prevent unemployment resulting from the considerable structural changes in the public sector (OECD, 1992, p. 87). Similarly, redundancies occurring in particular sectors of local government have often been offset by attempts to transfer the employees concerned to other areas of local government activity (Haggroth, 1993, p. 104).

Promotion

There is no career management in central government ministries and agencies; civil servants are responsible for the development of their own careers (MacDonald, 1992, p. 21). All vacant posts are advertised and individual civil servants must apply for them. Since advertisement is mainly internal, competition is mainly with currently employed colleagues (Jones, 1990, p. 153). An appeals system is in place to investigate claims that applicants should have been short-listed or appointed to a particular post (MacDonald, 1992, p. 21). In the 1960s the number of pay scales and classes were reduced and there are no barriers to promotion from one grade in the civil service to another.

Pay

Pay levels have traditionally been set by a process of national negotiation, which has maintained a very high level of equalization. From 1965 onwards levels of pay in central government were determined by a highly centralized and rigid system of grades applied to all governmental authorities (Schager, 1993). At the local government level, salaries were set by a process of collective bargaining between the Swedish Association of Municipalities and the Federation of County Councils on one side and the various public sector trade unions on the other. The strength of these collective bargaining procedures reflects the extent of unionization: around 90 percent of employees belong to a trade union.

In the past twenty years the system of determining public sector pay has become much more decentralized. Initially this was prompted, in part, by the problem of losing quality staff to the private sector. Pay differentials across the public sector are minimal and public sector pay, particularly at senior levels, compares poorly with other countries and with the private sector in Sweden (OECD, 1990a).

A more flexible system of pay was initially introduced in 1989 after a period of ten years during which the centralized system was eroded. This new system is now in full operation (OECD, 1992, p. 87) and the extent to which pay bargaining has been decentralized should not be under-estimated (Schager, 1993; Wise, 1993). Collective bargaining agreements now create pay funds rather than stipulating pay increases. These funds are then available for distribution as pay increases in the whole of the sector to which they apply (Schager, 1993, p. 116). The distribution of funds is carried out by managers at the local organizational level, although there are agreed minimum increases for each employee (Wise, 1993, pp. 80–1).

One legacy of the earlier policy of pay equalization is that there has been some resistance to the introduction of performance-related pay. However, most public sector unions have seen potential for pay gains and have there-fore agreed to more flexible pay systems (OECD, 1992, p. 117; Wise, 1993, p. 81). As a result of the greater autonomy given to administrative agencies in the 1980s, there have thus been significant moves towards individualized, performance-related pay within the nationally agreed framework (Mac-Donald, 1992). Within local government, pay is also controlled much more at the local level, with managers at the municipal level increasingly able to influence levels of pay (Haggroth, 1993, p. 94). Some incentive-based schemes have been introduced and parts of the wage bill are now more commonly distributed according to performance (Haggroth, 1993, p. 95). The introduction of these new pay policies in the Swedish public sector has been justified by a concern to improve efficiency and productivity (Haggroth, 1993; Wise, 1993).

Unsurprisingly, it has been questioned whether there is any real link between flexible pay and public sector productivity. As Wise (1993) makes clear, the emerging individualized pay system is a rejection of the 'soli-daristic' wage policies of the 1960s and 1970s. While the stated justification for more decentralized pay systems apparently stems from considerations of efficiency and performance, Wise suggests that they are mainly used by managers to give greater flexibility in recruiting and retaining valued staff. Managers have not developed appropriate measures to link performance and pay, and tend to use subjective judgements to allocate rewards (Wise, 1993, p. 84). In many cases, levels of pay tend to 'cluster' as man-agers refrain from using their discretion in the absence of agreed mecha-nisms (Wise, 1993, p. 83). Hence, individualized pay tends to be tacked onto the existing management framework rather than transforming it (Wise, 1993, p. 84).

Performance management

Methods of performance measurement are generally underdeveloped in the Swedish public sector, and this has caused problems where such criteria are linked to pay. There is some use of questionnaires and assessment interviews, but the general pattern is the use of measurable outputs (Wise, 1993). These outputs may, however, have tenuous links with performance. For instance, the performance of doctors may be measured according to the number of hours worked or factory inspectors by the number of sites visited. In the case of the latter, there is evidence that inspectors have tended to visit more 'compliant' sites in order to artificially enhance their performance (Wise, 1993). Attempts to link individual performance and organizational outputs are seen as 'sporadic' (Wise, 1993, p. 84).

In local government there are significant variations in the ways in which performance is assessed. In healthcare, as part of a general trend towards quality assurance, there is a growing use of quality circles as a means of groups of staff assessing their own performance (Berleen *et al.*, 1993, pp. 19–21). The experience of decentralization of blue- and white-collar pay bargaining at the level of the municipalities suggests that performance-related pay systems have worked best among small groups of professional workers, such as architects. In areas such as social welfare, however, there is often little distinction made between the performance of individual carers. Given that the majority of carers are women, there is a concern that flexible pay systems will reverse the process of pay equalization between the sexes. There is also concern that while collective bargaining agreements set out the general criteria according to which performance-related pay should be awarded, this has not been made clear to employees.

Training

Like recruitment, training is not centralized and training needs are determined in ministries and agencies through development talks (MacDonald, 1992, p. 21). Before 1992, many training and development activities were organized by the National Institute for Civil Service Development (SIPU). However, in July 1992 this institute was closed down, leaving the main responsibility to the agencies themselves (OECD, 1992, p. 273).

The extent of post-entry training in the public sector has recently been criticized for being too low. For example, the shortage of suitably trained personnel in local government has recently led to an expansion of in-house training (Haggroth, 1993, p. 94). The greater priority given to training in local government over the last five years has seen the proportion of municipal employees who receive training rise from 30 percent in 1987 to 49 percent in 1992 (Swedish Association of Municipalities, 1994).

Part II: Managing Change

The context of change

Taken as a whole, the process of change and reform in the Swedish public sector that has taken place over the past 10–12 years represents a dramatic break from the traditional model of social democratic governance. The 'Swedish model' which had emerged during the course of the twentieth century was based on a consensual political system of public administration and public policy, albeit an overtly social democratic approach to government. Essentially, this model was characterized by a centrally managed and directed system of government based heavily on rule-management and legal norms as well as continuous public sector expansion enabled through the steady growth in GNP. The strength of this consensus approach was shown by the practice of the centre-right government of 1976–82, which continued to govern according to social democratic norms and increased public expenditure during their six years in office.

Arguably, recent reforms have been prompted by two key factors. First, the Social Democrats' loss of power for the first time in over forty years after the 1976 election demanded that critical attention was paid to the traditional model of public management. Secondly, recurrent problems in the Swedish economy from the late 1970s and in the 1980s and 1990s undermined the implicit 'growth assumption' on which management of the Swedish public sector had hitherto been founded. In particular, the budget deficit grew at an alarming rate, reaching 13 percent of GNP in 1982 (Premfors, 1991, p. 86).

On their return to power in 1982, the Social Democrats faced similar problems as were being experienced elsewhere – the difficulties of managing a large and apparently cumbersome administrative system, a growing budget deficit and, hence, concern over the size of the public sector. While in opposition, Olof Palme, the Social Democratic leader, had seen through the adoption of a 'two-pronged strategy' for reform. This consisted of a 'crisis programme' intended to prevent further growth in the public sector as a proportion of GDP together with a 'new public administration policy' which was to be implemented by the new Ministry of Public Administration (Premfors, 1991, p. 87).

From 1982, a programme of economic reform termed 'the third way' was embarked upon. The programme was seen as an alternative to both Keynesian orthodoxies and neo-liberalism (Ryner, 1993, p. 6). It consisted of economic measures designed to boost the economy, maintain full employment and eliminate the budget deficit. Alongside this recognition of the need for greater austerity, a package of reforms aimed at the 'Renewal' of the public sector, including extensive decentralization of activities, was introduced. It was suggested that in the 1970s the machinery of government had been seen to be unwieldy and cumbersome, and the identification of these problems with the Social Democratic Party was regarded as one of the reasons for their electoral defeat in 1976. The Social Democrats' programme of 'Public Sector Renewal' therefore indicated a shift away from more traditional public administration and towards new public management (Aspegren, 1987). Whereas public spending and state intervention were previously seen as 'solutions', they were now, for the first time, perceived as 'problems' (Premfors, 1991, p. 86).

Important aspects of the 'Renewal' programme were to foster greater democracy, enhance freedom of choice, increase efficiency and improve the quality of the service to the public. Initially these goals were pursed through a process of delegation and decentralization. Private sector definitions of efficiency and productivity, which are concerned mainly with quantitative output, were judged to be inappropriate to the public sector where qualitative outputs such as equity and universality should be central (MacDonald, 1992). Measures to strengthen the position of the client when dealing with public services and to speed up procedures were also at the centre of the reforms (through the Administrative Procedures Act of 1986).

A paper published by the IPPR in 1992 praised the Swedish 'Renewal' programme as an alternative to the New Right orthodoxy in public sector reform:

> *Unlike the British drive to improve efficiency, narrowly conceived in terms of value for money, the 'renewal' of the public sector in the 1980s in Sweden was based on a proper understanding that the public sector, given the nature of the services it provides and the fact that provision must be both universal and equitable, cannot be measured by the criteria which apply to the private sector.*
> *(Macdonald, 1992, p. 15)*

An important product of decentralization under the renewal programme of the 1980s was the greater freedom given to local government. In 1984 the so-called 'Free Municipalities Experiment' was introduced, allowing nine municipalities and three county councils greater freedom from state control and direction. Later a further twenty-nine municipalities and an additional county were added (Haggroth, 1993, p. 44). The overall aim of the project was 'to put municipalities and county councils in a better position to adapt their decisions and measures to local conditions and needs' (cabinet proposal, 1983, quoted in Montin, 1993).

Although the project was formally brought to an end by the 1991 Local Government Act, amid mixed evaluations of success, experimentation in local government is still encouraged. The 1991 Act drew on the experiences of the experiment and granted municipalities more freedom in the design of committee structures and in budgeting. As a result, important changes in local government management and organization are currently taking place without central direction. Instead, the process of change in Swedish local government is that new ideas are applied within individual munici-palities or promoted by the Swedish Association of Municipalities and are then spread through the local government network. This extensive process of decentralization has meant that Swedish central government has had much less of a role in public sector reform than central government elsewhere.

However, decentralization has been interpreted by some observers as a tactical move designed to make local governments appear responsible for expenditure cuts. Wise (1993) sees decentralization as a form of crisis man-agement, while Garpenby (1992) argues that decentralization resulted from divisions in the Social Democratic party created by debates over internal markets and public sector competition. Rather than making radi-cal changes and cuts at the central level, the Social Democrats attempted to shift the need to make difficult decisions to the level of local government (Garpenby, 1992, p. 21).

Economic context

Sweden's resistance to the generally prescribed neo-liberal formula for pub-lic sector reform in the 1980s was echoed in its divergent approach to econ-omic policy. Unemployment was held down in Sweden, while it continued to rise to alarming rates everywhere else in the capitalist world, and the public sector deficit was apparently eliminated without unduly harsh cut-backs. From 1982 onwards, reductions in the budget deficit were achieved, and from 1987 the budget moved into surplus and a stabilization, rather than reduction, of public spending levels was made possible by increased tax revenues (Ryner, 1993, p. 8).

As a result of these reforms, Sweden in the 1980s seemed to buck the ubiquitous trend towards neo-liberalism. The Social Democrats, having re-turned to power in 1982, were re-elected in 1985 and 1988. Sweden in the 1980s thus became 'an international answer to the "new pessimism" con-cerning the future viability of the welfare state' (Olsson, 1990, p. 34). Some-how it seemed that political commitment to the Swedish welfare state was weathering the simultaneous storms of neo-liberalism and global recession, a point aptly advanced by Ryner (1993, p. 9): 'In one very important sense the Swedish Social Democrats proved the new right wrong: it was possible to restore macro-economic balance without giving up on a high social commitment to the welfare state.'

However, in the 1990s any reasons for cautious social democratic optimism seemed to evaporate, due principally to the re-emergence of economic difficulties. While budget surpluses had been recorded for four consecutive financial years (OECD, 1990b, p. 28), the 1990 Budget Bill presented in January of that year indicated that the balance was expected to move back towards a deficit in the 1990/91 financial year (OECD, 1990b, p. 118). The predicted budget deficit for 1994 was 13.6 percent of GDP (*Economist*, January 1993).

The value of GDP, which had grown at a rate of more than 2 percent annually from 1983 to 1989 (OECD, 1990b, p. 13), fell by almost 2 percent in 1991 (*Economist*, 1993, p. 54). Unemployment, which had been held below 2 percent throughout the 1980s, broke the symbolic 2 percent barrier, rose to 2.7 percent in 1991 (Statistics Sweden, 1993) and reached 9 percent in October 1993 (*Economist*, October 1993, p. 54). Finally, inflation rose to 10 percent in 1991, the highest anywhere in the developed world (Kelman, 1991).

These economic difficulties represent the key challenge to the Swedish public sector today. The growing budget deficit raises particular problems since, according to the 1993 Finance Bill, there is a significant structural element to this deficit.

Constitutional arrangements

Swedish constitutional arrangements provide an important context for public sector reform, as the principles of politico-administrative relationships established by the 1809 Constitution, and reiterated by its revision in 1969, are still in place today. There is thus a tension between a framework for public administration established originally in the early nineteenth century, which was intended to limit the power of the executive over the bureaucracy, and the type of administrative framework required to deliver a broad range of often complex services in a contemporary capitalist society (Pierre, 1993a, pp. 389–90). In particular, the division of policy-making and implementation in the Swedish system between the ministries and agencies 'is not conducive to co-ordinated and efficient – let alone politically accountable – government' (Pierre, 1993a, p. 390).

There is a conflict between the *Rechtsstaat* ideal on which the Swedish constitution is based and the reality of having to provide extensive public services, both of which are sources of legitimacy for the Swedish state (Pierre, 1993a, p. 388). Pierre argues that this conflict has led to 'goals being related to efficiency taking precedence over strictly legalistic goals' (Pierre, 1993a, p. 398). As a result there has been a need to make institutional changes in an attempt to re-establish legitimacy. This has principally been achieved through extensive decentralization and other attempts to make public services more accessible to the Swedish public (Pierre, 1993a, p. 389).

Since the administrative agencies are, in an international context, exceptionally autonomous (Pierre, 1993a, p. 390), they also represent a key problem for the direction of public sector reform. This is enhanced by the fact that agencies also have considerable resources, financial and human, available to them, particularly compared to the ministries, thus making them, in many cases, more powerful institutions than the ministries which are supposed to be overseeing them. The relative autonomy of the agencies is thus based partly on constitutional principle and on resource-based powers. However, the constitutional position is of key importance in public sector reform as it is virtually impossible for the ministries to direct agencies as they may wish to do so. This problem is amply illustrated in the case of the reform of the Swedish budget cycle.

Ideology

Arguably, public sector reform in Sweden has been far less ideologically driven than elsewhere and management reform is seen as an organizational rather than ideological issue. It could be argued that this has resulted from a culture of limited political interference in matters of management in the public sector. The relationship between politicians and managers has historically been characterized by trust and there is no perception of an innate conflict of interests as exists in many other countries. Reform has been carried out via a process of consultation and experimentation, with direct political intervention in public sector management being seen as unnecessary and undesirable.

It would, however, be naïve to suggest that there is no ideological dimension to public sector reform in Sweden, particularly following three years of centre-right government. In recent years the private sector has had an important influence on management practices, and this trend has recently been heightened with private sector managers displaying a growing interest in public sector management. Such approaches to management, with a stress on choice, competition and efficiency, are clearly underpinned by a management philosophy at odds with traditional approaches to public administration in Sweden.

In addition, although many reform policies have been supported by all the major parties, this support often rests on different ideological bases. For instance, decentralization policies were supported by the Social Democrats as a means of bringing about new forms of relationship between local citizens and politicians, while Conservatives saw decentralization as a means of dismantling the social democratic state and creating market relationships in service provision (Premfors, 1991, p. 92).

Consensus/majority on the direction of change

The reform programme of the Conservative–Liberal government was, in many ways, a logical extension of these earlier reforms. Concerns about economy, efficiency and effectiveness in the public sector were central to the Conservative–Liberal government's programme from 1991 to 1994. However, even before 1991, the Social Democrats' 'Renewal' programme had come to accept privatization and market definitions of efficiency.

During the early 1990s enhanced ideological conflict about the new directions in public sector management did emerge in key areas of public sector reform such as healthcare and care for the elderly. The populist New Democracy Party combined with the Social Democrats to defeat a government bill intended to liberalize healthcare by introducing further possibilities for private healthcare and patient choice (McIvor, 1994). Unsurprisingly, political disagreement is strongest where market-based reform threatens the principles on which Swedish public policy has traditionally been based, i.e. equality and universality.

None the less, there is a clear party political consensus regarding the need to curtail public expenditure which is reflected in the continuity of the approach to the reform of the budget process (see below). More generally, the shift from the Social Democrats' original reform programme in the 1980s towards one more recognizably neo-liberal in orientation in the 1990s, shows how, in comparative terms, there has been relatively little political controversy over changes in the public sector. Towards the end of the 1980s the Social Democrats' concern began to centre more on 'financial efficiency' as available resources continued to shrink.

There also appears to be a growing consensus in the Swedish population of the need for public sector reform and, in particular, to reduce public sector expenditure. Opinion polls carried out between 1982 and 1991 show that the percentage opposed to cuts in the public sector fell from 45 percent in 1982 to 23 percent in 1991, while those wanting to see a definite reduction in the size of the public sector rose from 38 to 50 percent in the same time period (Pierre, 1993a, p. 394).

Tradition

Traditionally, it can be said that public sector managers in Sweden have enjoyed a unique degree of autonomy with limited political interference and that this is particularly true of the administrative agencies. This autonomy has been made possible by the mutually reinforcing culture of trust, the transparent nature of the Swedish public sector and the highly developed appeals system through which citizens are protected from cases of maladministration and misjustice.

The authority and accountability of civil servants have historically been defined via a system of administrative law. However, recent reforms have seen a shift away from more legalistic conceptions of civil service towards more managerial definitions of autonomy and authority.

The importance of freedom of information, a long-standing principle in Sweden, is also highly significant. All governmental documents are considered official and available for public consultation (except in cases where protection of individual liberty or the interests of the state are deemed to override this principle). In addition, the Freedom of the Press Act means that the public sector is under close scrutiny from the media. As a result, the Swedish administrative system is based on a culture of openness and trust.

Cases of maladministration are investigated by the institution of the ombudsman, a system which has been adopted by a number of European countries. There are actually four ombudsmen who specialize in different spheres of activity and investigate cases brought to them by individual citizens or which appear in the media.

Public sector reform is not, therefore, guided by deep ideological or partisan motives. There has been a strong consensus on the need for reform and limited political controversy regarding the changes adopted. One important influence comes from the private sector which has taken an increasing interest in public sector management in recent years. Ideas have also been adopted from new practices in public management in Britain and the United States but without the ideological justification and conflict which has tended to accompany these reforms in the Anglo-Saxon countries.

REFORM OF THE BUDGET PROCESS

Changes to the budget process in Sweden since 1989 serve to illustrate how change in the public sector has been based on a broad consensus on the need for reform. Budget reform has been seen by all political parties as the centrepiece of public sector reform, illustrated by the fact that the Ministry of Finance took over the responsibility for public sector reform in 1991. Budget reforms are intended to encourage and enable long-term planning by moving away from incrementalist techniques and by replacing rule-based control systems with a stress on results and outcomes (see figure 2.1 for details of the process). Accordingly, the new Swedish budget cycle is one of several national budgetary reforms to be singled out for praise by Osborne and Gaebler (1992, p. 165) principally for its focus on longer-term planning through result-orientation and mission-driven budgetary control.

The reform of the Swedish budget cycle is an ongoing process of change and adjustment. The new budgetary process was tested on about twenty agencies between 1985 and 1988 and, despite concerns about its initial success, was introduced as a full reform in the Supplementary Finance Bill of

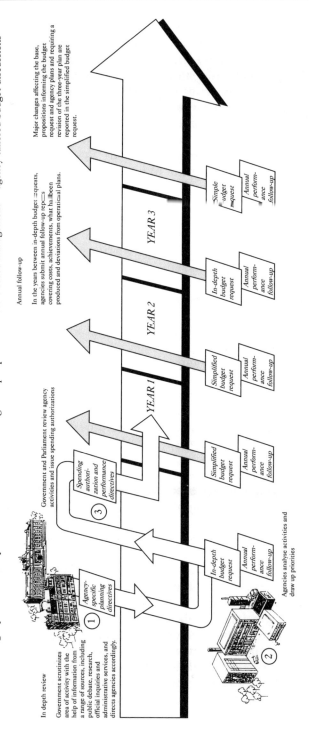

The budget process and how it works

The new budget process = in depth review of all activities +long-term perspective + result-based management – agency-tailored budget discussions

In depth review

Government scrutinizes area of activity with the help of information from a range of sources, including public debate, research, official inquiries and administrative services, and directs agencies accordingly.

Government and Parliament review agency activities and issue spending authorizations

Annual follow-up

In the years between in-depth budget requests, agencies submit annual follow-up reports covering costs, achievements, what has been produced and deviations from operational plans.

Major changes affecting the base, propositions informing the budget request and agency plans and requiring a revision of the three-year plan are reported in the simplified budget request.

① Agency-specific planning directives

② Agencies analyse activities and draw up priorities

③ Spending authorization and performance directives

In-depth budget request / Annual performance follow-up

Simplified budget request / Annual performance follow-up

YEAR 1

Simplified budget request / Annual performance follow-up

YEAR 2

In-depth budget request / Annual performance follow-up

YEAR 3

Simple budget request / Annual performance follow-up

Figure 2.1

1988 (Brunsson, 1993, p. 2). The need to introduce the new budget process was established to be a long-term concern and it was suggested that it might not apply to all government activity until 1996 (Brunsson, 1993, p. 2). The Ministry of Finance currently suggests that the full system may not be in place until 2005–2010, and Brunsson (1993, p. 14) proposes that the conversion to new methods and new ways of working may take ten years alone. A recent Ministry of Finance publication makes it clear from the outset that this long-term introduction of the system was always the intention, stating that the 1988 Supplementary Finance Bill made 'the matter one of successive changes and there was no question of imposing any given solution at that time . . . it was a question of initiating a process in a given direction' (Ministry of Finance, 1993c, p. 1).

As a result of this long-term approach, it is important to understand the guiding rationale for the new budget cycle as well as its features which are continuously being reviewed and amended as the new system is introduced. That the basic principles on which the reform was initially based continue to guide the process is evidence of the consensus which has directed this part of public sector reform. However, there has been considerable discussion about how the system should be designed to achieve the desired goals, and adjustments are continuously made in an attempt to correct the established failures within the system.

The rationale for the new budget cycle has always been to move away from an incrementalist annual budget process in order to take a longer-term view of the need to control public sector expenditure and enable a more effective management of resources. In addition, upon its introduction it was argued that, in contrast to incremental procedures, the new budget cycle would enable changes to be made in public expenditure priorities on a regular basis (Ministry of Finance, 1993, p. 1).

Although concerned with cost control and reduction, the change to the new budget cycle has not been based on direct central control over agencies. Rather than instigating new input controls, budget reform has centred on result-based management and scrutiny of agency outputs. Moreover, the budget reforms have been introduced alongside legislation such as the Public Administration Act and the Civil Service Ordinance, which have given agencies much greater freedom to determine their internal structure and organization and to appoint staff. In addition, agencies are now given block grants rather than specific grants which offer much greater freedom to determine internal spending priorities. As a result, political control over agencies has actually been reduced (Pierre, 1993b, p. 14).

The new budget process was initially based on a move to a three-year budget cycle, and to understand the nature of the new process it is useful to summarize its main features as well as briefly describe the timetable by which it was implemented. When first introduced in June 1989 the agencies were divided into three groups with each group working on a separate cycle. Cycle 1 was established to run from 1991/2 to 1993/4, cycle 2 from 1992/3 to 1994/5 and cycle 3 from 1993/4 to 1995/6. At this time (June 1989) two years before the three-year cycle was due to start, agencies from cycle 1 were given their specific planning objectives by the government. These directives consist of basic planning guidelines as well as proposed resources, expected outcomes, and requests for analysis and evaluation.

During the following spring, these agencies submitted a special report to the government providing a detailed response to the planning directives and indicating its overall policy decisions. In September 1990 this was followed by an in-depth budget request which provided an analysis of activities and achievements in the past five years, a full account of the agencies' proposed goals and activities (including a detailed budget-request for the first year), a resource budget for the next three years and proposed measures for result-based management. Directly afterwards the government reviewed agency activities and allocated spending authorizations in time for the 1991 Budget Bill.

It is at this point that the three-year cycle begins. The agencies are given their spending authorizations and performance directives and are then expected to perform their agreed activities and to achieve the defined objectives. Obviously, this process requires a clear definition and demarcation of roles and responsibilities. Under the new budget and management processes, the government is seen as 'the contractor' while agencies become 'providers'. As providers of government orders, the agencies take on executive responsibility, while the government has policy responsibility. Agencies are given considerable freedom to determine how to achieve the required objectives, but they must show each year how well they have performed their particular tasks. In the two years between in-depth budget requests, agencies submit an annual report, which details their performance over the past twelve months, as well as a simplified budget request for the next twelve months. These annual reports, the first set of which were submitted in autumn 1992, are evaluated by the National Audit Bureau (RRV). At the end of the planning period, agencies are expected to offer a full evaluation of the results of their activities.

Scrutiny of the first set of annual reports and reviews of the operation of the new budget cycle by the Ministry of Finance have pointed to several strengths and weaknesses in the system. The 1992 Finance Bill indicated that positive effects of the reforms included the development of a results-oriented culture in a number of agencies, and the involvement of the entire organization in a number of agencies when preparing in-depth budget-requests and future plans (Ministry of Finance, 1993b, p. 2). In addition, it has also been noted that the annual reports supplied in 1992 showed a significant improvement in providing the government with information on the results of agency activities (Ministry of Finance, 1993b, p. 2). The RRV has noted that the provision of such information has greatly aided the government's budget-planning process (Ministry of Finance, 1993b, p. 6). The RRV has also praised the way in which agencies have generally responded to specific government directives when providing information in their annual reports (Ministry of Finance, 1993b, p. 6).

However, it has also been found that in the case of some agencies the information provided has not been of high enough quality to enable decisions about the long-term direction of these agencies' activities (Ministry of Finance, 1993b, p. 4). In particular, there is a tendency for agencies to describe their activities rather than analyze their impacts. A study of a sample of in-depth budget requests by the Agency for Administrative Development has pointed to three further problems. First, agencies have not adequately related the declared results of their activities to the resources allocated to them. Secondly, much of the information submitted lacks relevance to the government's decision-making process. Thirdly, the activities of agencies are not broken down into areas of activity suitable for measuring results (Ministry of Finance, 1993b, p. 5). This means that information on productivity and unit costs is especially difficult to obtain (Ministry of Finance, 1993b, p. 6). In short, making the shift from input control to results-based management has proved difficult.

As a result, a number of changes to the budget process and the system of management by results have been proposed. The RRV has recommended clearer government guidelines for management by results, improved internal control of agencies and the development of follow-up systems within agencies. In addition, the RRV and the Agency for Administrative Development have been working on developing new methods for the analysis of public sector performance (Ministry of Finance, 1993b, p. 7). A new budget ordinance issued in the summer of 1993 should serve to tackle a number of the observed problems. In particular, the ordinance is intended to clarify the conditions of management by objectives and results, help enhance the role and importance of agencies' annual reports in the budget process with a stress on a more precise definition of results, and provide a greater focus on result analysis in the in-depth budget requests which are now to be submitted earlier (April rather than September) in the planning process (Ministry of Finance, 1993b, p. 8; Ministry of Finance, 1993c). It is also clear that in order for high standards to be achieved across the agencies, sanctions and incentives may have to be built into the system. Currently there are no such systems and so there are no established rules about how the information gathered from the agencies is to be used. The Ministry of Finance is currently exploring the possibility of using mechanisms which will provide some link between agency results and resource allocations.

A key change made in 1993 was to vary the length of the budget cycle. Despite the initial use of a three-year cycle, it was always the intention that budget dialog between the government and administrative agencies would be improved with a view to tailoring budgets to particular agencies. Under the centre-right coalition, budget reform was refined through a policy of allowing individual agencies to extend their budget cycle on an annual basis. Hence, agencies operating in a fluid and changing environment operate according to a one-year cycle, while those in a more stable policy environment have longer budget cycles of up to six years (Pierre, 1993b, p. 14).

However, there are further problems with the new budget process which will be more difficult to tackle. First, old ways of working remain deeply entrenched in several agencies but also at the parliamentary level. In sectors such as culture, arts and justice, where performance is particularly difficult to measure, very little progress has been made. There is also evidence to suggest that the behaviour of politicians has not changed and that there is little discussion of agency performance in parliament (Brunsson, 1993) Although this may be, in part, the result of politicians lacking suitable information, it none the less appears that 'the political leaders, and the members of parliament especially, do not seem to have been particularly concerned with the reform at all' (Brunsson, 1993, p. 16).

Second, the budgetary process is still guided by political and economic considerations and not by the rational objectivity of results-based management. Brunsson stresses this politicized, as opposed to rational, nature of the budget process which 'in practice could be carried out as the political leaders found best. The information provided by the agencies could be taken into account, discarded, or ignored' (Brunsson, 1993, p. 17). The tendency towards political intervention is heightened by the recurrent problem of the national budget deficit. Although most agencies now work on a three-year cycle, parliament must still make annual budget decisions and frequently disrupts agency plans through the need to make further cuts in periods of crisis. Patently, such interventions do not enable the desired long-term perspective to develop.

ACKNOWLEDGEMENTS

Olov Olson, Jon Pierre (Department of Political Science, University of Gothenberg), Ulf Bengtsson (Ministry of Finance), Karin Brunsson (Parliamentary Auditors), Ernst Jonsson (Institute for Local Government Economics, University of Stockholm), Maria Pernebring (Association of Swedish Municipalities), Soren Haggroth (Ministry of Public Administration), Kaj Essinger (Chief Executive, Stockholm County Public Health and Medical Services).

REFERENCES

Aspegren, L. (1987) Accountability in the Swedish public service. In Kakabadse, A.P., Brovetto, P.R. and Holzer, R. (eds), *Management Development and the Public Sector: A European Perspective*, Avebury.

Berg, S. *et al.* (1993) Local variations in old age care, *Health Policy*, vol. 24, pp. 175–86.

Berleen, G., Rehnberg, C. and Wennstrom, G. (1993) *The Reform of Health Care in Sweden*, SPRI, Stockholm.

Brunsson, K. (1993) Puzzle pictures: Swedish budgetary processes in principle and practice, unpublished manuscript.

Economist (1993) Farewell welfare, 23 October, pp. 51–4.

Fernow, N. (1992) Swedish elderly care in transition, *Current Sweden*, no. 392.

Garpenby, P. (1992) The transformation of the Swedish health care system, or the hasty rejection of the rational planning model, *Journal of European Social Policy*, vol. 2, pp. 17–31.

Haggroth, S. (1993) From corporation to political enterprise: trends in Swedish local government, Ministry of Public Administration, Stockholm.

Hedin, B. (1993) *Growing Old in Sweden*, Swedish Institute, Stockholm.

Holmgren, K. (1986) Sweden In Rowat, D.C. (ed.), *Public Administration in Developed Democracies: A Comparative Study*, Marcel Dekker, New York.

Huber, E. and Stephens, J.D. (1993) The Swedish welfare state at the crossroads, *Current Sweden*, no. 394.

Huntford, R. (1971) *The New Totalitarians*, Allen Lane, London.

International Monetary Fund (1991) *Government Finance Statistics Yearbook*, IMF.

Jacobsson, B. (1992) The public administration system of Sweden, unpublished manuscript, Stockholm School of Economics.

Jones, B.M. (1990) Sweden. In Kingdom, J.E. (ed.), *The Civil Service in Liberal Democracies*, Routledge, London.

Jonsson, S. (1982) *A City Administration Facing Stagnation: Political Organisation and Action in Gothenburg*, Swedish Council for Building Research, Stockholm.

Kelman, S. (1991) Swedish model on a diet, *Guardian*, 7 August.

MacDonald, O. (1992) *Swedish Models: The Swedish Model of Central Government*, Institute for Public Policy Research, London.

McIvor, G. (1994) Swedes revolt over health care, *Guardian*, 31 March.

Ministry of Finance (1993a) *Economic Policy Statement by the Swedish Government (Appendix 1 to 1993 Finance Bill)*, Ministry of Finance, Stockholm.

Ministry of Finance (1993b) *Management of Government Administration and Financial Control for State Agencies*, Ministry of Finance (Budget Department), Stockholm.

Ministry of Finance (1993c) *Ordinance Concerning the Annual Reports and Requests for Funds of State Agencies*, Ministry of Finance (Budget Department), Stockholm.

Montin, S. (1993) *Swedish Local Government in Transition: A Matter of Rationality and Legitimacy*, University of Orebro.

OECD (1990a) *Public Management Developments: Survey*, OECD, Paris.

OECD (1990b) *Economic Surveys: Sweden*, OECD, Paris.

OECD (1992) *Public Management Developments: Update*, OECD, Paris.

OECD (1993) *Public Management: Country Profiles*, OECD, Paris.

Olsson, S.E. (1990) *Social Policy and Welfare State in Sweden*, Arkiv, Lund.

Osborne, D. and Gaebler, T. (1992) *Reinventing Government*, Addison-Wesley, Reading, Mass.

Pierre, J. (1993a) Legitimacy, institutional change and the politics of public administration in Sweden, *International Political Science Review*, vol. 14(4), pp. 387–401.

Pierre, J. (1993b) Governing the welfare state: public administration, the state and society in Sweden, unpublished manuscript.

Pontusson, J. (1989) The triumph of pragmatism: nationalisation and privatisation in Sweden. In Wright, V. and Vickers, J. (eds), *Privatisation in Western Europe*, London.

Premfors, R. (1991) The 'Swedish Model' and public sector reform, *West European Politics*, vol. 14(1), pp. 83–95.

Riberdahl, K. (1992) *The New Swedish Local Government Act and its Impact on Swedish Local Authorities*, Swedish Association of Municipalities, Stockholm.

Ryner, J. M. (1993) *The Economic 'Success' and the Political 'Failure' of Swedish Social Democracy in the 1980s*, Swedish Centre for Working Life, Stockholm.

Saltman, R.B. and Von Otter, C. (1992) *Planned Markets and Public Competition: Strategic Reform in Northern European Health Care Systems*, Open University Press, Buckingham.

Schager, N.H. (1993) An overview and evaluation of flexible pay policies in the Swedish public sector, in *Pay Flexibility in the Public Sector*, OECD, Paris.

Sorensen, R.J. (1993) The efficiency of public service provision: assessing six reform strategies, in Eliassen, K.A. and Kooiman, J. (eds) *Managing Public Organisation: Lessons from the Contemporary European Experience*, Sage, London.

Statistics Sweden (1993) *Sweden in Figures*, Statistics Sweden, Stockholm.

Swedish Association of Municipalities (1994) *Kompetens och Uthildningsniva bland Kommunalt Anstallda*, Swedish Association of Municipalities, Stockholm.

Swedish Institute (1991) *Fact Sheets on Sweden*, The Swedish Institute, Stockholm.

Weyler, K. (1993) Big changes in Swedish education, *Current Sweden*, no. 399.

Wise, C. and Amna, E. (1992) Reform in Swedish local government, *Current Sweden*, no. 393.

Wise, L.R. (1993) Whither solidarity? Transitions in Swedish public sector pay policy, *British Journal of Industrial Relations*, vol. 31(1), pp. 75–96.

3

The United Kingdom

Norman Flynn

CONSTITUTION

The United Kingdom is a constitutional monarchy. The head of government is the prime minister who is the leader of the party with a majority of seats in the House of Commons. There is no written constitution in the United Kingdom, rather a set of laws and conventions which define the relations between government and citizens. Sovereignty lies with the Crown and Parliament, the House of Commons and the House of Lords. Parliament can change any laws and does not have to rely on precedent. There is no supreme council or other body overseeing changes in the constitution.

The House of Lords, which consists of hereditary and appointed members, has certain legal powers to delay legislation. Deliberation on proposed laws often results in their amendment. It is also the highest court for civil and legal matters.

The House of Commons is elected on a single-member constituency basis, using a 'first past the post' voting system. Normally the majority party takes all the government posts and ministries.

Between 1945 and 1979 there were six Conservative and six Labour administrations. Since 1979 there have been only Conservative governments (1979, 1983, 1987, 1992). Because of this single-party rule over a long period it has been possible for the government to implement a series of reforms.

STRUCTURE OF THE PUBLIC SECTOR

The government and Civil Service

The government is composed of the Cabinet of departmental ministers or secretaries of state, non-departmental ministers, ministers of state and junior ministers. All ministers are appointed by the prime minister, which gives that post a great deal of power.

The government is organized into the following departments:

Defence
Foreign and Commonwealth Office
Agriculture, Fisheries and Food

Trade and Industry
Energy
Transport
Environment
Home Office
Lord Chancellors' Department and other legal departments
Education and Employment
National Heritage
Health
Social Security
Departments for Wales, Scotland and Northern Ireland
Cabinet Office
Chancellor of the Exchequer's departments (covering tax collection)

The Civil Service is divided into departments and executive agencies which have been established since 1988. The report[1] on which these changes were based concluded that management of service delivery would be improved if policy formulation was separated from management. Agencies were to be given explicit performance targets and a defined framework of managerial discretion in which to operate.

About 60 percent of civil servants work in executive agencies which deliver services on behalf of their parent department. There are about 100 such agencies, which range in size from the Social Security Benefits Agency, with over 60,000 staff, to a conference centre with thirty staff. Customs and Excise (which collects customs duties and Value Added Tax and controls the cross-border flow of goods) and the Inland Revenue (which collects taxes) are organized on similar lines.

Each agency has a chief executive who is responsible to the relevant minister for the performance of the agency. However, since the chief executives are accounting officers they can be called to account by the Public Accounts Committee of Parliament and by departmental Select Committees of Members of Parliament. In principle, ministers are accountable for matters of policy and the chief executives are accountable for operational performance. In practice the distinction may become blurred, although accountability for the published performance targets is very clear.

Each agency is set targets by its minister, normally about service quality, financial performance, efficiency and volume of activity. These targets are public and each year each agency reports on their achievement.

Most chief executives are recruited by open competition, rather than only from within the ranks of the Civil Service. The principle is that the best people should be recruited to these positions and that they should be allowed to manage the agencies in the best way possible. As we shall see, there is continuing tension over the question of how much freedom to manage actually exists. There is a process of delegating the main instruments of management, such as the pay systems, to the agencies and to remove them from direct governmental control. By April 1994 over half of all civil servants were covered by local agreements on pay and pay-related conditions of service. By July 1994 all departments and agencies took responsibility for the pay of their 'industrial' staff.

Local authorities

Local authorities are responsible for the delivery of a dwindling number of services, including most school education, social care, some public protection, housing benefits, some public housing, public libraries, roads and transport, refuse collection and street cleansing, and land-use planning.

These services are run by directly elected councillors in county councils and district councils in England, thirty-six metropolitan district councils in the major cities in England, thirty-six London boroughs and the Corporation of the City of London. In Scotland and Wales there are (since 1995) unitary, multipurpose authorities. Northern Ireland has twenty-six district councils but specialist boards run most of the services provided by local authorities in Great Britain. Local government employs about 2 million people in the United Kingdom and accounts for about one-quarter of public expenditure. At the time of writing the structure of local authorities outside the major cities is being reorganized.

Local government is the only representative tier of government, apart from the national level. There are no provincial or regional levels of representation. Local government has no constitutional protection. All its powers derive from Parliament and there are no general competence laws which allow local government to do things: all powers are derived from specific statutes. In that sense the United Kingdom is a unitary state. No governments, other than the national government, have the power to pass laws.

Local government has been subjected to repeated reforms since the end of the Second World War. Central government has tried to contain local authority spending and to influence its activities. Less than 15 percent of local authority spending is financed by local taxation and the level of local tax is controlled by the central government. There has been a trend towards either the removal of powers and functions from local authorities or the development of elaborate control mechanisms through which central departments determine how services are managed. Examples of the removal of functions include the transfer of control of polytechnics and colleges of further education from local authorities to appointed boards, and the deregulation and privatization of public transport. Examples of central control include the legislation which forces local authorities to organize competitions for the delivery of services with the private sector, and the compulsory sale of municipal houses to their tenants.

Health

The National Health Service (NHS) was established in 1948 to provide healthcare free at the point of delivery. Family doctors ('general practitioners') were independent operators, contracting with the NHS for fees, while other medical practitioners were salaried employees of the service. The management structure of the NHS has changed many times during its history. In the past decade there have been attempts to impose managerial and cost control on the organization and to reduce the power and influence of the medical professionals, especially doctors.

The last reforms were introduced in 1991 and are based on central management by the NHS Executive in a headquarters and eight regional offices.[2] Below the NHS Executive are health authorities whose task is to ensure that healthcare is provided for the population of their areas. The chairs of these authorities are selected by the secretary of state for health. There are no elections to the health authorities. Budgets are allocated to health authorities for them to purchase health promotion and treatment from a variety of providers, including units directly managed by the health authorities, NHS trusts, which are semi-autonomous units providing acute, community and mental health services, and private sector providers. At the same time, general practitioners with relatively large practices also have budgets with which to purchase treatment for their patients.

Hence, the process of management is a combination of hierarchy and market: the secretary of state and the Department of Health make overall policy, while the service as a whole is managed hierarchically from the NHS Executive through the regional offices and health authorities, whose members are directly or indirectly appointed by the secretary of state and through general practitioners. Below that level, service provision is organized as a market: providers compete with each other for contracts with the health authorities and the general practitioners. Competition is based on price and quality. Unlike the Swedish healthcare system, however, patients do not have the right to choose from whom to obtain their treatment: while they have a choice of general practitioner (subject to capacity constraints) they can only get access to acute care by being referred to a hospital or clinic by their general practitioner.

THE STRATEGIC FRAMEWORK[3]

NHS Executive Headquarters develops a strategic framework including resources, human resources, performance management, information, market development and regulation, communications, and research and development. Health authorities carry out needs assessment and develop local health strategies within the context of the national strategic framework. This strategy work is carried out within the overall targets for the 'Health of the Nation' set by the secretary of state and the Department of Health. These targets include matters such as reducing morbidity from a variety of ailments, and improving health status, including mental and sexual health.

HUMAN RESOURCES

Employers, including trusts, are increasingly responsible for determining their employees' pay. Workforce planning starts with an NHS Executive policy framework, while regional offices commission education and training programmes for non-clinical staff. All education and development for this group of staff is also based on an internal market. For postgraduate medical and dental training, the NHS Executive Headquarters sets a framework within which postgraduate deans commission training.

PUBLIC HEALTH

Preventative public health programmes, including screening, control of communicable diseases and cancer registries, are functions of the health authorities. Regional Offices of the Executive provide support for these activities and for research and development, while NHS Executive Headquarters has responsibility for health outcomes assessment and clinical effectiveness.

Day-to-day management of the NHS consists of the relationship between the health authorities and general practitioners as purchasers of health treatments from their providers, within a hierarchical policy and management framework.

NON-DEPARTMENTAL PUBLIC BODIES

There is a category of organization which is not directly managed as a part of a ministry but carries out public service functions. These bodies are funded by public money, often in the form of a 'grant in aid', and have boards of management appointed by the government.

Non-elected quangos

There has been a growth in non-elected bodies which govern major parts of the public sector. All schools have boards of governors whose members are formally appointed, rather than elected. Health trusts are also appointed. Almost all social housing in the United Kingdom is now provided by housing associations, which are not elected; they are supervised, and to some extent funded, by the Housing Corporation, itself an appointed body.

Unlike other European countries, therefore, the structure of the public sector is highly centralized. Local government is largely controlled by

Table 3.1. Privatization proceeds, 1979–1995, £million

1979/81	1981/82	1982/83	1983/84	1984/85	1985/86	1986/87	1987/88	1988/89	1989/90	1990/91	1991/92	1993/94	1994/95
578	493	455	1139	2050	2706	4458	5140	7069	4225	5347	79	5460	6300

Source: Public Expenditure: Statistical Supplement to the Financial Statement and Budget Report 1995–96, Cmnd. 2821, HM Treasury, London, February 1995.

central government, health is controlled by boards appointed by the government and other functions are fulfilled by bodies subject to direct control by the government.

Nationalized industries

The major nationalized industries have been privatized and others are in the process of being prepared for privatization. In 1979 nationalized industries accounted for 11 percent of GDP and this proportion fell to 2.3 percent by the end of 1993. The remaining nationalized industries are candidates for privatization. The main remaining industries are the nuclear power industry (British Nuclear Fuels Ltd, Nuclear Electric and Scottish Nuclear), London Transport, British Rail and Railtrack, the Post Office, the Civil Aviation Authority and the British Waterways Board.

Privatization has reduced the government's commitment to provide subsidies for these industries and has produced considerable revenues for the government (see Table 3.1).

The implications of these structural arrangements for management

The high proportion of services which are under direct or indirect central government control means that there cannot be detailed supervision arrangements for all services. Most management is done at arm's length, through target setting and financial control.

The main control mechanism is financial performance in a series of markets or market-style mechanisms. In the health sector, there is competition among service providers for the contracts let by the purchasing authorities and the family doctors. The focus of managers in the provider units is therefore on successful competitive behaviour.

The lack of local political accountability gives a relatively high degree of discretion to managers, within the frameworks set out by central government. Even in local government, where there are local elected members, managers have a relatively high degree of discretion, especially in those areas which are subject to centrally imposed rules about competitive tendering.

The growth of managerial discretion has led to the development of what some people have described as 'managerialism'[4] or 'new public management'.[5] While there is not an identifiable, universal set of managerial behaviours, we can see some common themes across the public sector in the United Kingdom, in relation to competition, personnel management, pay systems and cost reduction.

MANAGEMENT PROCESSES

Budgeting

The budget process at central government level is an input-based, top-down, negotiated approach. The Treasury sets a 'control total' for public expenditure which includes local authority spending but excludes privatization proceeds, debt interest, and social security and unemployment benefits for people of working age (because these amounts are subject to cyclical fluctuations). The total is set for one year, with a projection for a further two years. The total is then divided among the departments in a series of negotiations.

Once the expenditure has been allocated, each department produces a budget accompanied by performance indicators and targets for the coming year. These indicators are usually output measures by which the department expects to be judged. For central government as a whole there are about 2500 performance measures.

Local authorities have a similar process. There is an annual budget cycle which takes account of the amount of central and local funding the government will allow each authority to raise. Budgets are normally historically based, each year representing marginal changes on the year before. Some authorities have a three-year budget cycle, in which items for year 1 cannot be accepted unless they previously appeared as bids for years 3 and 2. The purpose of the three-year plan is to make changes in the allocation of resources. The argument is that unless resources are expanding, it is impossible to make changes in resource allocation in the short term: in any one year resources are already committed. Local authorities also have performance indicators, which are published.

Cost information

Traditionally, government accounting has been on the basis of cash. In central government, all expenditures were treated as cash expenses in the year of account. No distinction was made between current and capital expenditure and it was not possible to produce a balance sheet of assets and liabilities. Local government expenditure has made the distinction between capital and current expenditure, mainly because the controls on these two types of expenditure have been different.

However, in recent years there has been a move towards accruals accounting and towards the use of cost accounting to identify the costs of activities or units of output. A White Paper, *Accounting in Government*, recognizes that the agencies and those parts of department which run trading funds have already converted to an accruals style of accounting. The Chancellor has persuaded the Cabinet that all central government accounting should be done on an accruals basis.

The implication of this is that there should be an asset register for all departments, so that the cost of capital can be identified in all activities. It also implies that capital expenditures will not be controlled as if all the costs of a capital project are incurred in the year in which cash is paid out. This should lead to more sensitive decisions in investments and in divestment of assets.

Policy evaluation

Not much policy evaluation is carried out at central government level. Since the Central Policy Review Staff, whose purpose was to look at policies which spread across more than one department and to be independent of departmental interests, was disbanded, there has been no central evaluation unit.

Individual local authorities have performance review units which often carry out evaluation studies as well as performance analysis. Individual government departments sometimes review the effectiveness of their policies. For example, the Home Office carries out reviews of the effectiveness of the criminal justice system. However, full-scale evaluations of the effectiveness of policy over a whole policy area are rare. For example, there is no departmental or independent evaluation of the effectiveness of the whole reform of the NHS.

Control (audit)

There are various inspectorates and audit bodies. Local government and the NHS are audited by the Audit Commission, an independent body which both organizes financial audit (carried out by public and private sector audit bodies) and carries out special studies of particular areas. The Audit Commission sometimes carries out studies which are very close to a policy evaluation, e.g. in the area of community care, rather than simply a value for money audit.

The National Audit Office audits central government departments and has some functions in auditing the NHS. These audits concern both probity and value for money.

MARKET ORIENTATION

Competitive tendering in local government

Local authorities have been obliged to use competitive tendering for a range of services since 1981. The Local Government Planning and Land Act 1980 imposed a regime of competitive tendering for building, maintenance and civil engineering work. The types of work covered were gradually extended in 1988 and 1992 to include other services, including street cleaning, gardening, building cleaning and catering, and professional services such as accountancy, architecture and financial services.[6,7]

Under these laws, the local authority must invite tenders if it intends to carry out work using its own workers in the defined areas of activity. When possible, three outside firms must be asked to bid and the tender should go to the lowest bidder, subject to a satisfactory appraisal of the capabilities of the winning company. The process has involved a change in the organization of local authorities, as those responsible for providing services, whether the in-house team or the company, are separated from those responsible for defining the work to be done, organizing the competition, letting the contract and monitoring the work.

On the provider side of the division there have been managerial changes to achieve increased efficiency to enable the bids to be successful. In many cases, new managers were employed who were used to working in a competitive environment. Their main task was to reduce costs. The first problem was to find out what existing costs were. Departments had budgets for expenditure under the usual headings – staff costs, materials, plant and buildings. However, it was difficult to allocate these costs to particular activities, and also to separate the costs of the 'purchasing' side of the organization from the 'providing' side and then to allocate central overhead costs first to each side and then to particular activities. In other words, the first task was to develop a costing system.

To reduce costs, there were a series of operations. Some involved accounting. All costs that had previously been allocated to an activity which was to be subject to competition but which were not strictly attributable to the activity were negotiated away. What this meant in practice was that many centrally allocated costs (legal costs, accountancy costs, personnel department costs) were exposed for the first time. Systems of cost allocation which operated pro rata to the numbers of people employed were questioned by the managers of the competitive units.

The second set of activities to reduce costs involved changing working methods. In the early days of competition it was possible to reduce internal costs by reducing the number of people employed in particular activities. For example, garbage collection crews would have fewer people; in the building trade people would do small amounts of work of people in other trades, rather than wait for, say, a plasterer to finish up after a plumber. Because most of these changes involved people working harder, the nature of the workforce changed. Younger and fitter people replaced the middle-aged workforce of pre-competitive times. The local authority had previously been seen as a place to go when you did not need to earn so much money but wanted a steady job. Now the competitive environment meant that this was no longer possible.

Often the changed working methods required different technologies. The competition encouraged people to think of using new equipment or a different approach to the work. In the early days this meant that French street-cleaning companies would introducing street-cleaning vehicles and methods previously unseen in the United Kingdom. Later it meant rethinking the kinds of computers required for collecting local taxes, as these services are also subject to competition.

One of the financial targets set for in-house operations which win bids is a return on assets employed (normally 5 percent). This led most of the in-house organizations to examine their asset holdings to ensure that there were no unnecessary holdings. In turn this convinced many to move into cheaper, less spacious premises and to dispose of plant which was not fully utilized. Sometimes these asset reductions were an accounting fiction: the 'ownership' was transferred to the 'purchasing' side, but in other cases they were real disposals of underused assets.

These efforts were really the introduction of market mechanisms only at the level of supply of services to the people under the control of the local authority. They did not establish choice for the users of the services. However, many local authorities have been making efforts to find out what sort of services their populations want and how satisfied they are with their delivery. In some cases, authorities established a contract with their populations, setting out the service standards which they could expect. York City Council and the London Borough of Islington were both leaders in the field of customer consultation and the publication of contracts. Many of these ideas were later taken up by central government in the Citizen's Charter initiative.

Community care

One of the reforms introduced in local government was a change in the way in which community care was provided. These services include residential care for older people, help in the home for older people and people with physical disabilities, services for people with mental illness and learning difficulties, and services for children with problems.

Social services departments have to make assessments of clients' needs and arrange to purchase services for them. A proportion of services has to be purchased from the private and voluntary sectors, through a series of contracts. While local authority provision is not compelled to enter competition with these sectors, there is an implication that if public sector provision is more expensive, work will be given to the independent sector. This has introduced an element of competition into the area of social care provision.[8]

Market testing

There has also been a programme of market testing in central government under the 'Competing for Quality' initiative. Market testing is a process whereby the in-house team bids against private sector competitors for an identified piece of work. There have been many cases of 'outsourcing' without an in-house bid. This is called 'strategic contracting out'.

The government claims annual savings of £116 million on activities subject to market testing of £594 million, a cost saving of about 20 percent.[9] There are some reasons to doubt the accuracy of these figures: in some cases the cost of the work to be tested had never previously been calculated separately; people involved in market testing were given target savings to achieve and the cost reduction may in fact be achieved through reduction in the volume or quality of work performed. However, there clearly have been some savings as a result of the market testing exercise.

The process has been slowed down by a series of rulings that the European Union regulations on the transfer of undertakings (Transfer of Undertakings Protection of Employment) apply when private companies successfully bid for work previously performed by public servants. Workers are entitled to protected terms and conditions of employment, at least immediately after the transfer. This made the option of cutting workers' pay and especially pension rights less attractive.

Protection of workers' terms and conditions of employment only applies to workers previously in employment and does not apply to new employees. For example, when London Buses was privatized by selling routes to private companies, cost savings were achieved by not giving pension rights to newly hired drivers.

Education reforms

The education system in the United Kingdom has decentralized management and centralized policy control. Schools have individual budgets which are managed by the staff and the board of governors. Some schools are funded directly by central government, according to a formula. Others are managed by local authorities. The core school curriculum is determined by the Department for Education and monitored by an agency of the department.

Universities are independent corporate bodies whose funding comes from central government and from students' fees. Funds are administered by a Higher Education Funding Council, which allocates funds according to a formula based on student numbers, the quality of teaching and research, and the balance of subjects taught. There has been a rapid expansion of higher education participation, with student numbers increasing by 53 percent between 1988 and 1994. To achieve this expansion, colleges were re-designated as universities and allowed to offer their own degrees. The last of these universities to be created, at Luton, grew from having 300 under-graduates to enrolling 9000 over a period of three years. This rapid growth and the competition for resources have required business-like management in the higher education sector.

Changes in the Civil Service

There have been a series of changes in the way in which the Civil Service is managed, designed to reduce costs or increase efficiency. Most of the ideas, of increased accountability, performance management and measurement, delegated authority and so on, were expressed long before the Conservative reforms were implemented. The Fulton Report of 1968[10] contained most of the themes but these had not been implemented because of a combination of lack of political will and resistance by the Civil Service. Only a strong government, keen to make an impact on the public sector and willing to make an effort to confront vested interests, could gather the will and power to influence the way in which the public sector was managed.

The Financial Management Initiative was an early attempt, from 1982, to delegate accountability and measure performance. This was a rather narrow initiative which concentrated on establishing costs and defining individual accountabilities. However, it started the process of making management a respectable activity for Civil Servants which would assist rather than hinder career progression.

The establishment of executive agencies was a more sharply defined way of establishing accountabilities and managerial authority. The framework documents which set out the relationships between the agencies and their departments were formal expressions of these. While the chief executives' authority and performance targets are explicitly established, similar steps have been taken within agencies for individual units.

The Citizen's Charter was mainly an attempt to get some of these matters into the public arena. By specifying performance targets and making them public, the benefits of the establishment and improvement in service stand-ards could be advertised. The Charter also contains specific ideas about how services should be managed, including a push towards performance-related pay which has now been introduced into most areas of the Civil Service.

In 'Competing for Quality', the government set out its ideas about introducing competition with the private sector. While local authorities had been compelled to engage in competitive tendering since 1981 (1982 in Scotland) and there had been experiments in the NHS since 1983 and the Civil Service since 1986, the White Paper encouraged the spread of 'market testing', and targets were eventually set for the proportion of work to be subjected to testing.

In addition to these major initiatives, there have been other pressures on the Civil Service generated by the government, such as annual unit cost reduction targets, which apply in addition to other targets. For example, Her Majesty's Stationery Office (HMSO) operates in a competitive environment for the supply of print, stationery and other services but has a unit cost reduction target as well as a commercial target.

The 'prior options' process, which occurs when executive agencies renew their agreements with their departments, questions the agencies' existence. They have to justify the function which they carry out, the need for that function to be conducted by government, and the reason for it being carried out by directly employed Civil Servants rather than contracted out to the private sector.

Stephen Dorrell, when Financial Secretary in the Treasury, embarked on what he called 'the long march down Whitehall'.[11] The purpose of the long march was to challenge whether government departments need to be directly engaged in all of their activities, especially if they are not part of the 'core business'.

In July 1994 the Government published a White Paper on the Civil Service.[12] Departments and agencies would have to draw up, each spring, an efficiency plan showing how they propose to reduce their running costs.

It was also proposed to extend the delegation of pay and grading below senior levels, from April 1996. While pay increases were not frozen, they have to be financed out of efficiency savings: budgets would not be inflation-proofed. The Chancellor of the Exchequer claimed that this was not a pay freeze. It was expected that this would result in delayering in the interests of efficiency.

The White Paper predicted that the Civil Service should reduce in size to a number below 500,000 compared with 748,000 in 1976, its peak level. However, it did not set targets for the numbers of employees. The Treasury would provide 80 percent of the funds required to achieve reductions in numbers if redundancies were necessary.

The following were the proposals for change in the way in which the senior Civil Service should work:

- Flatter management structures.
- Improved career management and succession planning to ensure interchange of people and that people with talent were promoted.

- Written employment contracts for senior civil servants.
- More flexible pay arrangements, to ensure recognition for personal responsibility, reward for performance and the retention of high performers.
- All senior staff (meaning grades 5 and above) should be recognized as senior civil servants.

Each department was asked to produce a new management structure which reflected these ideas.

At the same time as proposing improved management development for the senior Civil Service, the White Paper asked departments and agencies to consider giving civil servants more experience of the world outside the service and recruiting to the senior service from outside. Written contracts would be introduced for all senior people from April 1996. In general, fixed-term contracts were not favoured.

On pay, it proposed a more flexible pay structure to take account of the newly defined responsibilities, the likelihood of a less secure career and the need to accommodate open competition for senior jobs.

Recruitment and dismissal

The implications of the changes to the Civil Service for recruitment and dismissal is that appointments are being made to individual jobs, rather than recruitment to the service in general. This is reflected in the practice of advertising individual jobs, and in managers being able to choose the people who work in their units, rather than being allocated people by the personnel system.

At junior levels there is an increasing use of short-term temporary employment contracts. The state of the labour market in recent years, especially the persistence of unemployment among school and college leavers, has meant that it is possible to attract employees even with poor terms and conditions of employment. The other explanation for the increasing use of short-term contracts is that managers are faced with both reducing and uncertain budgets. Commitment to employ people on permanent contracts may endanger the budgets.

Promotion

Important proposals for change in the way in which senior civil servants were selected was announced in a report *Career Management and Succession Planning Study* by the Efficiency Unit at the end of 1993.[13] This report criticized the process by which experience in policy advice was the main route to the top, especially for people recruited to the 'fast stream':

All Departments seek to place their fast-streamers, recruited to the civil service as a whole by the Civil Service Commissioners on behalf of Departments, in testing posts which give them experience of policy making and support to Ministers. . . . But Departments are also conscious of criticism of the fast-streams – that they could encourage the worst aspects of elitism and without care might perpetuate a set of skills more suitable to the past than the future.
　(p. 31)

Apart from the fast stream, the report found that 'all Departments in our survey are increasingly encouraging the individual to take the opportunity to influence his or her own career development' (p. 37).

Moves from one job to another are frequent: 60 percent of people in the top three grades in 1993 had been in their current post for two years or less, and 80 percent for three years or less. This movement is intended to give people experience of different departments but it also has the effect of accentuating the generalist nature of policy work rather than specialism in one policy area. Given that ministers also change their portfolios quite frequently, it can mean that the people in charge of departments do not have long experience of them.

Performance, pay and incentive systems

Government policy in recent years has been to try to reduce the importance of national pay-bargaining in the determination of wages and salaries in the public sector. There has been a desire to introduce pay settlements which reflect the needs of the particular employer in each locality, and to reflect local labour market conditions.

However, a survey of pay determination in the public sector in 1990 showed that there had been little movement between 1984 and 1990 in the number of employees whose pay was determined at local level (Table 3.2).

This survey showed that there were hardly any pay settlements at the local workplace level. One percent or fewer employees have their pay

Table 3.2. Basis for pay increase in the public sector, 1984 and 1990[14]

| | Percentage of employees | | | |
| | Manual | | Non-manual | |
	1984	*1990*	*1984*	*1990*
Result of collective bargaining	98	92	99	90
Most important level:				
Multi-employer	74	72	87	76
Single employer, multi-plant	20	17	11	12
Plant/establishment	2	1	1	–
Other answer	2	2	–	2
Not result of collective bargaining	2	7	1	9

settled at this level. The survey did find, however, that there had been an increase in multi-stage bargaining especially for non-manual employees. A national agreement would be modified by the negotiations between employees and individual employers.

Since 1990 the government has attempted to reform the whole process of public sector pay determination and to control the level of expenditure on public sector pay.

The use of pay review bodies to determine pay has been extended. These bodies are independent of government and assess the labour market and determine the annual pay rise of about 1.4 million workers, including doctors, dentists, nurses, the armed forces, senior civil servants and judges. The review bodies do not always recommend low pay increases. In February 1995, for example, the review body which recommends the pay rates for senior civil servants recommended raising the maximum pay for top civil servants by 27 percent to £150,000. Nor does the government always accept the recommendations of the review bodies.

There is still collective bargaining for 500,000 Civil Service staff and for all local government workers apart from teachers. The government has to negotiate directly with the civil servants, but the local authorities are responsible for negotiating the pay of their workers. The government attempts to keep pay rises under control by controlling the amount of cash that local authorities have available to pay salaries. For example, in 1995 teachers were awarded a pay rise of 2.7 percent but the funding available to local authorities increased by between 0.5 percent and 1.5 percent. The only option that the local authorities had was to reduce the number of teachers to be able to meet the pay rise of their teachers.

The government is attempting to decentralize pay determination, both in the Civil Service and in the NHS. In the Civil Service, pay negotiations and pay scales are being decentralized to the executive agencies which are expected to design their own pay schemes and to conduct their own pay negotiations. In the Civil Service there has been a move away from automatic annual progression through pay scales. Progression now depends on a satisfactory appraisal.

In the NHS, the newly established trusts are expected to make local pay arrangements, based on local labour market conditions. In February 1995, hospital consultants were offered a pay rise of 5 percent on condition that they accepted the terms and conditions of their employing trusts. At the same time the nurses were offered a 1 percent pay rise and were told that they could negotiate with their trust employers for up to 2 percent more.

Performance-related pay and shorter contracts are also being introduced. All agency chief executives have fixed-term contracts and performance-related pay. A small element of performance-related pay is also being introduced for all agency employees. While newly appointed chief executives have been content to accept performance-related pay, there has been some resistance elsewhere. For example, chief constables (the local heads of the police service) have resisted the introduction of short-term contracts and performance-related pay. The president of the Association of Chief Police Officers refused a renewed contract on the new conditions. Announcing his refusal, he said:

> *I joined the police force out of a sense of public service . . . recognising the financial disadvantage. Had I wanted the principles of the market place, I would not have made that decision. . . . The notion that I will work harder or more effectively because of performance-related pay is absurd and objectionable, if not insulting.*
> *(The Times, 22 April 1995)*

As well as these changes in pay schemes and negotiating procedures there have been attempts to freeze pay rises. These have been expressed in two ways: in September 1993 the Chancellor announced that all pay rises would have to be funded from productivity increases, i.e. there would be no automatic compensation for price inflation. In November that year he announced that there would be an absolute limit on the amount of cash available of £80 billion. This effectively by-passed the pay review bodies, by setting a limit on funding, whatever the pay review bodies decided was an appropriate level of pay rise.

It is intended to decentralize all pay and grading to departments and their agencies: 'by April 1996, responsibility for the pay and grading of staff below senior levels should be delegated to all departments and the existing national pay arrangements replaced'.[15]

Training

There is no national scheme for training public servants, such as exists in France. There is a Civil Service College, which is run as an executive agency, selling training to government departments and agencies. The college offers specialist courses as well as management development activities for civil service managers. However, there is a 'fast stream' entry for the Civil Service in which individuals' careers are managed through an accelerated route to senior positions.

Some sectors also have their specialist training institutions, such as the fire service and the police service, both of which have their own colleges and a planned process of training linked to progression.

In local government, the only specialist training is organized within the individual professions which organize their own training and accreditation schemes, independently of the employers. Management training is mostly left to the market. While there is an organization called the Local Government Management Board, this is not the main provider of management development, which is mainly provided by institutes specializing in the public sector, or business schools which add the public sector to their repertoire of management education and training.

CONCLUSIONS

In some respects, the UK public sector is centralized: subnational government consists of local authorities whose powers and ability to raise funds are constrained by central government. Central government can impose policy on local authorities, including removing schools and colleges from local control, imposing competition and determining budgets. The NHS is run by a series of authorities and boards, all of which are staffed by people appointed by the secretary of state. In other respects, management is becoming decentralized. The executive agencies through which central government services are delivered are managed in an arm's length way by chief executives. Some elements of management, such as pay bargaining, are becoming more devolved to local managers.

There has been a move towards the use of various market-type mechanisms: internal markets, competition between the public and private sectors, and outsourcing without competition. Unfortunately, no systematic evaluation of the effects of these policies has been undertaken.[16]

NOTES

1. Efficiency Unit (1988) *Improving Management in Government: The Next Steps.* HMSO, London.
2. Between 1991 and 1994 there were adjustments to the structure, including changing the boundaries of health authorities and the abolition of a regional tier of health authorities, with effect from April 1996. The system described is that which was in place from April 1994.
3. For a description of the distribution of functions in the NHS, see National Health Service Executive (1994) *Managing the New NHS: Functions and Responsibilities in the New NHS*, Leeds, Department of Health.
4. Tony Cutler and Barbara Waine, *Managing the Welfare State*, Berg, Providence/ Oxford (1994).
5. For example, C. Hood.
6. For a technical account of the laws and the required processes, see Andrew Sparke (1993) *The Compulsory Competitive Tendering Guide*, Butterworths, London.
7. For an evaluation of the early experiences, see K. Walsh (1991) *The Impact of Competitive Tendering*, Department of Environment, HMSO, London.
8. For more detail on the reforms in community care, see Joanna Bornat *et al.* (eds), *Community Care: A Reader*, Macmillan, Basingstoke (1993) and Norman Flynn and Dominic Hurley, *The Market for Care*, Public Sector Management, London (1993).
9. *The Citizen's Charter*, Second report, 1994, Cmnd 2540, HMSO, London, p. 101.
10. Fulton, Lord John (1968) *The Civil Service*, Report of Committee, Cmnd. 3638, HMSO, London.

11. The French reforms have also been called 'The Long March': Celine Wiener (1991) *L'Evolution des rapports entre l'administration et les usagers*, Institut Français des Sciences Administratives, Economica, Paris.
12. Treasury and OPSS (1994) *The Civil Service: Continuity and Change*, Cmnd 2627, HMSO, London.
13. Efficiency Unit (1993) *Career Management and Succession Planning Study*, HMSO, London (otherwise known as the Oughton Report).
14. Millward, N., Stevens, M., Smart, D. and Hawes, W.R. (1992) *Workplace Industrial Relations in Transition*, Dartmouth, Aldershot.
15. Treasury and OPSS (1944) *The Civil Service: Continuity and Change*, Cmnd 2627, HMSO, London, p. 26.
16. The two major studies were inconclusive about the benefits of the market reforms, Walsh, K. (1995) *Public Services and Marketing Mechanisms: Competition, Contracting and the New Public Management*, Macmillan, Basingstoke and Bartlett, W. et al., (1994) *Quasi-markets in the Welfare State: The Emerging Findings*, Bristol, SAUS.

Case Study: Next Steps Agencies

INTRODUCTION: THE NEXT STEPS

One of the most significant reforms of public services in the United Kingdom has been the creation of executive agencies to carry out the service delivery functions of central government departments. The publication of a report by the Efficiency Unit in 1988,[1] called *Improving Management in Government – The Next Steps*, started the process of changing the Civil Service from a unified structure into separate, relatively autonomous entities responsible through their parent ministries and ministers to Parliament for the delivery of public services.

While this development may be seen as a turning point in the management of public services, there had been precedents for many of the ideas. The Fulton Report[2] had called for clearer accountability of civil servants and greater managerial autonomy,[3] and there had been attempts under a project called the 'Financial Management Initiative' to improve accountability at unit level in the Civil Service. However, the 'Next Steps' reforms were a comprehensive attempt to transform both management and accountability in central government.

The Next Steps report reached five main conclusions. The first was that the great majority of employees of the Civil Service were concerned with service delivery. However, the management arrangements in place were not geared to delivering services to the public. Secondly, senior management in the Civil Service consisted predominantly of people whose careers had been in the field of policy analysis and advice to ministers. The route to the top of the service was through a series of appointments in ministers' private offices, in policy divisions of ministries with possibly one or two periods of field experience. Hence senior management was dominated by people with limited service delivery knowledge or expertise. Those with such experience were in positions which made them subordinate to the policy makers, even for matters of operational management.

Thirdly, ministers were overloaded with work which was not about policies or policy making. Because of their direct accountability for the activities and actions of their departments they were involved in administrative details. There was a need to remove some of the detailed work so that ministers could concentrate on policy matters.

Because the management of the Civil Service was mainly carried out through the control of budgets and personnel, there was insufficient attention given to performance and results. While the Financial Management Initiative had had some impact on the generation of cost information and accountability for costs, there was not a coherent system for measuring and controlling performance, especially the production of outputs.

Finally, the report concluded that the Civil Service as a whole was too big and diverse to be managed as a single entity. A unified system of recruitment, pay scales and staff appraisal was inappropriate for the very wide range of tasks performed. Different tasks required different ways of managing, while managerial autonomy would necessitate more managerial discretion.

AGENCIES

The solution was to divide the Civil Service into those parts which were concerned with policy and policy making and those which delivered services to the public. This division implied a constitutional change in the role of ministers and their immediate advisors. In principle ministers would be accountable for the effectiveness of policy, while the managers of the operational units, or agencies, would be accountable for the day-to-day management of their units.

Each agency was to have a very clear set of guidelines under which to operate. A framework document was to set out the freedoms and limits of managerial discretion for each chief executive. At the same time, performance targets would be set, on which the chief executive would be held accountable, to the Permanent Secretary of the parent department, to the relevant Parliamentary Select Committee and to the Public Accounts Committee. Interviews with chief executives have revealed that the frequent, public scrutiny of their performance plays a large part in their working lives. Targets are taken very seriously and the process of accountability has increased the public exposure of individual civil servants who previously would have been anonymous to the public.

The framework document and the annual performance targets were designed to give greater clarity to the managerial tasks of the chief executives. Resources were defined, discretion identified and required outputs were made specific.

OTHER PRESSURES

At the same time as the process of establishing the executive agencies was begun, there were other pressures on managers. The government had a commitment to privatization of public services which was connected with the desire for efficiency but was rooted in different ideas. As we shall see, the belief that privatization was a desirable end in itself had an impact on the major managerial choices available to chief executives. Decisions on out-sourcing of services, whether peripheral such as cleaning and catering or core such as computer facilities management were made against the back-ground political assumption that the private sector was better than the public.

One expression of this tendency to privatize is the underlying policy of trying to reduce the size of the public sector, as measured by the number of people directly employed. From a peak of 748,000 employees in 1976, the government has reduced the size of the Civil Service to 533,000 by April 1994.[4] While there have never been publicly declared targets for the num bers of civil servants, the policy to reduce the size of the service has always been clear.

There has also been a constant pressure to contain expenditure, whether programme expenditure (such as social security benefits, construction costs of highways etc.) or running costs expenditure (the costs of maintaining the organizations and delivering the services). The creation of the executive agencies did not remove the tension between service quality and cost reduction.

THE PROCESS

Because of this mixture of pressures and the parallel policy ideas, the pro-cess of establishing and managing the executive agencies has not been sim-ple.[5] A project team was established, under the management of Peter Kemp, a senior civil servant, whose task was to establish the new agencies as quickly as possible. The team recognized that there were different types of agencies and therefore that individual framework agreements would be different. It also recognized that there were some departments which al-ready had systems of management and accountability which fitted easily into the idea of quasi-contractual relationship between an agency and a department. The process was therefore one of maintaining a central drive for implementation but recognizing that implementation should be carried out in different ways in different circumstances. In effect there were three main participants in the process: the department whose services were to be sub-ject to agency status, the Next Steps team and the Treasury. There have been disputes about whether the Treasury was enthusiastic about the delegation of managerial authority to agencies or not. The Treasury issued memoranda stating the delegations over pay and personnel matters which were available and under-used. Chief executives and managers complained that they were unduly constrained, especially when they wished to use their delegated authority to spend money in a way which might be interpreted by others as a precedent for more relaxed Treasury control. At a seminar at the London Business School in 1989 on the implementation of the Next Steps initiative, a Treasury spokesman showed a slide: 'True freedom is Treasury control'. The Orwellian irony was not lost on the agency managers present.

The criteria

For a unit to be made an agency, there was an examination of its activities against a long list of criteria. The first thing which ministers had to decide was whether the unit could be abolished or the function privatized. In other words, does the state need to be involved in the provision of this service at all? If the state had to be involved, the next question was whether the function could be contracted out to the private sector. Only when these questions were answered would a function be considered for agency status. This presumption in favour of privatization has continued during the periodic reviews of agencies, at each of which the same questions have to be asked.

The other criteria included whether the unit was delivering an identifiable service, whether it was big enough to warrant independent status (although this criterion was loosely applied: the smallest agency has 30 employees); whether it was possible to separate policy making from service delivery; whether ministers needed to have day-to-day involvement in the management of the unit.

In practice, there was a drive to create as many agencies as possible. The diversity of functions and types of agency shows that a wide range of activities met the criteria established.

FRAMEWORK DOCUMENTS

The agreement between the parent department and the agencies about how the relationship was to operate was initially drafted in framework documents (it is interesting that the French government adopted the same term, *Tableau de Bord* for its agreements between ministries and *centres de responsabilité*). These set out the chief executive's responsibilities to ministers; the agency's aims and objectives; the services provided; the financial arrangements, including financial objectives, planning, reporting and accounting; pay and personnel arrangements. A detailed definition of how the agency was to be judged was generally left to the annual operational plan, which is also agreed between the department and the agency. In the spirit of the age these operational plans are called 'business plans'.

The main difference between these framework agreements and contracts is that they are not legally enforceable. Since the agency and the department are both legally part of the Crown, there can be no legal agreement between them. While this may appear to be a legal technicality, in practice it does raise the question of what happens if an agency fails to meet its targets. In some cases, the targets have not been met and explanations are given. In practice, the only sanction for non-performance seems to be the level of performance-related pay of the chief executives and senior managers.

Appointing the chief executives
One of the advantages claimed for the establishment of the agencies was that the chief executives would have a clear management task, within a set of targets and managerial guidelines. It also provided an opportunity to appoint people through open competition. One of the criticisms in the Efficiency Unit report was that people in senior managerial positions in the Civil Service had mainly had experience of policy formulation. Open competition allowed the possibility of managerial experience being taken into account in the appointments.

Terms and conditions of employment were individually negotiated with the chief executives, rather than slotting them in to existing pay scales. All contracts were for a fixed term, normally of three years.

In the event there was open competition for 71 of the 113 chief executive posts filled by April 1995.[6] Of those appointed, 35 were from outside the Civil Service, although very few came from outside the public services in general.

COVERAGE

By April 1995, 108 executive agencies had been established and in addition, Her Majesty's Customs and Excise and the Inland Revenue had been reorganized into executive units and executive offices, operating on the same lines as agencies. In all, about 370,000 civil servants are employed in these units, or about two thirds of the Civil Service. There is a great variety of agencies included in these arrangements. The largest is the Social Security Benefits Agency which employs over 65,000 people, followed by the Employment Service, employing 42,000. The smallest is a conference centre run by the Foreign and Commonwealth Office, employing 30 people. The list includes a wide variety of functions, from prisons to laboratories and from issuing passports to training military personnel. The only departments which have not had a large proportion of their staff transferred to agency status are the Foreign and Commonwealth Office and the Treasury. Figure 3.1 shows the number of employees in executive agencies from 1988 to 1995.

The agencies represent a variety of types of state activity. The variables which represent the differences are:

- Whether they are 'trading' in the sense that they offer services to customers who can choose whether or not to deal with them.

Numbers employed in agencies

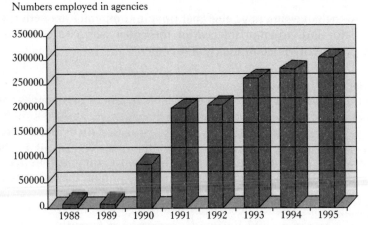

Figure 3.1. Number of employees in executive agencies from 1988 to 1995.
Source: Next Steps Briefing Note, April 1995, Office of Public Services and Science.

- Whether they are able to find customers and by so doing can grow their businesses.
- Whether they provide services direct to the public or only internally to government departments and their agencies.

These variables determine the degree of management ability required by the chief executives and boards in the field of marketing and customer orientation and produce commercial measures of success.

For example, the largest agency, the Social Security Benefits Agency, has a captive set of 'customers', i.e. people who apply for social security. While the agency has standards of customer service (speed and accuracy of processing) and has been very active in promoting customer care, it has to negotiate targets with the Department of Social Security. There are not immediate competitors who are able to provide the services to the people who claim benefits. Into this category fall most of the Employment Services Agency (especially those parts which deal with unemployment benefit/jobseekers allowance), Customs and Excise, Inland Revenue and the Court Service. Just over 60 percent of employees in agencies come into the category of not being in direct competition, unless competitive tendering exercises are organized for parts of their services.

Another category includes the Social Security Information Technology Services Agency, which provides the computer technology and support for the benefits system. Their customers are the other agencies within the social security system. Because of market testing, they are subject to competition from outside computer companies, but are not allowed to sell their expertise to other customers. Their managerial task is to satisfy their corporate customers and satisfy the Treasury that their service provides good value for money. However, like all computer operations in government, they are also subject to the government's belief that private companies are better than the public sector. Individual prisons within the Prison Service are also subject to periodic competition from private companies.

Other agencies are in a more 'normal' competitive position. Those agencies which run laboratories, for example, are sometimes able to find customers throughout Europe and compete for scientific and testing contracts within the European Union competition regulations. In that sense they are more like a commercial operation. In principle, there are no requirements for surrogate performance measures and standards: survival in the market place is a sufficient measure of success. In practice, their actions are limited by Treasury rules on investment and borrowing and on the use of assets and on a general presumption against the public sector.

Some agencies have moved from one category to another. The Central Office of Information, which provides information from the government to the citizens, was one of the early agencies. Initially it held the government's publicity budgets and could therefore determine how they were spent on behalf of departments. These budgets were then transferred to the departments themselves who could then choose whether or not to use the Central Office of Information as their advertising agency, or as their producer of television films etc.

Her Majesty's Stationery Office, another early agency, was initially protected from competition by rules about where departments should have their design, printing and stationery supplied. These rules have been gradually relaxed and the agency has increasingly to compete with outside suppliers of these services.

These distinctions are important because they help to shape the relationship between the ministry and its agencies. If the enterprises are mainly commercial, then the department is less interested in the details of their performance and accountability can in theory be related to some commercial 'bottom line'. If, on the other hand, there is no competition, nor need to find customers, surrogate measures of performance have to be defined and agreed. Where the services are provided to the public, market research techniques are used to discover which aspects of the service the public rate as important and which they are satisfied with. Where services are internal to government, internal customer surveys can be used to gauge satisfaction.

The question must be asked, whether the fact that there is a framework agreement between the service delivery part of the organization and its parent government department makes the relationship with the end users of services better. The government claims that they do, in three ways. The existence of the agencies, it is claimed,[7] produces greater clarity about objectives and targets, delegation of managerial responsiblity and a clear focus on outputs and outcomes. These effects are supposed to be, at least in part, a result of the separation of policy and managerial responsibilities. In what follows we examine the agencies under these criteria: are their objectives clear? Has there been a defined separation of policy making from management? Have managers been allowed to get on and manage? Has there been a focus on outputs and outcomes, as the government has claimed?

ASSESSMENT

Clarity of objectives

Next Steps Review 1994 (Cm2750) gives details of the targets and achievements of the agencies. Each agency has a set of key targets[8] which are negotiated between themselves and their parent department. These vary according to the nature of the work the agency does. For example, those which are operating in an environment where they have to generate income from customers have a target to recover all or a proportion of their costs from charges to customers. The Central Science Laboratory has a target of recovering all its full costs. The Civil Service College has had a target of achieving cost recovery after a subsidy of £1.3 million in 1993–4, with the subsidy reduced each year, until achieving full cost recovery in 1995–6. Companies House is required to achieve a 6 percent average annual rate of return on assets.

In addition to financial targets, agencies have quality, efficiency and throughput targets. For example, the Inland Revenue has a series of output performance targets, including: to respond to all correspondence within 28 days, to respond to enquiries within 15 minutes to at least 93 percent of people who call without an appointment. The Social Security Benefits Agency has a series of targets on response times and accuracy which are taken very seriously by all staff. The Prison Service has a series of quality targets, related to the number of assaults in prisons, overcrowding, the amount of time prisoners spend locked in their cells.

Efficiency targets include cost per prisoner per annum in the Prison Service, Inland Revenue had to reduce departmental running costs by 2.8 percent in 1993–4; the Passport Agency had a target to reduce the unit cost of issuing passports by 3 percent in 1993–4 and 3.2 percent in 1994–5.

Quality targets are less well developed and relate mainly to the time taken to provide a service, whether work is delivered on time (Central Office of Information), despatching benefits on the day that entitlement is agreed (Employment Service), clearing social fund crisis loan on the day that need arises (Benefits Agency). However, the Civil Service College has a requirement to meet customer satisfaction targets in their course evaluation procedure. Quality targets for the Central Statistical Office include a reduction in the number of revisions to key economic indicators such as changes in the gross domestic product and balance of payments.

As with all systems of performance measurement, it is possible to make criticisms of the agency targets. Some managers argue that the pursuit of the specific clearance time and accuracy targets in the Benefits Agency can distract from other aspects of customer care. Managers in the Foreign and Commonwealth Office have reported that because cases have to be dealt with in a certain time, files are not opened until a prospect of completion within the target time is apparent. Customers of the Civil Service College report that they feel under an obligation to their tutors to turn in positive customer feedback. However, there is no doubt that the use of the indicators has an impact on management. During 1993, for example, the Social Security Benefits Agency was criticized for poor performance on its accuracy targets while its speed of service targets were met. It was possible for managers to change the emphasis from speed to accuracy with measurable results within three months. The Passport Agency has dramatically reduced the average time to process a passport application.

It is impossible to evaluate whether this focus on outputs is a result only of the process of creating the agencies. In principle, the development and pursuit of targets would have been possible in a unified Civil Service. In practice, the process of producing an explicit framework document setting out managerial freedoms and the annual negotiation and publication of targets and of performance have focused managerial attention on the achievement of results.

Separation of policy and service delivery

The head of the Home Civil Service, Sir Robin Butler, said: 'We cannot expect to delegate management powers and continue at the centre of departments as if nothing had happened. The hardest part will be changing the functions and attitudes at the centre of departments and in central departments so as to develop a more strategic role, distinguishing between what is essentially central and what can be left to local management decision'.[9]

The job description of the chief executive of the largest agency (Social Security Benefits Agency) includes giving policy advice to ministers on social security matters. It has been accepted that those involved in service delivery should have a role to play in policy advice, especially on the implementability of policy. Both the Benefits Agency and the Employment Service (the second largest) have a large policy staff at their headquarters, in addition to the policy staff in their respective departmental headquarters.

At the same time, chief executives reported in 1994 that they have seen no reduction in the control functions with departments as a result of powers being delegated to agencies.[10] These questions had already been raised in a 1991 report[11] which had said that chief executives were too controlled by departments and should be given more managerial autonomy, especially over such matters as the use of support agencies.

The author's experience of working with officials of the Social Security Department and its agencies is that there has been a great deal of cultural

change in the agencies, as staff and management have become more concerned with targets and performance and with customer satisfaction. The
department has had less incentive to change. A large part of its work is still
concerned with policy making with ministers and with the annual financial
planning and bidding process. In these areas of work, the existence of the
agencies has led to little change. Only in those areas which interface directly
with the agencies has there been a need for change.

Sylvie Trosa, a French civil servant, examined the operation of the relationship between departments and agencies and found[12] that there was a
wide difference in culture, with suspicion on both sides of the divide: departments thinking that agencies were too autonomous, agencies thinking
that departments were too bureaucratic. She concluded that the agencies
were only semi-autonomous and were still to a large extent managed by
their parent departments. This was less the case with smaller agencies,
whose chief executives would have less contact with their departments than
those of the larger ones.

The route to the top (to Permanent Secretary or the two senior grades
below that) is mainly still via the policy process, not management. This may
be changing. In early 1995, the chief executive of the Social Security Benefits
Agency was appointed Permanent Secretary in the Department of Employment (not the agency's parent department). If this sets a precedent, there
may be a reduction in the cultural gap between departments and agencies.

Up to now, however, it would not appear that the great clarity of the
distinction between policy making and service delivery has been achieved.
As Barberis[13] said: 'So far, few firm and far-reaching consequences have
been manifest. There is some limited evidence that core departments are
adopting a more strategic role, though many – the Treasury included –
remain heavily involved in day-to-day supervision of agencies. There has
been some reorganization within those core departments in which agencies
have been more widely created, though there are no signs of the staffing
reductions called for in the Fraser report.' (pp. 115–16)

Delegation of managerial responsibility

One of the aims of the establishment of the agencies was to free the chief
executives and their managers from detailed control by ministers and civil
servants whose main role was policy making. There are two aspects of this
delegation: the freedom from interference in day-to-day management matters by the parent department; the ability to make decisions without Treasury approval, subject to conforming with the rules set out in the framework
document.

Elizabeth Mellon[14] reported that the two flexibilities which managers
most wanted were related to finance. The first was the desire to have

budgets controls in net rather than gross terms. In other words, rather than having limits placed on all cash expenditures, managers would prefer to be able to spend money to invest in technology or other improvements to reduce the net cost of providing services. The second was the desire to be free from strict annuality in budgets. This refers to the old custom of having to spend every allocated pound before the end of the financial year, lest it be given back to the Treasury. These two freedoms have been gradually extended: some agencies are now subject to net running cost control and there are small allowances for funds to be carried forward into subsequent years. Even when both flexibilities have been given, she reports, 'The 'spend it by the end of the year or your budget will be cut next year' mindset dies hard after many years of a more restrictive regime.'

It should be expected that the size of the parent departments would be reduced if they were no longer responsible for the day-to-day management of the delivery of services. In practice, the functions of control continued to be carried out, but the staff were transferred to the agencies. For example, the Department of Social Security transferred 2,800 headquarters staff (of 4,000) to the main Social Security Agencies, Benefits and Contributions. However, the size of the core departments (leaving aside functions which transferred, more or less unchanged, to the agencies) seems not to have reduced. Barberis[15] analysed the changes in the senior levels of civil servants and in the number of ministers in four departments, Employment, Social Security, Trade and Industry and Transport, before and after the creation of agencies. He found that the number of ministers had increased from 26 to 28 and the number of senior civil servants had remained stable at 401. Only Industry had reduced its number of senior civil servants, by 7 percent, despite an increase in responsibilities transferred from the Energy Department.

The other flexibility which was implied breaking up the monolithic Civil Service was in pay: avoiding national, rigid pay scales for all positions. While this has been the intention, especially when flexibility could bring cost savings, it has taken a long time to implement. Her Majesty's Stationery Office was an early agency to adopt a new grading structure and the Employment Service has introduced a modified pay scheme from April 1994. The White Paper of January 1995 which sets out the government's latest proposals for the Civil Service commits the government to the implementation of pay and grading delegation by 1st April 1996. Details of what this means are yet to be announced.

In interviews with chief executives of agencies[16] who had been recruited from the private sector, there was some frustration over external control over pay. One chief executive said, 'Pay and grading are stumbling blocks. The Treasury dominate and do not delegate. Executive agencies will falter because of lack of personnel freedoms.' Another said, 'I had wanted total freedom on personnel in the framework document . . . I can't recruit above AO (clerical) level.'

The impact of other initiatives on managerial authority

THE CITIZEN'S CHARTER

In 1991 the government published a White Paper called *The Citizen's Charter*[17] whose themes were quality, choice, standards and value. The mechanisms proposed were more privatization, competition, contracting-out and performance-related pay. In addition, services were expected to publish performance standards and performance results.

From April 1992 every agency and department had to produce a way of incorporating a performance-related element into their pay scheme. While the amounts offered, except at the top levels, were very limited, this approach to reward management became mandatory. In other words, whether managers believed that an individual performance-related pay element was the best way to manage and motivate staff or not, the approach had to be followed. In response to the White Paper *Continuity and Change* the Treasury and Civil Service Select Committee criticized the blanket use of performance-related pay: 'We recommend that the authority over pay delegated to departments and agencies includes the freedom for each organization to decide whether or not performance-related pay is appropriate to its needs and objectives' (p. 38).[18] In response, the government maintained its belief in performance-related pay but said that it did not want to impose a single system.

PRIVATIZATION

One of the criteria for the establishment of an agency was that the activity was not suitable for privatization. It was expected that, once agency status had been granted, the question of privatization would not be raised again before the agency's review. However, the 1994 *Next Steps Review*[19] stated that some agencies had been created with a view to privatization at some point in the future. This is another case of a separate government policy (maximizing the transfer of activities to the private sector) overriding the managerial autonomy of those managing the agencies.

COMPETING FOR QUALITY

The competition policy was restated in another White Paper in 1991 *Competing for Quality*.[20] Departments and agencies were expected to subject a proportion of their work either to 'market testing', i.e. inviting a competition between the private sector and the in-house teams to bid for existing work or to what was known as 'strategic contracting', i.e. an invitation to outside firms to tender for work without an in-house bid. By the end of 1993, 389 market tests had been completed. The results were as follows:

- 25 resulted in a decision to abolish all or a substantial part of the activity.
- 3 activities were privatized.

- 113 activities were contracted out as a result of a strategic decision to employ an outside supplier. No in-house bid was permitted in these cases.
- Where there was an in-house bid, 82 activities were contracted out and 147 were awarded to the in-house team.
- 6 activities were restructured without a formal test.
- 13 tests were withdrawn and efficiency gains made internally.

The private sector was awarded £855 million of this work. Of this, £768 million was contracted out with no in-house bid. Around £525 million of this was accounted for by two reviews, 'The Atomic Weapons Establishment in the Ministry of Defence' and 'Inland Revenue Information Technology Services'.[21]

These tests were demanded of agencies and departments by the Office of Public Services and Science. They represent a managerial initiative which cut across the managerial judgement of those who had been put in charge of the agencies, who may or may not have decided to hive off parts of their functions. Since 1994, managers do not have to comply with this particular instruction but rather have to produce efficiency plans which show that they have taken account of the possibility of market testing among other ways of achieving efficiency improvements.

Accountability

The final criterion by which the programme can be judged is whether it improved the accountability within the system: when ministers are allowed to concentrate on policy and managers on management, there should be greater clarity about who is accountable for what. O'Toole and Chapman[22] argue that the changes in accountability are confused. The prime minister stated, when announcing the creation of the agencies in 1988, 'The structure of accountability will remain the same, in the sense that there will be reporting through ministers to Parliament and there will be . . . no change in that' (p. 125). However, Michael Heseltine suggested that the new arrangements should produce different patterns of accountability: 'If you really want accountable units, you want them as far removed from the disciplines of the classical public sector arrangements as possible'.[23] In practice it has been difficult to separate the accountability for policy and accountability for the management of operations.

There are three reasons for this: first, managers of the operations have a role, as we have seen, in advising on policy. Secondly, it is sometimes hard to attribute the causes of matters which go wrong to policy or management. Thirdly, ministers in effect retain the right to interfere in the management of agencies.

One example of the second problem was the Child Support Agency, established as a new organization to ensure that estranged parents contributed to the upkeep of their children. The agency became unpopular, partly because it concentrated on pursuing those parents who were already making some contribution, rather than those who made none at all. There were some problems with the management, record keeping and operations of the agency. However, it had been set a target of the amount of money to be collected and therefore saved to the taxpayer in social security payments, which it attempted to meet in the most efficient way possible. Who should be accountable for the unpopularity of the actions of the agency? The minister? The government as a whole for setting the policy framework which was itself unpopular? The minister and the civil servants in the core department for setting the performance targets? The chief executive for pursuing the targets? In the event the chief executive was replaced.

On the third point, the association which represents senior civil servants has expressed the view that ministers will continue to interfere in the day-to-day management of agencies for political reasons, but that when things go wrong, the senior civil servants will be used as scapegoats.

The official position is that ministers are accountable to Parliament for matters of policy and the allocation of resources and that they have delegated the responsibility for managerial and operational matters to the chief executives of agencies. In practice, the distinction between these categories is not completely clear, especially as it is up to ministers to define what they have delegated and therefore what is managerial and operational in character. Perhaps it is in the nature of politics that ministers will wish to accrue as much power as possible and to shrug off as much accountability as possible when things go wrong.

NOTES

1. Efficiency Unit, (1988), *Improving Management in Government: The Next Steps*. HMSO, London.
2. Report of Fulton Committee, (1968) CM 3638, HMSO.
3. For a history of reforms and attempted reforms, see Peter Hennessey *Whitehall*, (1989), Secker and Warburg, London; Patricia Greer, (1994), *Transforming Central Government: The Next Steps Initiative*, Open University Press, Buckingham; Andrew Cox and Frances Lamont *L'Amélioration du Management dans L'Etat: Effets de l'Initiative dite des 'Etapes Suivants' sur l'efficience de l'administration au Royaume-Uni*, Politiques et Management Public, Vol 11, N.2, (1993).
4. *The Civil Service: Continuity and Change*, Cm 2627, HMSO, London (1994).
5. Diana Goldsworthy, (1991) *Setting up Next Steps* London, HMSO, for an official account of the establishment of the agencies.
6. Next Steps Briefing Notes, April 1995.
7. *The Civil Service: Continuity and Change*, Cm 2627, HMSO, London (1994).
8. Targets and their achievement are published in the annual reports of the agencies and are collected together in the Next Steps Annual Reviews. The examples

which follow come from *Next Steps: Agencies in Government, Review 1994*, Cm 2750 (December 1994).

9. Elizabeth Mellon (1994) *Executive Agencies in Central Government* in Anthony Harrison (ed.) *From Hierarchy to Contract*, Transaction Books, New Brunswick and Oxford.
10. Price Waterhouse (1994) *Next Steps Review*.
11. Efficiency Unit (1991) *Making the Most of Next Steps*, HMSO, London.
12. Sylvie Trosa (1994) *The Next Steps: Moving On*, OPSS, Cabinet Office, London.
13. Peter Barberis (1995) *Next Steps: Consequences for the Core and Central Departments*, in Barry J. O'Toole and Grant Jordan (eds) *Next Steps: Improving Management in Government?*, Aldershot, Dartmouth, pp. 115–16.
14. Ibid., note 9.
15. Peter Barberis (1995), ibid., note 13.
16. Elizabeth Mellon (1993) *Executive Agencies. Leading Change from the Outside-in* Public Money and Management, Vol 13, No 2.
17. HMSO (1991) *The Citizen's Charter: raising the standard*, Cm 1599.
18. HMSO (1995) *The Civil Service: Taking Forward Continuity and Change*, Cm 2748, p. 38.
19. Chancellor of the Duchy of Lancaster (1994) *Next Steps Review 1994*, Cm 2750, HMSO.
20. HMSO (1991) *Competing for Quality*, Cm 1730.
21. HMSO (1994) *The Citizen's Charter: Second Report*, Cm 2540, 1994, p. 93.
22. Barry O'Toole and Richard Chapman (1995) *Parliamentary Accountability*, in Barry O'Toole and Grant Jordan (eds) *Next Steps: Improving Management in Government?* Dartmouth, Aldershot.
23. Ibid., p. 25.

4

The Netherlands

Martien Kuitenbrouwer

INTRODUCTION

Scale

The size of the public sector in the Netherlands has been the subject of many studies. The Dutch public sector is similar to Scandinavia when it comes to public expenditure. After Sweden, Denmark and Norway, the Netherlands is the fourth largest spender (56 percent of GNP). Like the Scandinavian countries, Dutch government revenue is also more than 50 percent of GNP (51 percent).

However, when it comes to employment, the Dutch public sector shows a different picture. While it has always been believed that the Dutch public sector was both huge in terms of expenditure and size, recent studies have offered a different outlook. A recent study, conducted for the Dutch Ministry of Internal Affairs, which wished to put an end to the many myths on the size of the Dutch public sector, has shown that employment in the Dutch public sector, defined in the most broad possible way, is smaller than that of Britain.

Public sector employment is here defined as the civil service plus employees of institutions dependent on government subsidies or grants, the non-profit sector or the NIS sector (nationally insured and subsidized). This sector is rather comprehensive, since it includes institutions from the educational sector, social security, health, etc. (see below, under PGOs) (Tilburg, 1994).

Public sector employment is concentrated at the local level (nearly 60 percent of total government employment). Administration of the public sector is concentrated at the central level while service delivery is first and foremost the concern of the municipalities.

Scope and structure

Public expenditure covers many areas. Social security takes up the bulk of the expenditure (over a third). Both healthcare and education account for around one-eighth of the total budget (Kuipers, 1992).

The characteristics of the Dutch public sector are formed by the characteristics of the Dutch state. First, the Dutch state can be described (Lijphart, 1985) as a 'pillarised pacification democracy'. Traditionally, the Dutch pacification democracy was divided into a small number of antagonistic pillars with religious or political bases. These 'subcultures', as Lijphart describes them, led completely separate lives. A Catholic child went to a Catholic school, played at a Catholic football club (which played on Sunday, unlike the Protestant clubs which played and still play on Saturday), the parents read the Catholic daily newspaper, subscribed to the Catholic broadcasting organization, watched the programmes broadcast by this organization, and so on. Mixed marriages were very rare.

Lijphart distinguishes four characteristics of Dutch consociational democracy: executive power sharing or grand coalition, a high degree of autonomy for the different segments, proportional representation and a minority veto. Compromises between the different pillars are based on a positive-sum principle. In order to reach this to full extent, policy decisions are shared and there is a large degree of (functional) decentralization, not so much to the local authorities as to the different para-governmental organizations (PGOs, see below).

Since the early 1960s, Dutch society has become increasingly 'depillarized': the strict divisions between the different pillars have disappeared. This is mainly the result of the process of secularization and increased individualization. However, although Dutch society is no longer strictly divided into different isolated subcultures, Dutch politics and policy are still very much consensus oriented. The fundamental characteristics of the consociational democracy are still intact.

Another characteristic of Dutch society that influences policy-making is the (neo)-corporatist structure. In the Netherlands, there are many councils and organizations in which social partners come together. The groups are not unitary, but consist of an assemblage of organizations which reflects the 'pillarized' structure. Trade unions can be Protestant or socialist in origin, for example. However, more and more of the smaller trade unions are now merging. The Socio-Economic Council (SER), a tripartite body, of which the third element comprises government representatives, is the summit of official corporatism and one of the government's most important advisory bodies.

Finally, the Netherlands is often referred to as a 'decentralized unitary state' (H. Versnel, quoted in Gladdish, 1991, p. 147). Policy-making in the Netherlands is not concentrated in one centrally based institution. Not only do municipalities have wide-ranging powers, policy decisions are often made within largely autonomous 'policy sectors', composed of interest groups, advisory boards of a government department and specialized committees in Parliament. This 'functional decentralization' is characterized by the large number of neo-corporatist institutions and PGOs and the absence of a unified civil service (Andeweg, 1993, p. 164).

The post-war commitment to indicative central planning was undertaken by a set of non-corporate bodies: the Central Bank (nationalized in 1948), the Central Bureau of Statistics (set up in 1899) and the Central Planning Bureau (1945). Together, they comprise 'a system of rational, pragmatic and strategic inputs into a crucible of orderly, democratic national decision making' (Gladdish, 1991, p. 139).

As a result of this complex network, the Dutch public sector consists of a government sector and a 'non-profit sector'. The government sector consists of four tiers of government: central government, the provinces, the district water boards (or 'polderboards') and the municipalities. The provinces and the district water boards are very small and relatively powerless. Public sector expenditure is concentrated in the central government and the municipalities.

At the central level, the executive authority is in hands of the Cabinet, with a relatively weak role for the prime minister (the Dutch state is a constitutional monarchy, with a parliamentary system of government). There are thirteen ministries or departments, each headed by a secretary-general. The departments are subdivided into several directorate-generals, which are again subdivided into policy units. The departments are very autonomous. The Ministry of Internal Affairs and the Ministry of Finance have some coordinating tasks. The director-general for public management of the Ministry of Internal Affairs is formally charged with the promotion of efficiency, effectiveness and democratic quality of public administration. The tasks have become limited as a result of growing decentralization over the last decade. The director-general for the state budget of the Ministry of Finance coordinates the financial management of the different ministries and advises on the general financial management of the civil service. Prior to 1993, the Ministry of Internal Affairs conducted the central wage-bargaining process with the unions for the public sector as a whole. Now, wage bargaining has been decentralized, and is subdivided into eight separate sectors.

The relationship between central and local government is both very centralized and decentralized. Relationships between national and subnational government are not strictly hierarchical. The constitution guarantees the competence of subnational bodies to govern domestic affairs. The Netherlands is divided into twelve provinces. The provincial council is directly elected by proportional representation, and forms the provincial equivalent of the second chamber. Each council elects an executive, for four years. The tasks of the provinces are rather small, compared to the central government or the municipalities. The main tasks lie in the fields of physical planning, transport, environment and supervision of the district water boards and municipalities.

The district water boards or 'polderboards' date from the thirteenth century. They are concerned with 'management' of water: dams, drainage and waterhouses. There are currently 128 'polderboards'.

There are currently 647 municipalities, with extensive responsibilities. They are autonomous in fields such as traffic, recreation and culture, and co-governmental in fields such as physical planning, housing, (public) education, police and social aid. All municipalities are governed by a municipal council, directly elected for four years, and the executive – a board of aldermen and burgomaster.

The current financial relationships between the different tiers of government are the result of long-term historical processes. In 1805, the minister of finance united the eight different district tax systems. This 'grand design' marked the end of the federal state union of the Netherlands and the beginning of the Dutch unitary state. In 1850, another level of decentralization was introduced, bypassing the provinces, which made the municipalities and the central goverment the most powerful layers of government. Nevertheless, financial freedom of the municipalities is limited. Only 10 percent of their budget is raised out of local revenues (taxes and charges). The remaining 90 percent is provided by central government. Central government money is divided into a general municipalities fund (funded by national taxes) and special grants. The money is allocated to the municipalities on the basis of set parameters such as number of inhabitants and area. The municipalities' fund money can be spent freely and accounts for 28 percent of the municipalities' income. The bulk of the municipalities' income comes from specific grants paid by the different central government departments (education, transport, etc.). These specific grants must be spent according to specific guidelines set by these departments. The amount of money allocated is based on the level of activity of the municipality in this specific sector. The level of activity in a specific sector is decided by the local council (burgomaster and aldermen).

In 1991 a decentralization initiative was introduced, which consisted of a large transfer of tasks and responsibilities from central government to lower levels of government. The transfer amounted to 8000 million guilders, and saved the central government 500 million guilders at the same time. An important program in this context is the 'social renewal' program. This program enables municipalities to improve the situation of deprived citizens and make innovations in the field of labour, education, environment and public safety.

While a large percentage of the GDP is allocated by the government, only around 15 percent of public expenditure is directly controlled by the core government. Public tasks which are not directly executed by the core government are managed by PGOs (Aquina, 1988). This is called the NIS or non-profit sector.

There are many PGOs: 775 at national government level in 1982 (Aquina, 1988). Their size and influence vary, as does their legal status. Around two-thirds of them are corporate bodies, with their own legal identity. However, appeals against a PGO may be heard either by a public or private law court;

there are no general rules. The independence of most PGOs is fairly limited, since they are dependent on government money, and in many cases central government can appoint board members and veto decisions. So, since the government provides 50–100 percent of non-profit sector finance, its grip on the PGOs is large, despite their independent status. However, the status of PGOs is different to that of the agencies, which are now being set up by the central government as independently operating executive organizations. The PGOs, unlike the agencies, are not a formal part of the government.

PGOs are found mainly in the areas of social security, healthcare, education, agriculture and justice. Management in the PGOs, and the degree of government control, differ but there are general trends within each 'family group' or sector.

Social security is financed by a mixture of contributions from households, employees and payments from central and local government. The core government collects the money and formulates the policy, while the PGOs distribute the funds, give advice and share in the supervision. Legal arrangements which decide the expenditure of these funds are made by Parliament. The Cabinet decides upon the size of the contributions. An important part of the medical insurance fund is paid for by private insurance companies; the expenditure of these funds therefore only shows a part of real health expenditure in the Netherlands. Different areas of social security, such as unemployment insurance, sickness insurance, widows benefits, etc., are covered by different social security funds. The Socio-Economic Council, a tripartite organization, is the supervisory umbrella organization. It supervises the implementation of social security Acts and advises the Cabinet on matters such as premium rates. The members of the board of administration of each fund are appointed by the unions, employer organizations and central government.

Health expenditure is organized in the same way as social security. Medical insurance funds handle the money paid by employees, employers (compulsory) and government, and pay doctors and hospital bills on behalf of the claimants. Here, too, a council which consists of doctors' organizations (doctors are independent professionals), trade unions, employer organizations and central government is charged with supervision, coordination and advice to the government. The Cabinet fixes premium rates. Previously, the medical professionals determined the total volume of expenditure. This has, however, been limited with the introduction of budgeting to hospitals.

Healthcare delivery is mainly in the hands of 'pillarized' institutions, which are private. GPs are also private entrepreneurs, however, and their charges are regulated by the Cabinet and the Central Hospital Tariff Council. This Council consists of representatives of the core government, insurance companies, trade unions, and other social and professional organizations.

In 1982, the Health Care Law (which dated from 1956) was renewed: the structure of non-governmental hospitals and clinics remained, but governmental control was increased, by decentralized planning and increased coordination from regions and municipalities.

Education is provided in private and state schools. The former are attended by around 28 percent of all schoolchildren, and take up around one-third of total expenditure. The public schools are maintained by municipal authorities. Public schools are attended by around 72 percent of all schoolchildren. Most private schools have a religious or special pedagogical outlook (teaching according to Montessori methods, for example). The administration is in hands of school boards which are accountable to the local authorities or to the private organizations which run them. The state sudsidizes this 'special education' often up to 100 percent. The schools are subject to educational legislation which is enforced by the minister of education and science. The government sets the teachers' wages (they are civil servants), and lays down the curriculum format and outline; furthermore, it controls the quality of schools (though not universities) through inspectors. Private schools may select teachers and pupils according to belief.

The procedure for decisions on expenditure, quality standards, etc., resembles that of other sectors. The Cabinet ultimately decides, but consulting bodies which represent both government and private education influence the shape of policy. They have no formal power, however.

The existence of the large number of PGOs in the field of welfare delivery can be explained by the pillarized nature of Dutch society. The PGO system enabled a system of service delivery according to various religious beliefs. Furthermore, it was a practical way of providing social services 'close to the client'. The social security system represents a compromise between socialist preferences for a full 'state' system, liberal preferences for a system fully accountable to Parliament, and Christian preferences for a system to be handled by autonomous employer–employee organizations per industry (Aquina, 1988, p. 100). Secularization and 'depillarization' have left the PGO system largely intact, but the grip of the government on the PGOs has in most cases tightened over recent decades. Furthermore, central government has played an increasingly important role in welfare delivery.

The Dutch public sector is thus far from unitary. The Dutch government is a large money-provider but has a limited role in service delivery.

MANAGEMENT PROCESSES

Goals and objectives setting

In 1992, Parliament and the government agreed on revision of management rules. In a report *Towards More Result Orientated Management*, proposals for greater devolution of authority and the introduction of independent executive agencies were made.

The idea of greater authority at microlevel, which is linked to goals and objective setting, was not new. The idea of contract management in central government was born in 1983, after the publication of the yearly 'reconsiderations report' (see p. 94). A committee for the introduction of management contract experiments was set up. In 1990, the final report was published. In the first instance, the experiments were not very successful: most departments were satisfied with their traditional style of management. However, as a result of more budgetary pressures and cost reduction, contract management in central government has been given new attention and has been introduced extensively over the last four years.

The extent to which contract management is used differs by department, and each department can decide for itself. The management contracts, made between the political and civil service top and the lower management, lay down the period (usually one year) and the conditions (the policy framework and the legal context), the tasks and the means. The contracts have no legal basis; failure to reach targets cannot be the basis for dismissal.

Since central government is preoccupied with policy-making and administration, goals and objectives are often defined in a qualitative rather than a quantitative way. This makes control at the end of the contract rather difficult.

At the municipal level, management contracts have also been introduced since the mid-1980s. Agreements are made between the central administration (board of burgomaster and aldermen) and the different sectors. In general, the contracts are made annually. The contracts contain agreements, attached to the budget, on the services and products to be delivered. Furthermore, the contract lays down certain 'rules of the game'; the competence of the service towards personnel policy, financial and social policy, and the way in which contracts are to be evaluated. The contracts do not have a legal status. The way the contracts are monitored differs for each service and for each municipality. The extent to which contract management is used in the municipalities differs. Some municipalities are quicker than others (Tilburg and Delft are two middle–large municipalities where contract management has been introduced on a large scale). In Amsterdam, contract management has been introduced in sectors which are relatively easily measured by output, such as housing and water supply. For social services, the development of contracting has not gone as far.

The prime reason to introduce contract management at both the central and local level is to increase cost consciousness. The public sector is subject to cuts everywhere.

In the health sector, goals and objective setting are becoming increasingly important as well. There is, however, no clear or systematic procedure as yet. As everywhere, development towards goals and objective setting is linked to changes in the budget system (see below).

Planning

Because of the pluralistic nature of the Dutch public sector and increased decentralization, central planning is rare. There is no systematic planning procedure for the whole of the public sector. Central indicative planning is done by the non-corporate advisory boards such as the Central Planning Bureau.

The most important kind of planning at all sectors/levels is the budget plan. The annual budgetary proposal of the central government (*Miljoenennota*) is presented by the Staten Generaal (Parliament) as a legislative proposal divided into chapters according to the ministries.

Like goals and objective setting, planning in the Netherlands is linked to budgeting procedures. Here again, planning is more developed in the executive services, which are output-oriented, than in the policy-making units of central government. Introduction of budget-holding at the policy-unit level within the different departments of central government has increased the scope of planning. As for goals and objective setting, the departments are free to decide upon the introduction of planning; there is no set standard procedure. With the move towards independent agencies, planning and control have been given a new dimension. However, since the development of agencies is still very premature, set procedures for planning and control have not yet been developed (see case study for more information on agencies).

In higher education, the minister of education makes a two-year plan, based on the institution's own plans. The same system is introduced in adult and further education. However, in primary and secondary education there is no central planning procedure.

Budgeting

As a result of the decentralization wave of the mid-1980s, there is an overall tendency to increase the scope of lump sum budgets together with increased autonomy at almost every level/sector.

At the central government level, lump-sum budgeting has been introduced on a large scale. Departmental secretary-generals (heads of the departments) delegate budgetary powers to directorate-general level; the directorate-general managers can then delegate the budget further down if they wish. Managers have a large amount of autonomy in spending the budget. Recently, material costs and personnel costs have been joined together: managers are free to decide whether to hand out a bonus or to buy a computer.

Over the last ten years, the relationship between general funding of municipalities by central government through the municipalities fund and specific grants has changed in favour of the former. However, there have been cuts in the municipalities funds. There have also been talks to increase the tax limit of the municipalities, giving them greater freedom to raise their own revenues. Although, in general, the municipalities welcome the greater financial autonomy, sector-responsible aldermen are worried that their special interest is overlooked when a lump-sum rather than a specified budget is increased. As for increasing the tax-raising possibilities, many municipalities are worried they will be blamed for rising costs and expenditure cuts; these plans are therefore not welcomed with undivided pleasure (Kuipers, 1992, p. 105).

As a result of cuts in the municipalities fund, (which has not yet really led to recentralization) and because municipalities have become more autonomous in their expenditure of the central government budget, there is an increased scope for budgeting and contract managment of the different services at the municipal level. However, there is a difference between the different municipalities. The southern municipality of Tilburg is the model for modern public management at the municipal level in the Netherlands. In 1989, the budget procedure was changed as a result of a complete reorganization of the service delivery structure. The traditional sector model was replaced by a 'concern model'. The different municipal services became more autonomous and competent, with the main policy developments being directed by a central 'concern staff'. Management reports were introduced; these were responsible for reporting information from the services to this central staff. As a result of the introduction of the 'concern model', the budgets became output based instead of function oriented. The budgets were no longer subdivided according to services, but based on three factors: strategic policy, finance and management.

Other municipalities, such as Amsterdam, have not yet gone this far. In Amsterdam, there is a difference between easily quantifiable and less quantifiable services. Whereas the former services are budgeted on an output basis (such as transport), the latter often still have an open-ended budget (such as social services). There are no central guidelines, and each municipality develops its own methods.

Budgeting of hospital and nursing homes has changed greatly over the last ten years. The system of automatic process-financing (open-ended) was changed to input budgeting in 1983. This, however, emphasized the unequal starting positions of the hospitals, which was regarded as unfair. This led to the introduction of 'function-oriented budgeting'. This 'task-setting' budget is bound to a maximum, calculated on the basis of a maximum level of activities (operations, for example). When the maximum level of activities is overstepped, these activities will not be covered by the government. So above a (historical or political) maximum, budget and activities are separated. The introduction of this kind of budgeting seems to have been effective; there has been a decline in costs and volume. However, other developments in the health sector may have been important as well.

In higher education, a system of output-based budgets was introduced in 1989. In 1993, this system was altered and has become even more output based. At the same time, the universities have been given more freedom in the spending of their lump-sum budget.

Primary and secondary education makes use of the so-called 'formation-budget'. This separates the budget into personnel and material costs. The personnel budget is based on a standard/centrally formulated system of 'average personnel costs'. In 1996, this kind of budget is to be replaced by a lump-sum budget, leaving the schools to decide whether to spend money on staff or on a new roof. In the health sector, there are also plans to move towards a more lump-sum style budget. The big insurance companies and the government are still negotiating.

Costs and costs information

An increase in cost awareness can be detected in all sectors, as a result of the changing budget procedures. Contract management has also increased cost awareness. The central state budget is, however, based on expenditure rather than on costs. Limits are set by public deficit and the ability of the public to pay.

In 1986, the financial accountability operation was launched, as part of the several 'great and small operations' executed by the government (see case study). This operation aimed at making each ministry primarily responsible for the structure and organization of their accounting system. The supervisory role was left to the minister of finance. The main objectives of the operation were the establishment of an accounting system at the departmental level, permitting efficient and legitimate implementation of budgets, and the establishment of a system to supply financial information between the different departments and the Ministry of Finance, and between the civil servants and Parliament in order to provide information rapidly and efficiently. Furthermore, the operation adjusted the structure of the draft budgets and budgetary statements and accounts so that Parliament can exercise its right to approve the budgets more easily.

The financial accountability operation was completed in 1992. The operation has led to the adoption of proposals on the introduction of more independent agencies. Furthermore, there was a reassessment of the rules governing financial and personnel management which was implemented in 1993 and 1994.

In the health sector, costs are decided centrally at the COTG (Central Hospital Tariff Council and Cabinet). There is thus no room for price competition.

Evaluation

At the central level, Parliament monitors the government. When there is a problem, there is some kind of policy evaluation; Parliament can undertake oral or written inquiry. This kind of evaluation is not systematic. Its function is largely political – in order 'to point out the guilty'.

The Central Audit Office, a central independent organ like the other High Councils of State (Parliament, the Council of State and the Ombudsman), is charged with researching the income and expenditure of central government. Over the last decade, its task has widened from inspection of legitimacy to inspection of efficiency in the form of operational research and evaluation policies.

In 1981, a new type of evaluation at central govenment level was introduced, as part of the 'Great Operations' (see case study): the 'reconsideration' (*heroverweging*). Thirty important fields of policy were selected to be checked to see if all activities undertaken at these fields were efficient and effective. Efficiency was formulated as the achievement of results with as few losses as possible, and effectiveness was measured by looking at whether the targets had been reached. The 'reconsiderations' are supposed to lead to an overview of possible expenditure reductions, between which the government can choose. The reconsiderations are a structural part of the ongoing activities of the Ministry of Finance. So far, over eighty policy fields have been 'reconsidered'. The yearly *Miljoenennota* (central government Budget plan) contains the results of the most recent outcomes.

Other than this, arrangements to evaluate ongoing reforms are scarce. A big evaluation programme set up recently is the evaluation of the 'social renewal programme'. The social renewal programme enables municipalities to improve the situation of deprived citizens and to make innovations in areas such as employment, education, environment and public safety. The evaluation programme, implemented by the Social and Cultural Plan Body consisted of ten case studies in ten municipalities. The results have recently been published. Another big evaluation programme was set up to investigate the high sick-rates and absenteeism in the Dutch labourforce.

The government has started a programme to stimulate policy evaluation. The ministries are obliged to set up institutional arrangements to coordinate and stimulate policy evaluation. Since 1992, ministries have been obliged to report on their policy-evaluation programmes, with the emphasis on budget explanation (financial accountability operation). The overall aim is to offer Parliament a better insight into the implementation of policy evaluation at the ministerial level. Since 1991, the Ministry of Finance has been working on the improvement of performance measurement; it wishes to develop measures to plan and control efficiency productivity and the effectiveness of policy processes in ministries. Nevertheless, evaluation at the policy-unit level with the different managers of central government is not very well developed. Looking forward remains a lot more more popular than looking backward. The lack of evaluation is seen as a fault, but a kind of 'prisoner dilemma' can be detected at the same time: who will go first in setting up evaluation procedures (interview with Mr Vos, director-general of public management, Ministry of Internal Affairs)? The introduction of agencies in 1994, however, has resulted in increased interest in performance measurements. Scope for individual evaluation has increased enormously, through 'performance talks' and 'assessment talks' (see pp. 101–2).

In education, there is increased scope for evaluation procedures, which is linked to the increasing institutional freedom (which is the result of 'functional decentralization'). There is a division between performance measurement/evaluation by measurable targets (percentage of graduates, percententage of Ph.D.s, for example) and non-measurable performance. The latter is evaluated by special 'visitatie commissies' (search committees) and self-assessment procedures.

In most municipalities, there is no central evaluation procedure which is applied to all services, apart from control of the budget. However, some municipalities are now switching from the traditional sector model of service management to a 'concern model' (see budgeting). The 'concern model' links increased autonomy to a great deal of control and extensive evaluation procedures. The evaluation reports are the basis for the budget. In order to promote transparency, standard procedures for reports were introduced. In 1991, Tilburg introduced a new public management instrument, the 'effectiveness measurer'. The measurement of effectiveness is both *ex post* and *ex ante*. *Ex post* measurement is done by specific research into the effect of one specific subsidy. *Ex ante* is a more structural and integral way of measuring the effect; criteria of effectiveness are formulated within the budget itself. The latter is becoming increasingly important. Thus, the level of development of evaluation procedures at the municipalities level differs.

Market and customer orientation

The most important body involved in checking customer satisfaction of public services is the Ombudsman. The institution offers supplementary protection (next to legal protection) against unacceptable behaviour by public authorities. Furthermore, the Ombudsman aims at promoting structural improvements in the functioning of public bureaucracy. The institution of the Ombudsman was introduced in 1982. The Ombudsman is appointed by Parliament for six years. The National Ombudsman is one of the High Councils of State like the General Audit Chamber. All these institutions are independent from the executive. The tasks of the National Ombudsman are limited to the central government but many of the larger municipalities have appointed their own Ombudsman.

The judgements of the Ombudsman are not legally binding, nor does he test lawfulness or efficiency. Administrative and ethical decency is the criterion used. The most common complaints are about active provision of information to the public and promptness (in particular the length of time to deal with matters) (The National Ombudsman of the Netherlands, annual report 1993, summary). In most cases, the advice of the Ombudsman is followed.

In 1992, experiments with the concept of 'civic service centres' started. The civic service centres aim to improve public service to customers. The centres are a concentration of contacts between the government and the citizens of all kinds of administrative services. The centres are an attempt to integrate counter and desk functions of different government bodies.

In the development of market orientation, there is, of course, a split between the policy-makers and the service-deliverers. The service-deliverers (at the municipal level mainly) are increasingly liable to market forces. (Amsterdam is the main example: the city has been slow with the transformation towards more market-oriented services because of the traditionally strongly social-democratic council. However, developments in Amsterdam are the same as everywhere, only the scale and speed are different.) As a result of central government cuts in funding to the municipalities, the municipalities had to change the way they ran their (costly) services. This has led to an enormous wave of complete privatization, and semi-privatization through increased self-sufficiency and contracting-out of municipal services everywhere. The latter especially is used extensively. The 'truck-system' has been abolished in Amsterdam in 1990 (all municipal services were obliged to use each other's services). The council remains a shareholder in these services.

The level of market orientation of the publicly owned services left depends on the nature of the service. Some services have to compete freely with other services on the market, like the service for land development, and must tender together with private companies. The council is obliged to ask the municipal service to make an offer but it is not obliged to use its services. Other services, such as social aid, are not really market oriented. Services like the latter are trying to become increasingly client oriented through questionnaires, etc. Furthermore, these non-market-oriented services are compared (by the Ministry of Social Affairs in most cases) with services in other municipalities. The development of market orientation is also dependent on the attitudes of the municipal council. In the health sector, customer orientation is becoming increasingly important. Market orientation is a lot less developed as the tariffs in the health sector are laid down centrally, and there is not much room for open competition on the basis of costs. This limits the scope for private clinics.

As in Britain, the GP in the Netherlands is the 'gatekeeper' between the client and the customer. A hospital's budget is partly based on the so-called 'adherent area' (the area/amount of patients covered by the hospital). Since the hospitals are dependent on GPs for their patients, they have become increasingly customer oriented (towards the GP).

An interesting case of customer/market orientation in the sense of customer choice is the Dutch school system. The system of school choice has traditionally been free. Private schools (though publicly funded) were usually based on religious outlook. This settled school choice, which was consequently based on religious conviction. However, with the secularization of Dutch society, the system of 'obvious choice' has largely disappeared. This has led to an increased system of competition between schools. In order to provide parents with 'objective' information, schools are now obliged to publish a school guide according to centrally set rules. The guides provide information on graduation percentages, extracurricular activities, etc. Schools also produce pens, sweatshirts, bags and other 'freebies' provided at the 'open-day' of the school in order to attract pupils. The Dutch system of free school choice attracts many American and British academics and managers.

Personnel policy

The Netherlands does not have an institution like the British or French civil service. The Law on Civil Servants determines that the government, provinces, municipalities and district water boards must regulate appointments and take responsibility for dismissals, and other employment conditions, as well as regulations with the civil service trade unions. A civil servant is a person who is 'appointed by the government to be active in public service' (Tilburg, 1994). Teachers, whether employed in public or private education, are also regarded as civil servants in the Netherlands. The employment conditions for the civil servants of the central government are laid down in the ARAR (General Central Government Civil Servants Regulations) and for the central government officials in the BBRA (Pay Agreement for Central Government Civil Servants).

Whereas previously, employment conditions of all civil servants in all sectors were negotiated between the minister of internal affairs and the trade unions, since 1993 agreements on employment conditions have been decentralized. Negotiations are now being made at eight different sectors: central government, provinces, municipalities, polderboards, defence, police, education and justice. The decentralization concerns both primary and secondary employment conditions. Differentiation of employment conditions is considered necessary 'in order to create conditions which are more compatible with the different circumstances of each sector' (Kurvers, 1994). This development has thus put an end to the unitary status of the Dutch civil servant. However, the differentiation of labour negotiations is not expected to lead to great discrepancies in the immediate future – employers still have to negotiate with the same civil service unions.

The position of Dutch civil servants has undergone some changes over the last ten years as a result of the 'normalization' process. The aim of this normalization is to make the position of civil servants as comparable to employees in the private sector as possible. The focal point of normalization has been the review of the consultation procedure on labour conditions, including the way in which negotiations on pay, pensions and related matters are conducted. The government has codified the protocol in which the formal requirement to reach an agreement is embodied. Central government has also set up a personnel reduction operation (the -2 percent operation, later named the 'slimming' operation, see case study). Between 1983 and 1986, the civil service was reduced by 6,100 positions. Between 1987 and 1990, another 20,000 positions were abolished.

The decentralization of personnel policy and the European legislation on the free movement of capital have led to the privatization process of the Dutch general pension fund (ABP) – the second largest capital investor in the world – to be completed in 1996. The privatization of the pension fund, combined with the integration of civil servants into the general insurance scheme (to be completed this decade) are regarded as important steps in the normalization process.

RECRUITMENT AND DISMISSAL

There is no central recruitment system for Dutch civil servants. Recruitment policy is decentralized, with each department or institution recruiting for itself. A new civil servant at central government is usually appointed on a temporary contract for a trial period of two years. The 'slimming' operation has led to minimal external recruitment. Recruitment for open positions is always internal at first. For central government, vacancies are announced in other departments as well. Only when it has proved impossible to find someone from inside will the vacancy will be advertised in the large daily newspapers. Candidates can be invited for an interview on the basis of a letter or an application form. A psychological test is almost always part of the application procedure, and this is the only thing the departments have in common, in terms of recruitment.

Apart from the diplomatic service, recruitment is almost always on the basis of a job, not a general service. However, since July 1993, top civil servants have been appointed for general service in central government. This deovelopment is linked to the idea to set up a British-style civil service within which top civil servants are mobile, and move places every so often (see case study).

In 1988, a market-related allowance or bonus was introduced to recruit (or retain) certain difficult-to-obtain civil servants. In August 1994, this arrangement led to a scandal when it was found out how much the head of the Amsterdam police force was paid as a result of this special arrangement.

There are special arrangements to encourage the recruitment of ethnic minorities, women and the disabled. Target figures have been set: 5 percent of total personnel for ethnic minorities and disabled in 1995. For women the target figure was 30 percent in central government by 1995 (Ministerie van Binnenlandse Zaken, 1993). Target figures are in no way binding. The recruitment of disabled and ethnic minorities does not so far seem very satisfactory at any sector/level.

Dismissal is always difficult since civil servants are protected by special law. However, dismissal procedures have become more flexible, with a greater freedom for the manager. An appointment can be ended on the completion of a temporary contract; a permanent appointment can only be ended on grounds laid down in the ARAR. There are several grounds on which a civil servant can be dismissed. These include pensionable age, bad health, inadequate performance, termination of the position, surplus of staff and at personal request. A civil servant can also be fired as the result of a reorganization. There is a special hierarchy for dismissals in this case, those with more than thirty five years of employment are the first to go, followed by those under the age of thirty-five, with the fewest years of employment. Officially, civil servants can still be dismissed for 'anti-state' action (this is used to include membership of the Communist Party) but this has practically fallen into disuse. When dismissal is 'honourable' and not at personal request, the civil servant is entitled to a special benefit, 'waiting money'. The amount of this benefit is dependent on the length of the previous working period; minimally three months and maximally 4.5 years, unless the person in question is over 57.5 years old, in which case the 'waiting money' is paid until the pensionable age (65) is reached. The amount paid is 93 percent of the salary for the next nine months, 73 percent for the following four years and 70 percent for the time after that. The 'Great Efficiency Operation', a great cost-reduction programme (see case study) has as one of its aims the reduction of the amount of people claiming the costly 'waiting money'. This led to renewed intensity of 'replacing policy'. Since personnel policy had been decentralized, each manager is primarily responsible for the 'replacement' of redundant staff and for the 'failure' of this: the 'waiting money' expenses.

'Malfunctioning' or inadequate performance can also lead to dismissal. Managers now have a relatively high level of freedom in this. The decision to fire on these grounds can only be decided upon after several assessment talks (see performance management section).

PROMOTION

There is no strictly organized career-development policy, and there are no nationally set targets for promotion or career development. Promotion can normally only be made by application for internal vacancies. In a survey conducted by the Ministry of Internal Affairs, it was estimated that 79.5 percent of current personnel in central government had at least had one promotion with the current employer. On average, promotion is made after nine years of employment (Ministerie van Binnenlandse Zaken, November 1993).

Pay rises are, however, 'automatic', once a year (see pay section). Mobility, not specifically vertical, is stimulated. The Ministry of Internal Affairs has set up a temporary exchange program for civil servants in central government to change place for a set period of time, after which they can return to their old post if requested. However, the initiation of the exchange depends on the personal request of the civil servant in question. The aim of programs such as these is to break through the 'vertical' departmental structure (*verkokering*: the formation of 'silos' or 'tubes' in central government – see the case study for more on this).

Some departments have a system of 'career-planning talks' between managers and employees. In these talks, the wishes of the civil servant and possibilities within the organization are discussed.

PAY

Prior to 1993, pay negotiations were made between the Ministry of Internal Affairs and the unions. Pay bargaining has now been decentralized, and negotiations are now made in eight separate sectors: central government, the provinces, the municipalities, defence, police, justice, education and Polderboards. Agreements are made for a period of two years. According to the PUMA review of the OECD, civil servants' pay in the Netherlands is the lowest in the whole of Europe (OECD, 1993a).

Payment for civil servants is based on a system of scales and grades. Depending on the nature and level of the appointment, the civil servant is put in one of eighteen salary scales. The nature and level of the job are specified according to a job-ranking system. If a civil servant does not agree with the outome of the ranking-system, he or she can file a complaint. Each scale is subdivided into around eleven steps/grades. At the start of a job, one usually starts at the lowest possible step, depending on factors such as previous salary. Furthermore, civil servants receive holiday payment of 8 percent of the gross salary. At the end of the year, there is a special bonus, which is 0.3 percent of the yearly salary. When performance is normal/ satisfactory, each employee moves up one step each year until the top of the scale is reached. When performance is regarded as outstanding, two steps can be made at once. When performance is regarded as inadequate, the automatic progression can be withheld. Managers have great freedom to decide upon this. Withholding the 'automatic' pay increment is, however, rare.

If a civil servant has reached the maximum pay-step, and performance is regarded as outstanding, his/her manager can decide to hand out a 'performance allowance'. This is temporary, for one year. Under special circumstances, the 'performance allowance' can be awarded for longer than one year. The allowance can be at most 10 percent of the salary. The manager can also decide to award a special bonus for outstanding performance. This is a one-off payment, for a special achievement, to be given at any time. There are no set rules on the amount – this is up to the department, to the unit manager who holds the budget to decide. Normally, the bonus is around

20–25 percent of the monthly salary. Higher awards are possible, though when it is more than 50 percent of one month's salary, permission of the secretary-general (head of the ministry) is requested.

Next to the monetary awards are the 'tokens'. A book or a bottle of wine may be given for a special achievement. This is very common. Again, the manager has complete freedom to decide upon this.

In 1989, greater freedom for the different departments to decide upon the size and distribution of performance-related bonuses was introduced. Budgets for perfomance-related pay have become bigger and managers have been given special training in the implementation of these special awards. Since 1989, the additional budget allocated to the departments for performance-related pay is around 0.25 percent of the salary base budget Furthermore, departments are allocated 1.5 percent of the basic salary for automatic pay increments and 0.5 percent for performance-related increments. The number of awards paid is unlimited; it is up to the manager to decide. The departments can decide to award more for performance-related pay by taking money from other areas, such as training. They are free to decide. There are no central agencies involved in the auditing of the special pay schemes: the departments are fully responsible for the implementation of these.

The introduction of greater pay flexibility in 1989 was reviewed in 1991. The results showed that there was a great deal of diversity in the implementation of performance-related pay between the ministries (OECD, 1993c). However, these differences seem to have evened out (Mr van Baarle, director-general personnel management, Ministry of Internal Affairs, interview 18 August 1994). Furthermore, it was concluded that performance-related pay was awarded much more often to senior level grades than to lower grades. Finally, it was concluded that the performance-related pay system demotivated employees who did not receive performance-related pay. Other complaints include the lack of openness on the decisions made by management and the use of wrong criteria on which performance-related pay is based.

PERFORMANCE MANAGEMENT

Individual performance measurements are becoming increasingly popular. The procedures are applied widely, and are the same for all civil servants in all sectors. There are two kinds of talks between management and personnel. 'Performance talks' (*functioneringsgesprekken*) between the civil servant and the manager are about the general performance of the civil servant. These talks have no legal consequences. Although it is not compulsory, the Ministry of Internal Affairs recommends that these talks should be held at least once a year. Performance talks have been used widely for a few years, and have become increasingly common in all sectors.

'Assessment talks' (*beoordelingsgesprekken*) are meant to judge the functioning of the civil servant. This can lead to legal action, if it is decided the civil servant has not performed adequately (this kind of talk is usually preceded by a performance talk). Some departments hold these talks regularly, others only when there is a direct reason to do so. In the educational sector, the introduction of assessment talks has been prevented by the unions. Assessment talks are not used as widely as performance talks but are gaining ground everywhere. In general, the municipalities which are more positive towards new styles of public management have introduced assessment talks more widely than other municipalities.

The decisions on the awarding of special allowances or bonuses are made on the basis of these talks. Group performance measurement is very rare. However, bonuses, such as bottles of wine, can be given to a group, after a successful project.

TRAINING

Like the rest of personnel management, training of civil servants is decentralized at institutional level and departmental level. There is hardly any special kind of training for civil servants, either before or after recruitment. Special training for specialized staff such as documentation or computerization is becoming more important.

Departments and institutions are free to decide what to spend on training. According to the yearly review on employment in central government, central government spends more money on training than the private sector (Ministerie van Binnenlandse Zaken, 1993). Overall, training costs account for around 4.5 percent of the total labour costs for central government, while this is only 1.7 percent for the private sector (on average). There are large differences between spending on training between the different departments. The highest spender, the Ministry of Social Affairs and Employment, spent four times as much as the lowest spender (General Affairs) in 1993.

The most common kind of training is in computerization and management. Around 85 percent of these courses are taken within working time. The average course lasts around six days. There is also the possibility for employees personally to request a course, the cost of which can be refunded by the employer. There used to be a central training institute for all civil servants working for central government, though this has now been privatized. Although it is still called the State Training Centre and is specialized in training civil servants, departments can choose freely whether to use its services or not.

In the education sector, training has been completely decentralized as well. Previously, for primary and secondary education, there was a national 'refresher' training program, paid for by a national budget. This has been abolished, and schools now each get a part of the 'refresher' budget, which they can spend almost freely. At the moment, schools are obliged to spend the budget at the old training institutions, but with the introduction of the lump-sum budget, this obligation will disappear. There are no central guide-lines on training.

MANAGING CHANGE

Economic context

The rapidly increasing budget deficit and unemployment form the economic context in which the changes in public management in the Netherlands must be placed. Until the late 1970s, the Dutch economy was booming. The com-mitment to the 'magic pentangle' of full employment, economic growth, reasonable income redistribution, balance of payment equilibrium and price stability was maintained until the late 1960s. The post-war reconstruction was very successful and the Netherlands benefited from its membership of the European Community and Benelux.

In the late 1970s, the situation deteriorated. The crises which hit all indus-trialized economies hit the Netherlands particularly hard, since the Dutch economy was very open to external pressures. On top of that, the Nether-lands had to cope with the so-called 'Dutch-disease'. 'Dutch disease', now an internationally known economic term, refers to the use of temporary income to finance permanent expenditures. This results in increased govern-ment expenditure and hard currency. 'Dutch disease' was the result of the discovery of a large natural gas reservoir in Groningen in the late 1960s. At first, the discovery led the Netherlands into a period of economic euphoria. However, the strong guilder eventually put the Netherlands at a disadvan-tage. Dutch products became increasingly expensive at the same time as the oil crisis hit the world economy. The income from the gas production was not invested in permanent economic structures, but mainly used to finance increased welfare expenditure. In order to become less dependent on gas revenues, expenditure had to be reduced.

At the end of the 1970s, unemployment started to become a serious political problem. For a long time, the post-war aim of full employment had been fulfilled. (It should, however, be noted that Dutch 'full employment' has never meant 100 percent participation rates. Throughout the twentieth century, there has always been a low participation rate for women. So even when there was a situation of official 'full employment', there was always a large number of people not working and not officially looking for work.) However, unem-ployment had started to rise in the late 1960s, and continued to rise through-out the 1970s. In 1983–4, unemployment reached a peak of approximately 17 percent of the labourforce. This figure was only exceeded by Belgium, Turkey, Ireland and Spain from the OECD countries (Andeweg, 1993, p. 192).

By the late 1970s, public expenditure in the Netherlands had risen to Scandinavian proportions. Between 1955 and 1975, the net national income had increased by a factor of 2.3. Public expenditure on education, science and culture had increased by a factor of 4.6, and public expenditure on housing and physical planning by 5.6 (OECD economic survey of the Netherlands, quoted in Gladdish, 1991, p. 141).

Unlike the Scandinavian countries, the increase in public expenditure cannot be explained by a long-term dominance of the Social Democrats. The increase in public expenditure from the late 1960s onwards can partly be explained by the economically favourable circumstances. Post-war reconstruction had been accompanied by restraint. When the natural gas supply was found, however, constraints seemed to be forgotten. However, the most important reason for the enormous increase in public expenditure in the 1960s and 1970s must be sought in the depillarization process. With the secularization and depillarization of Dutch society in the late 1960s and the 1970s, the grip of the government on welfare delivery increased. As a result of these processes, the focus of Dutch paternalism transferred from the religious subcultures more explicitly to the secular state. As Gladdish (1991, p. 142) puts it, Dutch society had long been paternalistic, but through secularization and depillarization, this became obvious through a sudden increase in government expenditure. However, the pillarized structure was by no means completely dismantled. The state simply became more involved in welfare delivery.

Even though the discovery of the gas increased revenues, the government was still forced to borrow money, since revenues were still not compatible with expenditure. This led to an enormous increase in the budget deficit. The Dutch national debt increased from 43.8 percent of national income in 1982 to 71 percent in 1991 (Andeweg, 1993, p. 209). The deficit reached its peak in 1982 when it was 10.7 percent of net national income. Discussion on the size of the budget deficit and ways to reduce it has preoccupied Dutch political parties for over a decade. The reduction of this deficit has become even more important in the context of the EMU criteria. At the moment, the deficit is still over the limit.

The deteriorating economic situation in the Netherlands of the early 1980s led to 'a general feeling that action was necessary to call a halt to further increases' (Andeweg, 1993, p. 199).

Constitutional arrangements

Constitutional arrangements in the Netherlands leave little room for the prime minister to undertake action on his own behalf. There is no strong central leadership in government reorganizations. The British situation of central, top-down leadership where the prime minister and the secretaries of state have wide powers, unchecked by Parliament, is unthinkable in the Netherlands.

Furthermore, the Netherlands has a strong tradition of a democratic *Rechtsstaat*. This gives the government and the state a relatively strong legal root in society. The legitimacy of the government in the Netherlands is relatively high.

Ideology

The discussion on public management renewal has been influenced remarkably little by ideology. It is important to realize that the rise of the Dutch welfare state and the increase of public expenditure were also not led by (social-democratic) ideology. The financial economic situation in the early 1980s was the primary reason for change – a fact that has been accepted by all major political parties. There has been relatively little rhetoric on the blessings of the free market as opposed to the public sector. Privatization in the Netherlands has been promoted as an aim for administrative efficiency and budgetary reduction rather than 'an ideological crusade for free market capitalism' (Andeweg, 1993, p. 200). It is interesting in this context that the Dutch Social Democrats had already dropped their clause on the nationalization of industry in the 1930s. Since the process of privatization lacked any 'new right' style ideology, the Dutch Social Democrats have had little difficulty in accepting privatization.

The discussion on public sector renewal is, however, not completely free from ideological rhetoric, but a more ideological discussion on the 'make-ability' of society only took off when the 'Great Operations' (the Dutch renewal programs) were already in action. Also, Dutch government memoranda are not free from new public management jargon, often literally copied from American and British programs. However, ideology does not take such a central place in the Dutch discussion on public management renewal, and seems a lot more subtle. A more ideological discussion on the role of the state and government did not automatically create fierce defenders of the free market. The ideological discussion on the role of government emphasized the importance of quality rather than quantity. However, a severe cutback of the state in favour of private enterprise was not advocated by anybody.

Ideology has never had a strong place in Dutch policy-making. As Lijphart (1985, p. 123) explains, Dutch politics is business, not a game.

Consensus

Traditionally, Dutch policy-making has been very much consensus oriented. Changes in public sector management and public sector expenditure reduction are largely based on consensus. Only 'Green Left', one of the smaller left-wing parties which embodies the former communist and socialist parties, opposes most plans on welfare expenditure cuts. The first and second 'Christian–Lubbers' Cabinets (1981–9), which introduced the 'Great Operations', were coalition cabinets of the Christian Democrats and the Liberals. The last one (1989–93) was a coalition between the Social Democrats and the Christian Democrats. As mentioned above, public sector renewal has been introduced largely out of financial necessity. This is something all major parties could agree on. The government, which came to power in August 1994, a coalition of the Social Democrats, the Liberals and the Democrats (the first government without the Christian Democrats since the 1930s), announced more changes in public sector management, more or less following the initiatives taken under the former government.

Furthermore, there has been a general acceptance by the public of the unpleasant measures. The 1992 wage agreements where the trade unions agreed to wage restraint symbolize this (Andeweg, 1993, p. 210).

Changes in management of the public sector in the Netherlands started to take off in the early 1980s. Unlimited public sector growth, in terms of size and expenditure, was brought to a halt. At least, this was the aim of the centre-right Cabinet which stayed in office from 1982 until 1989. The reasons for the 'no nonsense' government policy, introduced by Lubbers, the Christian-Democratic prime minister in 1982, were first and foremost an attempt to reduce the budget deficit. Only when the 'Great Operation' was in action did a more ideological discussion on the role of the state and the government start to develop. However, a strong Anglo-Saxon style, 'new right'-led discussion has never taken place in the Netherlands.

Case Study

THE 'GREAT EFFICIENCY OPERATION' – THE REORGANIZATION
OF THE CENTRAL GOVERNMENT SECTOR

The 'Great Efficiency Operation' was introduced by the centre left government which took office in 1989. The 'Great Efficiency Operation' aimed to increase the efficiency of the central government by reducing its tasks and improving organizational structure. It was in fact a follow-up of the 'Great Operations' which had been introduced by the centre-right Cabinet during the 1980s.

In 1982, the centre-right Cabinet led by Ruud Lubbers, a Christian Democrat, took office. The government undertook activities which have subsequently been named the 'Great Operations'. While the first aim of the 'Great Operations' was the reduction of public expenditure, the improvement of quality of public policy and service delivery became increasingly important as a centrally formulated aim. Following developments in the United States and the United Kingdom, the role of the Dutch government was increasingly questioned.

The 'Great Operations' can be categorized as decentralization, reconsideration of government expenses, deregulation, reduction in the number of civil servants, privatization, and reorganization. The 'Great Operations' were introduced at the central government level, the municipal level and in the non-profit sector.

The measures introduced under the 'Great Operations' were not altogether new. Decentralization, the first 'Great Operation', was not a new goal. Decentralization refers to transfer of power from central government to local and to functional institutions (functional decentralization).

The second 'Great Operation', 'reconsideration of government expenses', had already been started in 1981. Two factors are important: increasing efficiency and attaining goals. These 'reconsiderations' are aimed at reducing public expenditure. Different policy fields are selected and compared in terms of the two factors mentioned above. These reconsiderations have become permanent on-going procedures at the Ministry of Finance.

Deregulation was introduced as a 'Great Operation' in order to reduce strict government regulation in the private sector. Originally, the deregulation operation was supposed to improve private sector development; however, the improvement of the legal system and the abolishment of costly and unnecessary rules became increasingly important as a goal of deregulation.

The reorganization of the central civil service, the fourth 'Great Operation', was also not a new item. Discussion on the organization of government dates back to the 1960s. Originally, the aim was to increase the steering capability of central government. However, since the mid-1980s, emphasis has moved to the 'management policy' of central government. Several activities have been introduced in order to increase the efficiency of the central civil service.

Reducing the number of civil servants, the fifth 'Great Operation', was introduced under the first Lubbers Cabinet in the form of the '-2 percent operation', referring to the aim of reducing total government apparatus by 2 percent. Under the second Lubbers Cabinet, the reduction in the number of civil servants was named the 'slimming operation'. Between 1983 and 1986, the -2 percent operation led to a total reduction of 6,100 positions. The 'slimming operation', which covered the period between 1987 and 1990, made 20,000 positions disappear. This development was mainly the result of the privatization operation.

Privatization, the last 'Great Operation', took several different forms in the Netherlands. Tasks of the government were taken over by the private sector by contracting-out, by the complete hiving off of government duties to the private sector and by giving independence to governmental organizations. The first form has been particularly popular.

With the change of government from centre-right to centre-left in 1989, the emphasis of the activities previously introduced under the 'Great Operations' changed somewhat. The new Minister of Finance, the Social Democrat Kok, was hesitant about continuing the privatization activities undertaken by the former government.

Furthermore, the 'slimming operation' came to an end in 1990. The third Lubbers Cabinet decided to introduce the 'Great Efficiency Operation', which was in fact an amalgamation of some of the 'Great Operations' of the 1980s. In order to reach its goal of increased efficiency, several possibilities were mentioned in the 1991 budget plan: hiving off executive services, decentralization, deregulation and rearrangement of tasks within the central civil service (Mierlo, 1993, p. 9).

The 'Great Efficiency Operation' was first and foremost an economy measure on a very large scale. The budget deficit was still a problem, and with the formulation of the EMU criteria, the reduction of this deficit became increasingly urgent. Originally, the goal of the 'Great Efficiency Operation' was to save 300 million guilders by 1994. In 1991, compromise was reached and it was decided to increase this amount to 600 million. The departments (where the savings were being made) were allowed to keep 20 percent of the saved expenses to spend on the reorganization of personnel. The Ministry of Finance and the Ministry of Internal Affairs were given important coordinating roles. In line with the increased efficiency, the meetings of the secretary-generals were given more substance to ensure a more streamlined reorganization. Whereas prior to 1991, the meetings of the secretary-generals were not much more than an informal lunch club, now they were given a separate secretarial bureau.

Several key developments can be distinguished as being initiated by the 'Great Efficiency Operation'. First, the development towards 'core departments': departments are supposed to concentrate on their central policy-making task. Secondly, linked to this is the development towards independent 'agencies', or 'internal gain of independence' (Kickert, 1992) which will be 'steered at a distance'. Thirdly, the promotion of a central, defragmented, more unified civil service. A first step in this direction is the 'General Management Service' (Algemene Bestuurs Dienst).

The development towards core departments, where policy is made by a unified civil service and where the executive tasks are left to the agencies is very much based on the British 'next step' developments. However, the developments in the Netherlands have not gone as far yet. At the moment, in most departments, discussion as to what constitutes the 'core tasks' is still going on.

The setting up of agencies is one of the ways to separate policy-making and executive services. The agencies have more freedom than the policy directorate-generals or line management units. The minister remains, however, fully responsible for the policy and administration of the agency. Since January 1994, three agencies have been formally established; the Ministry of Justice has set up a separate immigration and naturalization service; the Ministry of Economics has set up an independent service centre; and the Ministry of Agriculture has given its centre for 'botanical diseases' the status of an independent agency. Together, these agencies involve around 1,250 positions. In 1995, the Ministry of Justice will install an agency responsible for youth delinquency and detention centres. This involves 1,310 positions. The introduction of another two agencies, one within the Ministery of Internal Affairs (which will provide information for civil servants) and one within the Ministry of Transport, are being discussed.

The Ministry of Finance together with the Ministry of Internal Affairs has set up a coordinating team for the introduction of the agencies, which will try and trace potential bottlenecks. The 'steering at a distance' model demands new ways of planning and control. Some departments are more developed than others in this respect. The setting up of agencies is a form of 'internal gain of independence'; the agencies remain formally part of the department and the employees will continue to have the status of civil servants. Their employment negotiations now fall under the central government sector. At the same time, some services are being given 'external independence', in the form of 'self-administrative organizations' (ZBOs) or completely privatized organizations.

The 'General Steering Service' (ABD) is defined as 'the apparatus of a core-task central government which is concentrated on strategic policy questions'. The new government (which took office in August 1994) has stated it will press ahead with the creation of a 'General Management Service'. The idea is to create a civil service which will be flexible and able to concentrate on policy processes that may overlap different departments ('integral management').

The service will cover two levels. Top civil servants are expected to rotate between departments every five years. A program intended to increase mobility between top civil servants is currently functioning under the name 'Intertop'. Next to this, there is the departmental route of function exchange, which is meant for persons in high positions but lower than directorate managers.

So far, the 'Great Efficiency Operation', which really has been set up as a large cost-reduction programme, has been quite successful. The cuts in personnel and the so-called 'task-setting budgets' have reached their aims. The savings target of 600 million guilders has been reached.

The 'Great Efficiency Operation' and the other 'Great Operations' are remarkably similar to developments in Britain and the United States. However, there are some characteristics which make the operations typically Dutch. First, it must be noted that the operations have not been accompanied by a great deal of ideology in terms of the free market vs. public sector. An important reason (apart from the reasons mentioned above under 'Ideology') for this is the fact that the basic role of the government is no longer being discussed, it is only its organization which is being questioned. The 'Great Efficiency Operation' has not led to US situations of 'bureaucrat bashing'.

However, this is not to say the operations have been free of rhetoric; quite the contrary. The jargon used is often borrowed from Britain and the United States, and often left untranslated. This is in fact another characteristic of the operation(s): the large amount of rhetoric and the remarkably slow real developments. Many of the aims set by the 'Great Operations' were not achieved by the time they finished. Only in the last two years, it seems, have things really started to move more significantly; the *ad hoc* character of new style public management has made way for a more general pattern. The 'Great Efficiency Operation' has been rather successful.

The 'Great Efficiency Operation' is also an example of an operation supported by all major political parties. This reflects the consensus character in Dutch policy-making. This also explains the lack of 'new right' ideology.

One of the most important aims of the 'Great Efficiency Operation' – to lift the fragmented departmental system – is also typical of Dutch public management. The largely autonomous departments have each developed their particular 'culture'. This is partly the result of the important role of interest groups in Dutch policy-making. Departmental ministers are often recruited from these interest groups: the Minister of Agriculture is often recruited from an agricultural interest group, the Minister of Social Affairs from the trade union world, the Minister of Economic Affairs from an employers' association and so on. Signs of distinct departmental cultures are the use of different jargons, and the different dress codes for each department: corduroy at the departments of Health and Welfare, blue blazers at Internal Affairs and pin-striped suits at the Foreign Office (Gladdish, 1991, p. 144).

In August 1994, the 'purple coalition' took office. This coalition of Liberals, Democrats and Social Democrats is the first without the Christian

Democrats in the post-war period. In their program, they have announced that things will continue along much the same lines.

References

Andeweg, R. (1993) *Dutch Government and Politics*, London.

Arntzen, H. L. (1992) De gemeente in ontwikkeling: naar betere beheersing en effectiever sturing, *Openbaar Bestuur* no. 2, pp. 9–14.

Aquina, H. (1988) PGOs in the Netherlands. In Hood, C. and Schuppert, G.F. (eds), *Delivering Public Services in Europe*, London.

Braam, A. van (1993) Vernieuwing van de rijksdienst, 'a continuing story' in Nederland, *Bestuurswetenschappen* no. 4

Breunesse, J. (1993) Over het eindrapport van de commissie-Wiegel, *Openbaar Bestuur*, December, pp. 8–15.

Deloitte & Touche, Public Affairs Consultants, (1992) *Zoekwerk of Maatwerk. Conclusies naar aanleiding van interviews over Bestuurlijke Vernieuwing.*

Gladdish, K. (1991) Governing from the center. In *Politics and Policy-Making in the Netherlands*, Gladdish, Hurst, London.

Kam, C. A. de, en de Haan, J. (1991) *Terugtredende Overheid, Realiteit of Retoriek?*, Schoonhoven.

Kickert, W. (1991) Meer aandacht voor management. Verzelfstandiging van uitvoerende overheidsdienst hier en overzee, *Openbaar Bestuur*, January pp. 6–13.

Kickert, W. J. M. (1992) Verzelfstandiging bij de rijksoverheid, *Bestuurswetenschappen*.

Kickert, W. J. M. (1993a) *Verandering in management en organisatie bij de rijksoverheid*, Alphen aan de Rijn.

Kickert, W. J. M. (1993b) Nieuw publiek mangement; ideologische mode of zinvolle trend?, *Openbaar Bestuur*, no. 12, pp. 19–26.

Kuipers, R. I. J. M. (1992) en Postma, J. K. *De rijksbegroting in perspectief*, den Haag.

Kurvers, R. (1994) Ambtenaren CAO's, gestandaardiseerde differentiatie, *Personeelsbeleid*, no. 2.

Lijphart, A. (1985) *Consociational Democracy*, Mimeo.

Mierlo, J. G. A. van (1993) Grote operaties in de publieke sector, bestuurlijke vernieuwing of politieke symboliek? In Hemels, J. M. H. J. (ed.), *Besturen en Innovatie: Handboek voor Bestuurders en Managers*, Houten.

Ministerie van Binnenlandse Zaken (1991, 1992) voortgang Grote Efficiency (interne nota).

Ministerie van Binnenlandse Zaken, *Rechtspositie Rijksambtenaar* (November 1993).

Ministerie van Binnenlandse Zaken, *Overheid & Arbeidsmarkt 1993*.

Ministerie van Binnenlandse Zaken, DG PM, *Koers naar de Algemene Bestuurdienst* (interne nota) (April 1994).

Ministerie van Binnenlandse Zaken, *Mensen en Management; dl. 1 Beleid* (October 1994).

Nispen, F. K. M. van, en Noordhoek, D. P. (1986) *De Grote Operaties. De overheid onder het mes of het snijden in eigen vlees*, Deventer.

OECD, PUMA profile update 1992.

OECD, PUMA, survey 1993.

OECD, PUMA country profile 1993.

OECD, *Performance Related Pay* (1993).

Postma, J. K. T. (1994) Verzelfstandiging; aansturing en terugkoppeling essentieel, *Openbaar Bestuur*, June, pp. 2–5.

The National Ombudsman of the Netherlands: A Brief Introduction, Ombudsman den Haag, Netherlands Government, 1991.

Tilburg, IVA (1994) *Public Employment: A Comparison of Six European Countries*, Tilburg.

Verkooijen, W. (1993) Personeelsmanagement in de Britse Civil Service, *Openbaar Bestuur*, June/July, pp. 24–8.

5

France

Norman Flynn and Franz Strehl

CONSTITUTION

The Fifth Republic, established in 1958, set up a strong executive centred on the presidency. The president, elected for seven years, appoints the prime minister and the government. Parliament is elected for five years. There are two chambers, a directly elected National Assembly and a Senate indirectly elected from local government.

There is a close relationship between senior politicians and senior civil servants. Between 1958 and 1993 eight of the eleven prime ministers had served in the civil service. Parliament legislates and makes the budget, but the majority of legislation is originated by the government. In practice the constitution allows a strong executive presidency, which is supported by an élite civil service of the *grands corps*, trained in the *grands écoles*, the state graduate schools.

MANAGEMENT PROCESSES

There have been many efforts to improve the management of public services in France since the economic recession of 1983. There have been four major themes: improving decision-making and accountability through devolving responsibilities; the need to increase productivity and limit or reduce the number of employees; a desire to change the way in which people are managed; changes in 'customer service' to produce better levels of public satisfaction. The last of these has also had an emphasis on citizenship and democracy, rather than purely customer orientation. The idea has been to enhance participation in decision-making, not just improving service quality.

These themes have recurred in many campaigns (for a detailed description of the campaigns, see Barouch and Chavas, 1993). From 1984 there have been targets to reduce the number of public employees by various percentages (e.g. 1 percent in 1984 and 1985, 1.5 percent in 1986–8).

There has been constant reference to devolving accountability and developing responsibility. Since 1985, successive reports and ministers have called for a modernization of human resource management, arguing that an over-juridical approach did not lead to high performance. A national quality campaign in 1987 called for a reform in the way people are managed, including individual career management, better training, better individual evaluation and more participative management.

Deconcentration

The last ten years have seen an attempt to devolve responsibility from central government to local authorities. There were Deconcentration Acts in 1982 and 1983 designed to start this process of shifting both accountability and tax-raising for a proportion of social services and education expenditure. The deconcentration policy was adopted during a period of trying to contain expenditure and the numbers of people employed in the public sector. The process has continued since then. A major element of policy towards the public sector since 1988 has been two sorts of decentralization: the decentralization of managerial accountability and certain aspects of decision-making to individual accountability centres, whether units of government, schools, universities and so on; and the devolution of powers and responsibilities for services to the local geographical level, especially the prefecture.

Accountability centres (*Centres de Responsabilités*, CDR) have been set up since 1990. The idea is that the chief executives negotiate a set of objectives and targets with their parent department, and engage in a dialog about the budget required to deliver those targets. Some responsibilities for personnel matters and procurement are also devolved to the managers of the individual centres.

In 1992 the government passed a law and a charter on decentralization. These measures set out the competences of the tiers of government (central, regional, department and arrondissement) based on the principle of subsidiarity. The prefect is the central figure in the organization of local services.

Michel Rocard started a campaign to improve public services in 1989. He said that the public service mission should be redefined to include 'equality, equity, solidarity and the public interest'. As with previous reforms programs, a central theme was a move towards people accepting responsibility for their actions, rather than simply following procedures, and the development of a trained, committed workforce. A commission was established on 'the effectiveness of the state' which set out four main areas for change:

1. A policy of new work relationships
   Training and dialogue
   Valuing people
   Decentralizing negotiations
2. A policy of developing responsibilities
   Decentralization

Service projects
Experimental CDRs (responsibility centres)
An examination of accountability procedures
3. A duty of evaluation of public policies
4. A new policy of service to the public
Better information
Better relationships between service users and service providers

There were two main implications of these moves for management. First, the managers of the accountability centres require competencies in management which are different from those required to administer a centrally controlled system. Secondly, managers' orientation has to switch from keeping the *grand corps* (powerful central government departments) happy to satisfying regional and local management.

Goals and objectives setting

The central administration sets objectives, establishes programs and evaluates service delivery. Since the decentralization initiatives of 1989 (*déconcentration*) service delivery has been formally devolved to territorial authorities, especially in education, land use planning and social action (OECD, 1993a).

The establishment of accountability centres defined the locus for policy and objective setting. The prime minister's letter of 25 January 1990 set out the principles behind this initiative: management responsibility should be devolved to a chief executive and a management team, and the sponsoring Ministry should make policy, set service guidelines and then negotiate a contract and budget with the CDR.

The process followed is that an agreement is reached, covering a three-year period, between the accountability centre, the parent ministry, the Ministry of Economy, Finance and Budget, and the Ministry of Public Functions and Administrative Modernization. By 1994 there were 150 accountability centres.

The contract is for three years at a time with central government to deliver services, within a negotiated budget. Targets are set out in a framework document (*tableau de bord*) (framework is the term used for the agreement between ministries and agencies in the United Kingdom) and the accountability centres are given more autonomy in management in exchange for external scrutiny of their performance.

The framework includes a set of objectives and performance targets, which are quantified wherever possible and set out in a schedule. Performance is interpreted through quantitative outputs as well as processes, such as measurement of how much training a centre carries out, what its absenteeism levels are and so on (Direction Générale de l'Administration et de la Fonction Publique, 1991).

Planning

In addition to the framework document, a three-year plan is negotiated between the ministry and the accountability centres. The intention is that the plan, known as 'Plan of Objectives and Means', sets out specific proposals on how the overall objectives will be achieved, volumes of activity, staff to be employed and the priorities to be met in the coming three years.

In practice, managers report that there are difficulties associated with the planning system. First, ministries find it difficult to be sufficiently specific about objectives to enable them to be translated into a detailed operational plan. Secondly, there are difficult negotiations about the accountability centres' room for manoeuvre in their operational plans to meet the objectives.

Budgeting

In France, there has been a change in the process of setting the running cost budgets for the CDRs (Ministry of the Economy, Finance and Budget and the Ministry of Public Functions and Administrative Modernisation, 1992). Before the establishment of the centres, there was a detailed central allocation of budgets which often did not reflect the actual spending needs.

The devolution of detailed budgeting is based on the assumption that each organizational unit is better able to identify its needs than its parent ministry. However, the chief executive of each unit is held accountable by an *ex-post* accounting mechanism.

Since the establishment of the centres, budgets are negotiated between most of the centres and their parent ministry. However, the negotiations do not include the main item of expenditure, the number of staff to be employed, since this is determined by law. In principle the budget allocations are linked to the objectives agreed in the framework document, although in practice this was only the case, in 1992, in 50 percent of the centres.

Evaluation

Ministries monitor and evaluate policy and management changes. In addition there are two bodies, the Interministerial Committee on Evaluation and the Scientific Council on Evaluation, which assess the impact of public policy. From 1990/91 these bodies have assessed policy in a wide range of fields, from wetland protection to policy on drug trafficking and abuse.

Market and customer orientation

France has a public service charter (*Charte des services publics*) which was adopted in March 1992 (Soisson, 1992). Announcing the charter in 1992, the minister, M. Jean-Pierre Soisson, said that the intention was to add to the traditional principles of French public service, which are equality, neutrality and continuity. The new principles were to be transparency, participation and simplification. The charter was intended to allow every citizen to measure how well the administration was performing, to improve the quality of customer service (*accueil*) and to simplify and make the procedures more accessible.

The charter is in three parts:

1. Principles upon which modern public administration should be based.
2. 'Golden rules' for public service in the main areas of state intervention: employment and training, education, health, social security, security and justice, the environment, transport and communications.
3. Definition of user rights in public services.

Five objectives were set out:

1. Take account of users' needs, and welcome, explain and help them with the procedures.
2. Adapt the administration to the evolution of the population, especially in the suburbs and rural areas.
3. Develop participation by citizens: to make the functioning of the administration more democratic, especially by creating 'user conferences' and improving the information available to the public.
4. Cut delays and simplify procedures, replying to correspondence more quickly, increasing the number of cases in which no response implies a 'yes' rather than a 'no', and reducing charges for services, especially those payable by businesses.
5. Increased accountability, especially through quality indicators, removal of the protection of anonymity and more recourse to conciliation and arbitration with regard to disputes.

PERSONNEL MANAGEMENT

Recruitment/dismissal

Recruitment to the public service is essentially by open competitive examinations. This is considered to produce equality of access and recruitment on merit. For a few jobs there are selection commissions, rather than competitive examinations.

Entry to the public sector from the private can be done either through contractual arrangements or by taking the third competition to enter the Ecole Nationale d'Administration (ENA), which is now open to anyone with eight years' professional experience in the private sector.

Exit from the civil service was traditionally known as *pantouflage* (putting on slippers), whereby senior civil servants joined the private sector at the end of their career to enhance their pensions and last few years' pay. More recently people have left temporarily to earn more money, or even left permanently at an early stage to make faster career progress. Rouban (1994) reports in his study of 500 senior French civil servants that a high proportion of civil servants wished to leave public office by the beginning of the 1990s. And younger people were more likely to want to join the private sector:

> When asked if they were ready to leave the state service, 28.5 percent of those questioned said 'yes'. The younger they are the more likely they are to plan to leave; 38 percent between 41 and 50 and 59 percent between 25 and 40.
> (Rouban, 1994, p. 95)

Promotion

Promotion within a grade is generally based on age, although there is a possibility of accelerated advancement on merit. Promotion to a higher grade is done by promotion boards, after competitive examination.

Pay

There is a minimum wage for public sector workers, which is slightly higher than the minimum in the private sector, and mean salaries are about 5 percent higher than those in the private sector. At the higher levels, civil servants are paid on scales which are supplemented by between 200 and 300 different types of bonuses (Rouban, 1994). An OECD report (1993b) describes the bonus system as 'highly complex and obscure'.

In recent years the value of the bonuses as a proportion of the total pay has risen: between 1988 and 1990 bonuses rose by 38 percent while basic pay rose by 8.2 percent. By 1994 they represented 11.6 percent of total civil servants' rewards, although they are unevenly distributed: at the higher levels those in the top 5 percent receive 40,000FF per year while the bottom 5 percent receive 1,220FF per year.

There are also variations between occupational groups. The OECD (1993b) reports that after five years' service social workers receive on average a bonus equivalent to 3.5 percent of basic pay, while civil engineers receive 64.3 percent. The prestige of the corps in which an officer works also affects the amount of bonus paid; thus a high prestige corps such as the Inspectorate General of Finances is thought to pay an average of 45 percent of basic salary to its senior people. While the total amount available for bonuses is decided by the Ministry of Finance, how this money is distributed is left to departments. Furthermore, while there is a rule that officers should not receive a bonus which exceeds 100 percent of their basic salary, this rule may be broken on some occasions.

Bonuses are not based on a formal, universal system of performance appraisal. Employees can ask for an interview in which the manager is asked to justify the performance bonus rating, but this is not necessarily done as part of a performance appraisal system.

Performance management

Performance appraisal, outside the bonus appraisal, is supposed to be based on an annual appraisal interview. In practice these conversations, when they have taken place, have been retrospective.

Currently, accountability centres are developing a system of evaluation interviews which links the accountability centres' objectives to individual performance. These interviews are supposed to be forward-looking, to identify individuals' potential and training needs and critical tasks in the next period.

Training

There are about seventy schools of administration, besides the teacher training and military schools. The ENA trains the highest level of public servants. The Ecole polytechnique and the engineering schools train the high-level technical grades and there are five Instituts regionaux d'administration for grade A administrators. (The top 12,000 civil servants are organized into grades A–G.) Then there are schools which provide specialist qualifications.

There are three sorts of training programs: pre-employment training, preparation for promotion and personal development training. In addition to technical training there are programs in management, human resource management and specific training in customer care, communications, etc., as part of the program of reform in customer relations, training in new technologies, policy development and law.

CRITIQUE

Fialaire (1993) has argued that the implementation of the accountability centres has not produced the management freedoms which were expected when they were established. He argues that there is, in practice, still a great deal of *a priori* budgetary control by the Ministry of Finance which has been reluctant to move towards global running cost budgets because such a change would challenge the power of that ministry.

He argues that there have been few examples of the real adaptation of the financial framework to the needs of the service and that where this has been achieved it has been 'at the expense of interminable negotiations' (p. 41). He also reports that evaluation based on objectives has had little impact on the budget allocation process and that many chief executives of accountability centres have their budget imposed on them by their parent ministry. This has held back the devolution of managerial control to and development of participative management in the centres.

Fialaire argues that the hostility to devolution of control can be explained as 'a counter strategy which seeks to defend territory. They frequently refuse to concede to chief executives powers which would give real managerial autonomy, such as the right to recruit, freedom to use "efficiency savings", changes in remuneration arrangements' (p. 45).

A further explanation is offered by Gibert and Thoenig (1993), who argue that the training offered by the ENA is not conducive to the development of devolved management and management innovations: 'Its competitive selection process contains nothing about public management as such. It does not produce integrated teaching in "action sciences"' (p. 15). They argue that while the courses cover questions of the modernization of public management, such matters are dealt with in a descriptive, factual and formal way. This leads to a formal and mechanistic application of the basic ideas of the reforms. In turn this produces uniformity in approaches, rather than diversity representing the different needs of different services: 'what is good for one part of the administration is good for the rest' (p. 17).

Fialaire predicts that the only way to counter the powers of the *grands corps* is to develop integrated approaches to management at the prefecture level. The fragmentation of centres at local level, with each accountable to and controlled by its central ministry, means that there is neither a genuine devolution of managerial control nor a territorial decentralization.

Education

The national education service in France has been going through a series of modernization and decentralization processes since 1965. The circular of 9 January 1991, which encouraged decentralization of certain aspects of management in all ministries was based in part on the experience of decentralization in the national education service. The process started as one of consultation with service users (parents, pupils and representatives of the professions) and then made local authorities partners in the education management process.

The framework agreements which have more recently been introduced in other ministries have been used as a management tool in education for thirty years.

In addition to devolution to local directors of education, establishments such as colleges and schools have progressively acquired more control over certain managerial matters, such as recruitment of some personnel, use of supplementary hours, and some educational initiatives.

There is a tension between the desire to have a system of some local autonomy combined with participation and consultation in decision-making, while at the same time maintaining some national coherence in the education system. Champaigne *et al.* (1993) argue that the processes appear to be centralizing: 'This desire for coherence may seem centralising: general application of systems across the whole territory, uniform coverage of functions in a formalised chain of command, use of a common language and procedures' (p. 94). While a uniform information system may imply centralized control, they argue that the information collected is itself modified by discussions at all levels, and that in any case only aggregated information is passed up to the ministry.

The main tools for decentralization, the framework agreements, include 'globalized' budgets which should give greater autonomy to local managements and to individual institutions. However, the autonomy is exercised in a contractual framework:

> *Globalisation, accompanied by a clear definition of mission, puts responsibility in the hands of the unit responsible for implementation. It is the response to the centre's wish to change the relationships between those responsible for setting missions and objectives and those responsible for implementation. This relationship goes from being a hierarchical one to a contractual one. The creation of accountability centres reinforces this change, but the power relations in sectors, and their financial implications, do not go away.*
> (p. 97)

As in the other ministries, it seems, the change to a contractual relationship does not necessarily reduce the power of the centre. In the case of the universities, for example, the system is supposed to produce continuity of funding, subject to compliance with reaching preset objectives. However, Champaigne *et al.* are of the opinion that the contractual relationship is actually still blurred for two reasons: nobody knows what would be the results of either side failing to meet its part of the contract; and the lack of proper methods of evaluation.

Their conclusion on the distribution of power within the education service is as follows:

> *Deconcentration has done little, up to now, to modify the structures and the control mechanisms have not lost their technocratic character, normally associated with centralised structures. . . . Today the problem is much more difficult because it asks the central administration to limit its activities to those which are essential to its mission. . . . Decentralisation based on a sharing of competencies is not accompanied by a sufficiently clear definition of the role given to state services.*

UNFINISHED REFORMS

In 1993, Prime Minister Edouard Balladur set up another investigation into the responsibilities and organization of the state. The results of the investigation support the conclusion that the reforms which have been put in place in France have had limited impact (Mission sur les responsabilités et organisation de l'état, 1995). In all the main areas of management of the public sector, the report calls for more changes.

The major emphasis on decentralization, for which much has been claimed, has not produced the desired results. For example, the administration of education was supposed to have become less centralized and rigid. The prime minister's report suggests that the system is still centralized:

> National education has made efforts to decentralize, but this has not touched the essential element: the centre still directly controls secondary school teaching. . . . This is incompatible with good human resource management. The lack of decentralization cannot allow real development of responsibility. Central administration has not sufficient capacity for coordination and guidance, mainly because it is divided into ten directorates, none of which understands all the problems to be dealt with.
> (p. 60)

An explanation for the lack of real decentralization is offered by Celine Wiener, the chief inspector of education (Decentralisation and National Education Services', in Gilbert and Delcamp, 1993). First, she argues that the constitutional guarantee of equality of access to education for both children and adults implies that there should be national standards and therefore centralized control. Secondly, she argues that people who work in the education service, especially rectors and inspectors, think of themselves as part of a national, not local service. In practice, the only functions that have been decentralized are professional training and transport.

The prime minister's report did not call for a transfer of responsibility for education to local authorities, as this would cause more problems than it solved. It did call for clearer objectives and more managerial autonomy at local level. The list of suggestions is similar to those of many reports since the decentralization started:

1. Replace rigid and uniform norms with objectives. The objectives should be stated as knowledge to be acquired at various stages and local management and professionals should be able to adapt their teaching methods to local circumstances.

2. Give establishments more autonomy. There should be contracts with individual establishments, the administrative councils of establishments should be revised and managers should have more freedom to manage. At the same time there should be safeguards for children with learning difficulties and establishments should be encouraged to cooperate with each other.

3. Evaluation should be strengthened but should concentrate on results and not methods and should aim to bring about improvement not punishment of failure.

4. The role of the central administration should be revised and limited to the setting of national objectives, setting an overall human resource policy, coordinating management and legal matters, and providing an information and evaluation system for establishments.

The fact that this report could still be calling, in 1995, for a more autonomous approach to establishments and a more strategic role for the centre shows that the decentralization program is not complete. This conclusion echoes that of Albert Mabileau: 'The general impression remains that the dynamic of decentralisation is still far from being achieved and that its evolution will still take a long time' ('La Décentralisation en Retard: Principes et Normes, Comportements et Mentalités', in Gilbert and Delcamp, 1993).

The second aspect which indicates disappointment in the reform programme is customer orientation. Despite the Charter and various efforts at introducing quality and customer care campaigns, the report concludes that customer service is still poor in many areas and that 'In truth, the administration seems oriented towards its employees more than towards service users' (Mission sur les responsibilités, p. 150). Its recommendations are essentially centralist: that there should be a minister for customer service and that communications with customers of public services should be centrally controlled.

There are similar conclusions in the area of human resource management, where the lack of a performance orientation is criticized: 'When unemployment hits one in six of the working population, it is difficult to understand why those who benefit from security of employment should be the only ones not subjected to the constraint of results' (p. 139).

While recognizing that employees need protection from the arbitrary use of power, there should be more sanctions and incentives for good performance. Managers should have more control over who is appointed to positions and there should be a pay system which includes basic salary, allowances according to the responsibility of the job and bonuses for good performance.

The current pay system is heavily criticized: 'Nobody knows the number of allowances and bonus payments. According to one estimate of the directorate general of the public sector, there are more than 3000. Confusion is great and confidentiality, jealously guarded, will not reduce it' (p. 143).

As well as criticizing bonus payments, the report is also critical of the proliferation of pay scales, claiming that there were 1700 potential different pay rates in existence and 1000 currently in use. In fact, the tendency in some other countries is to move away from unified scales towards individual pay for people doing particular jobs.

In general, the report concluded that the public sector had not yet responded adequately to the demands made on it to change, although it would have to:

> There are no longer any protected sectors. The opening of the borders exposes all our collective functions to international competition. It is time that the State, in its turn, changes its habits and works with current methods. The State should not be a brake on the modernization of the whole country.
>
> (p. 105)

CONCLUSIONS

Since 1983 there have been many attempts to reform the French public services. The themes of the reforms have been similar to those of other European countries: improved accountability through increased responsibility; changes to the pay system to make people more performance-oriented; clarification of objectives and managerial authority; improved customer service; increased efficiency and productivity.

However, there seem to have been obstacles in the way of change. First, there have been technical difficulties in defining and measuring objectives and outputs with sufficient confidence to enable the various elements of the 'centre' to allow real devolution of managerial control. Real decentralization involves a bargain in which control is devolved in exchange for performance delivery.

Secondly, the tradition of a strong central government makes it unlikely that power will be truly decentralized. Without pressure from subnational government, power is likely to remain centralized. When the elements of subnational government have a stake in the centre (regional inspectors, local arms of ministries, etc.) their actions will tend to reinforce centralization.

Thirdly, the politicians and the *grands corps* of civil servants have a shared interest in maintaining their power. This interest consists not only of political and administrative power in its own right. There is also a strong material self-interest. Politicians are able to join and rejoin the civil service as their political careers ebb and flow. Michel Rocard, for example, returned to his civil service post several times during his political career, including when he ceased to be prime minister. Such movements require powerful jobs to occupy. Élite civil servants are themselves well respected and well paid through a system that is not very open to public scrutiny. There is also a possibility of a move to even more lucrative employment prior to retirement. Such privileges for the élite do not provide many incentives to reduce the centre's power and influence.

Practical Example

Management instruments are presented in the circular letter of 23 February 1989 as being essential for the modernization of the public sector. Of course, there has been a tradition of the use of management instruments in the public sector. The improvement in the area of efficiency makes it necessary to know production costs and to be able to control them. These requirements are increased by decentralization and devolution of the decision-making power of the federal administration. This holds especially for situations in which the administrative units face increasing degrees of competition from local institutions concerning service quality, efficiency and professionalism of service delivery.

The new aspect in the context of the modernization is the approach to implementation and use:

- The development of management instruments is primarily based on a bottom-up approach and not a hierarchical top-down aproach.
- Each hierarchical level develops the appropriate instrument suited to its needs.
- There has to be a coherent overall information base.

The management instruments apply to the following areas:

- Planning, definition of goals and objectives
  - Strategic analysis and planning
- Organization, programming
  - Allocation of resources
  - Relationship between goals/objectives and resources
  - Cost–benefit analysis
- Steering, coordination, control
  - Cost accounting
  - Indicators of resources
  - Indicators of results
  - Integrative control devices
- Evaluation
  - Measures, indicators

The two main management instruments for integrating these areas are the following:

- Plan objectives/Resources (*plan objectifs-moyens*)
- Management information instrument (*tableau de bord*)

These instruments have been widely developed and implemented in the Ministry of Equipment (whose main responsibilities are to provide infrastructure – roads, ports, airports – transport, urbanization and public constructions) within large-scale reorganization projects, which are organized in four main phases.

Phase 1

Increasing competitive pressure is put on the subdivisions by regional and local decision-makers, who demand the best service performance at the lowest cost. This led to 'Operation CLAIRE' which had two main goals:

- To respond in a simple, clear and pertinent way to the information requirements concerning the management of the central organizations and regional subdivisions.
- To develop practical, easily usable instruments for steering and control based on common and consistent data permitting to know the overall costs and the economic functioning of the units.

This management and control system is aimed at the managing units within the ministry (about 100) which are organized in regional subdivisions – so-called responsibility centres – (about 1300) and deliver services to the federal level (35 percent), the regional level (45 percent) and the community level (20 percent) (Serge Vallemont, Le développement de gestion au Ministère Français de l'Equipement, unpublished paper).

Phase 2

In phase 2 the main goal is the further development and implementation of the systems for the regional subdivisions and is intended to support the managers concerning the following issues:

- How best to use personnel, equipment and material?
- How to measure results and to know service efficiency?
- How to measure as accurately as possible the cost of service delivery?

The second goal is the development and diffusion of a 'management culture' in the overall system, both at the top and well down the hierarchy.

The main method of attaining these goals is to build hierarchically overlapping working teams assisted by an external consultant. The results are made accessible to all users, thus creating an integrated learning loop.

The overall result is the implementation of an instrument called CORAIL, which is simple and accessible to all decision makers, permitting them to follow the activities of the subdivision and to have a full picture of costs and revenues. Overall, this gives a better basis for improved organization, planning and accountability.

Phase 3

The decentralization process is supplemented by a policy of conferring management responsibility on the chief executives, resulting in the implementation of contractual relationships between the centre and the decentralized regional services. This contract is based on an analysis of the status quo and defines the expected improvements and progress based on objectives.

Phase 4

Operational implementation of the overall management system and instruments. The main two instruments are the following:

- Management information instrument (*tableau de bord*)
- Plan objectives/resources (*plan objectifs-moyens*)

which are described below in more detail.

MANAGEMENT INFORMATION INSTRUMENT

The management information instrument presents the key information elements of the management of the responsibility centres in their specific context (the responsibility centre concept will be characterized below). It presents not only the financial data but also a quantitative and qualitative description of the activities. The combination of these measures and indicators shows the resources used, the results achieved, the changes in the relevant environment and may also describe (social) indicators of the internal situation of the centre. Emphasis is given to visualizing the data in order to facilitate decision-making. For the same activity there may be several different descriptions and diagrams adapted to the (hierarchically) different users of the information.

The methods constitute a combination of various planning and control instruments, e.g. network technique, milestone charts, planning and control diagrams, task and work package structure, scenario techniques, cost-monitoring table.

There are basically two types of instruments to be found in centres (especially those belonging to the Ministry of Equipment):

- Information instrument for the overall management of the centre. This serves primarily to monitor and control results for the chief executive, and thus contributes to transparency. A precondition for full use is the clear definition of goals and objectives at all hierarchical levels.
- Project-information instrument. This serves first the project managers to monitor and control project schedules, performance (as measured against project objectives) and cost.

The information instrument refers mainly to non-strategic aspects of the centre and focuses on day-to-day operations. Reports are usually generated on a monthly basis for the different domains and projects, and a synopsis is presented to the chief executive.

This documentation permits the following:

- Managers being informed in a concise way on the status of activities and results.
- Visualization and presentation of the data according to the target groups on different hierarchical levels.
- Identification of the results in the different domains (plan against degree of realization; inputs against outputs).

Key factors for the successful implementation and use of these instruments are as follows:

- Determination of the functional requirements.
- Observation of the preconditions for implementation (organization, culture, training).
- Development as a professional instrument.
- Secure, practical and simple to use.
- Integration with existing information systems (e.g. CORAIL – see below).

PLAN OBJECTIVES/RESOURCES

A systematic instrument for planning activities and priority setting is being developed in a situation of scarce resources and increasing complexity both in the overall system and within responsibility centres. This instrument is characterized as a necessary and useful basis for defining the relationships of the responsibility centre with the ministry and the negotiation of goals, the achievement of control and resource allocation – and is, thus, an important dimension of the contract between the responsibility centre and the ministry.

The optimum timeframe for the definition of priorities and the development of the respective actions is considered to be three years (this holds for the specific situation of responsibility centres belonging to the Ministry of Equipment).

The plan is based on the strategic policy and resource decisions and states precisely the following:

- The expected developments for each domain in terms of objectives, volume (work, output), resources (means), quantity and quality of staff (positions).
- The activities having priority according to the objectives.

The main issue is seen in the agreement between mid-term ambitions and the given restrictions. It is important to identify the 'room for manoeuvre' needed to realize the plans. This only can be achieved by an iterative, process of small steps, adapting objectives, priorities and means.

'Room for manoeuvre' involves the following:

- Identification and measurement of productivity gains per year.
- Optimization of the management of given resources, especially staff positions.

This requires an inventory of existing resources, analysis of probable developments and plans for recruitment, training, mobility and personnel development.

The strategic objectives of a responsibility centre are derived from the national (ministerial) overall policy determined by Parliament and take into account the various stakeholders and the specific contingencies under which the centre operates.

Generally the strategic goals are ill defined, which leads to difficulties with the concrete definition of objectives in the ministries. However, this varies and not all objectives can be operationalized in the same way. There are indications that this concept still has room for improvement but it is considered essential that it is applied. The organizations involved are on a learning curve, and the concept should be continuously improved.

The concept of plan objective/resources integrates and organizes existing management instruments. It develops and combines the various approaches of activity and resource management at the responsibility centre level based on the overall national (ministerial) policy.

The overall concept is summarized in Fig. 5.1.

As a first important instrument to promote the realization of management tools – especially control – the information system CLAIRE was developed for the responsibility centres belonging to the Ministry of Equipment.

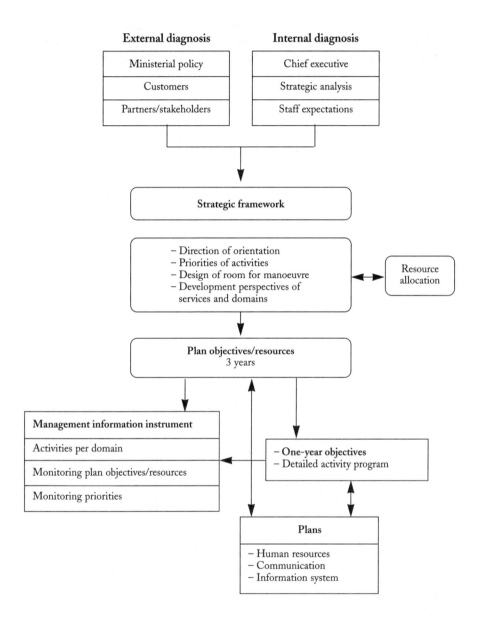

Figure 5.1. The plan objectives/resources approach.

CLAIRE was implemented in 1988. Its primary purpose is to respond to the information requirements formulated by the regional authorities. The second purpose is to have a simple, easily accessible instrument to integrate information given by the management information instruments. CLAIRE was the first approach to identify the global costs and the economic performance of responsibility centres.

A second step (the CORAIL system) focuses on the regional levels of the centres (subdivisions covering the regional infrastructure). This is a logical consequence of the overall decentralization approach, and also aims at increasing the awareness and motivation of civil servants at local level. CORAIL provides management with detailed as well as aggregated information on activities at local level, thus integrating management tools at this level.

RESPONSIBILITY CENTRE CONCEPT

A circular letter from the prime minister is the normal basis for the establishment and the management of responsibility centres and, thus, of contracts and agreements.

The prime ministerial letter of 25 January 1990 describes the responsibility centre concept as characterized by a close association of personnel with the organization, a more efficient, customer-oriented service, more rigorous management and the publication of measurable results with respect to quantitative and qualitative criteria.

The letter describes the characteristics and the areas of autonomy and responsibility, and identifies the themes to be specified in the contract and agreeement:

- Real autonomy and full responsibility within the overall policy framework. The details are defined according to the specific contingencies under which a centre has to function.
- The relationships between a centre and the parent ministry are regulated by a three-year contract.
- The conditions of the establishment and the operating rules are determined by an agreement – within the contractual framework – between the centre, the parent ministry, the Ministry of Economy, Finance and Budget, and the Ministry of Public Functions and Administrative Modernization.
- Matters of personnel management and social matters.
- Credits for running costs – global budget – budget for equipment.
- Collective returns on efficiency gains.
- Scope of responsibilities concerning the following matters:
  - Development of a service project.
  - Goals and objectives.

- Budgeting and cost management.
- Internal evaluation.
- Evaluation of the centre by the parent ministry (annually).
- Evaluation of the centre at the end of contract.
- Globalization of specific running cost budget elements.
- Financial control.
- Responsibilities of the parent ministry
  - Management control.
  - Ensuring coherence of information and reporting of the centres.
    Reporting to the Ministry of Economy, Finance and Budget (annually).
- Establishment of an interministerial group to control the realization and implementation of the circular letter and the contracts.

REFERENCES

Barouch, G. and Chavas, H. (1993) *Où va la modernisation? Dix années de modernisation de l'administration en France*, Editions L'Harmattan, Paris.

Champaigne, P., Cottereau, Y., Dallemagne, G. and Malan, T. (1993) Processus de modernisation dans l'administration de l'education nationale, *Politiques et Management Public*, vol. 11, no. 1.

Direction Générale de l'Administration et de la Fonction Publique, (1991) *Cahiers du Renouveau*, la Documentation Française.

Fialaire, J. (1993) Les stratégies de la mise en œuvre des centres de responsabilité, *Politiques et Management Public*, vol. 11, no 2.

Gibert, P. and Thoenig, J.-C. (1993) La gestion public: entre l'apprentissage et l'amnésie, *Politiques et Management Public*, vol. 11, no. 1.

Gilbert, G. and Delcamp, A. (1993) *La décentralisation dix ans après*, Librairie Générale de Droit et Jurisprudence, Paris.

Ministry of the Economy, Finance and Budget and the Ministry of Public Functions and Administrative Modernisation, (1992) *Enquête sur la mise en place des centres de responsabilités. Rapport de synthèse.*

Mission sur les responsabilités et organisation de l'état (1995) *L'Etat en France: servir une nation ouverte sur le monde*, Documentation Française, Paris.

OECD (1993a) Public management, *OECD Country Profiles 1993*, Paris.

OECD (1993b) *Private Pay for Public Work*, Paris.

Rouban, L. (1994) France: political argument and institutional change. In Hood, C. and Guy Peters, B. (eds), *Rewards at the Top: A Comparative Study of High Public Office*, Sage, London.

Soisson, J.-P. (1992) Ministre d'état, Ministre de la Fonction Publique et de la Modernisation de l'Administration, Conseil des ministres, speech, 19 February.

6

Germany

Part I: Public sector modernization in Germany – recent trends and emerging strategies

Helmut Klages and Elke Löffler

OVERVIEW

Federalism, local self-government and division of power are the dominant principles of the administrative structure in Germany. The five levels of German administration are: the federation, the *Länder* (states), the government districts, the rural counties and county boroughs, and the communes and the commune associations. The federal government makes use of the administrative institutions of the states and the municipalities (communes) on the level of the *Länder* and the local authorities.

In Germany exists a very special situation in contrast to modernization trends and programs in other countries: the modernization of the public administration has to be understood in terms of a bottom-up evolution. Local governments are focusing on an enormous variety of modernization strategies. The starting point of the new movement of guidance and steering was the Dutch city of Tilburg. Tilburg and several other Dutch communes were suffering from striking financial problems at the end of the 1970s – start of the 1980s. This led to an increasing demand for more quality, efficiency, effectiveness and openness to markets.

The special German situation allows current trends in public administration to be treated from the point of view of several German experts.

The aim of the first section of this chapter, 'Public sector modernization in Germany – recent trends and emerging strategies' by Klages and Löffler, is to give an overview of the present trends of the modernization process in Germany with a particular focus on modernization strategies. They use the notion of 'bottom-up revolution' and discuss the implementation of the so-called 'new steering model' by local governments, illustrating potential deficits of this model. (The notion 'new steering model' is used to express new management concepts at local level.) An interesting aspect is the recently developed 'Speyer Quality Competition Award'. The applications for the second 'Speyer Quality Competition Award' in Germany show that a large number of communities are engaged in new management activities. They are trying to implement special management practices of the private sector and perceive themselves at the same time as service-providers. Counties and county boroughs lag a little behind local governments (some pioneers are Baden-Württemberg, Berlin and Schleswig-Holstein).

The opening of the border in November 1989 brought some specific problems facing public administration in East Germany: former Eastern administrative institutions had to fulfil the postulates of a legalistic bureaucracy. In organizational terms the East German civil service, which was renewed to a large extent, had to fulfil many new functions on the basis of new laws. But there are also variables that hinder the full functioning of new public management in East Germany and that cannot be changed in the short term. Referring to this dimension Klages and Löffler also discuss the social cultural patterns of East and West Germans and their consequences for modernization processes.

In the next section Pracher focuses on specific aspects of German administrative areas from a different point of view. The explanations are concentrated on the administrative structure of Berlin and the main features of the new model of guidance and steering.

Concerning the implementation of modernization processes in Germany, Reichard discusses 'new steering models' in German local government and provides a case study of implementing public management concepts in local authorities. By comparing various issues of steering some main points can be differentiated: decentralized structures with semi-autonomous units; contract management; steering by output; guidance at a distance; thinking in terms of 'products'; decentralized responsibility for resources and results; global budgets, a stronger orientation towards citizens; market-type mechanisms to improve competition in general. In these areas an enormous variety of modernization strategies used by local governments can be identified. The 'new steering model' is recommended to local governments by the consulting agency of local governments, located in Cologne.

INTRODUCTION

It is no accident that Germany is the native country of Max Weber. Given the strong impact of the concept of the *Rechtsstaat* (judicial state) on German public administration, Max Weber's bureaucratic organization as an ideal type exists here – or rather existed here from today's perspective – as a real form of administrative organization (Klages, 1994). This rule-oriented administrative culture may be interpreted as an endogenous variable impeding reforms from within the administrative system. In contrast to this, the German traditions of federalism and local self-government can be seen rather as an exogenous variable, leaving experimental fields to administrative organizations and thereby allowing for reforms.

The reformers of the 1960s, however, did not make use of this liberty to test different administrative models. Consumed by Keynesian planning euphoria, politicians tried to implement PPBS (Planning, Programming and Budgeting System) on the federal level and on the level of the *Länder* (regions). At local government level a territorial reform could be accomplished but a functional reform never followed. These attempts to increase the efficiency of the public administration were followed by a general disillusionment about the 'reformability' of the public sector. In the 1970s some reforms, such as internal reform (management models), political steering of the administration and reform of the civil service, were on the political agenda but the results were rather meagre. In contrast to Great Britain, the Netherlands and the Scandinavian countries in the 1980s, there was even a reform-moratorium in Germany.

Maybe the complex task of German reunification with all its implications, together with the deepest recession since World War II gave the necessary impetus to German public administration to catch up with the public administration of more progressive neighbouring countries.

The aim of the chapter is to analyze the present trends of the modernization process in Germany with a particular focus on modernization strategies. We base our analysis on data and information obtained 'first hand' by the foundation of so-called 'innovation circles' directed by Professors Hill and Klages, Speyer Postgraduate School of Administrative Studies. These circles are a forum for innovative administrations to exchange experiences and problems of administrative modernization. This sort of 'round table' exists for small, medium-sized and big cities, the counties and county boroughs (*Kreise*), and government districts (*Regierungsbezirke*).

CURRENT TRENDS IN THE MODERNIZATION OF THE PUBLIC ADMINISTRATION IN GERMANY

A bottom-up revolution

In contrast to modernization programs in countries like the United Kingdom (Hogwood, 1993, p. 207) and France (Commissariat Général du Plan, 1988) aimed at restructuring central government, the modernization of public administration in Germany has to be understood in terms of a 'bottom-up' revolution: there are essentially no reform initiatives at the federal level, at least some German *Länder* show up as modernization pioneers, but the truly new entrepreneurs in the field of modernization are the local governments.

The incoming applications to the second Speyer Quality Competition Award show that a large number of communities are 'on the move'. They perceive themselves as service providers and try to implement the management practices prevalent in the private sector. The counties and county boroughs follow a bit behind the local governments. However, the state administration is much more cautious. On the level of the German *Länder* there are some pioneers such as Baden-Württemberg with the reform initiative 'Public Administration 2000' (Staatsministerium Baden-Württemberg, 1993), Berlin (Hoffmann and Dill, 1993) and Schleswig-Holstein (Die Ministerpräsidentin des Landes Schleswig-Holstein, 1994).

The implementation of the 'New Steering Model' by local government

An enormous variety of modernization strategies is used by local government. Nevertheless, the so-called 'New Steering Model', which is also recommended to local governments by their consulting agency (*Kommunale Gemeinschaftsstelle für Verwaltungsvereinfachung* in Cologne: KGST), gives them an orientation (KGST, 1993). The elements of the 'New Steering Model' that local governments put into practice are the following:

- *Result-oriented budget:* in most cases only applied to certain business fields (pilot projects) but there are also examples like the county of Soest and the city of Osnabrück which have a result-oriented budget for all activities.

- *The search for the costs of administrative products:* within the budgetary framework most local governments try to calculate the true costs of their products. At present this is only done for the direct costs, but some cities also aim at using the concept of indirect costs.

- *Introduction of commercial bookkeeping:* this is a logical consequence of the innovations mentioned above. The present laws for budgeting still force local governments to use the classical *cameralistic* system (a Prussian tradition of hierarchy and a single line of accountability) so that at present enterpreneurial cities such as the city of Passau have to run two bookkeeping systems (*Die Zeit*, 1994, p. 24).

- *Decentralized resource accountability:* former departments which are partly restructured become autonomous agencies with more responsibility for their tasks and the resources they are using. Here again the city of Passau acts as a model.

- *Definition of indicators for quality standards:* in order to improve and maintain the quality of administrative products, complex indicators have to be defined. In this area no ready solutions are available yet in Germany.

- *Customer orientation:* quality of administrative products also means customer satisfaction. Therefore most local governments set up decentralized citizen offices where citizens can address all their wishes and problems.

- *Outsourcing/contracting-out/privatization*: this is a field where local governments have become most active. Municipalities in East Germany in particular face the dilemma of a diminishing local tax base and an increasing
  mountain of new duties. Private capital thus becomes vital for local self-
  government.
- *Openness to 'competition'*: the high rate of participation in the first
  and second Speyer Quality Award in 1992 and 1994 shows that there
  is an interest and willingness on the part of public administrators
  to find out 'how good they are' in relation to other administrative
  organizations (Haubner, 1993, p. 54). Another proof is the success
  of the Carl Bertelsmann Prize 1993, which attracted an international
  entry.

Even though this is a brief summary it shows that most local governments
tend to follow the Tilburg model. In other words, at the German local level
there is a trend to be more efficient, effective and open to the market.

Local exceptions showing up potential deficits of the 'New Steering Model'

This general orientation of private management strategies is valid for all
modernizing local governments in Germany. However, there are some cases
that show that there might be some deficits inherent to the concept of an
'enterprise city'.

The city of Passau, for example, has developed a new personnel management with a focus on 'personnel development and organizational development'. This field of modernization usually does not get much attention from
municipal administrations. In addition, the county of Main-Kinzig and
initiatives at the level of the *Länder* of Rheinland-Pfalz and Baden-
Württemberg can be cited as exceptions with respect to the general non-
application of new personnel management methods.

Furthermore, most German municipalities ignore the opinion of their citizens when restructuring their products and the way in which they are
offered. Here again the city of Passau takes the lead by working on a (new)
corporate identity together with its citizens, city council and staff. The city of
Duisburg should also be mentioned in this context for its regular citizen
surveys.

The exceptions mentioned above suggest that the orientation towards
private management methods is a necessary but not a sufficient condition
for the modernization of the public administration in Germany. This seems
to be especially true when analyzing the challenges to local governments in
East Germany.

AN EAST–WEST DIVISION IN THE MODERNIZATION APPROACH

The specific problems facing public administration in East Germany

As in West Germany, public administration in the former East Germany has also undergone far-reaching changes. However, the transition from a real socialist public administration to a classical European public administration has another dimension and quality different from the current modernization process in West Germany. This is why it is more accurate to refer to the restructuring of the public sector in East Germany as a transformation process (König, 1991a, p. 177). As we will try to point out, this transformation process can be interpreted as a special kind of modernization process with specific challenges, problems and solutions.

The transformation process in East Germany can only be understood against the background of the structure and functioning of the public administration in the former German Democratic Republic. This public administration was anti-Weberian in the sense that it fulfilled the postulates of a legalistic bureaucracy such as the obligation to act according to the legal rules, a clear division of competences, and the provision of professional education. The main reason for this can be seen in the competence of the Socialist Unitary Party (SED) which established the principle of the democratic socialism – with the emphasis on central – as the working principle of the public administration.

As a consequence, the traditional German institution of municipal self-government was eroded more and more, so that by 1952 the functional reform of the East German public administration had already been achieved (Bernet, 1992, p. 15). The 'administrative and territorial reform' decided by the SED at a party conference on 9–12 July 1952 meant the official liquidation of municipal self-government in East Germany. As a result of the new law the five *Länder* were substituted by fourteen districts (*Bezirke*), including East Berlin, and from the existing 132 counties and county boroughs, 217 smaller ones were created. More importantly, the municipalities and districts became the instrument of central government. In fact, in most cases the mayor had been delegated into the office by the SED (Schmidt-Eichstaedt, 1993, p. 3). Thus communities were subject to the principle of double control (Schneider, 1993, p. 18). In contrast to liberal reforms in the state and local administration in Hungary, the administrative system in East Germany remained frozen until the opening of the frontier in November 1989.

When the Berlin Wall came down, the 'general systemic frontier' (König, 1991b, p. 16) that had been separating the political systems in the East and the West became apparent. The contradictions between the systems which had to be removed by the transformation process affected the public administration as a whole and not only parts of it. König (1991a, p. 177) distinguishes the following categories of the overall transformation task:

- *competencies: from the holistic planning authority to the balancing function which is typical for a market economy;*

- *civil service: from the 'cadre administration' with political qualifications to a civil service based on professional qualification;*

- *organization: from the unity of powers to the horizontal and vertical separation of power; and*

- *procedures: from the guidance principle of the Party to legalistic administrative behaviour.*

In organizational terms, public administration in East Germany faced a complex challenge: the East German civil service, which had been extensively renewed, had to fulfil many new functions on the basis of a new legal framework. At the same time, territorial reform was inevitable due to financial reasons which would threaten the existence of many municipalities and districts.

How did the political and administrative actors answer these challenges? With the reunification with West Germany on 3 October 1990 the central administration of the GDR merged with the federal administration of the Federal Republic of Germany and the five former *Länder* (existing since 1952) were reconstituted in East Germany (Hausschild, 1991, p. 217). As a result only the local level of the administrative system of East Germany remained. This made the territorial reforms a very delicate matter since the local level became an important element of continuity for the former GDR citizens for whom everything – from the welfare system to the job situation – had changed.

However, after reunification it soon became obvious that, given their size, the municipalities and districts in East Germany could not fulfil their role of municipal self-government and take over the responsibilities transferred to them by the state. Finally, there was political consensus in all the so-called new *Länder* that territorial reform had to be undertaken with the second municipal elections (in Brandenburg on 12 May 1993, in Mecklenburg-Vorpommern, Sachsen, Sachen-Anhalt and Thüringen on 12 June 1994). This territorial reform reduced the districts existing in 1989 to 87 new districts. Compared to the district reform in the West German *Länder* between 1968 and 1978 scientific methodology played a much smaller role in the current territorial reform, which was driven by politicians, civil servants and consulting firms from the corresponding partner *Länder* (Bernet, 1992, pp. 31, 33).

Whereas the number of inhabitants are increased in the districts, none of the five new *Länder* has so far dared to initiate a territorial reform of the communes. There is agreement that the present size of municipalities is inadequate as far as the low density of population and modern technologies are concerned. On the other hand, given the deindustrialization and high unemployment rate in East Germany, bigger municipalities would not have the financial power to deal with their own affairs without financial transfers and other aid. Therefore it seems that at present the socialization argument is given preference over the efficiency argument in the sense that politically and socially functioning municipalities are considered to be more important than efficient administrative units (Schmidt-Eichstaedt, 1993, p. 14).

Nevertheless, as a result of the first local elections on 6 May 1990 there was a far-reaching exchange of political élites. The new mayors often came from non-administrative professions and tried to compensate for their lack of experience and knowledge with enthusiasm and initiative. This new personnel input in the public administration could become an important factor for public administration in West Germany which has a monopoly of lawyers.

Another specific element of the modernization process in East Germany has to be mentioned in the context of local government. Communities in East Germany face the dilemma that they have to take care of problems formerly handled by the state or by mass organizations, whereas their financial resources are extremely limited. This problem is also known in the West but is much more acute in the East. In this situation East German local governments see no other solutions than staff reductions and massive privatization. It remains doubtful whether privatization measures taken out of financial constraints and not out of economic considerations are the optimal solution to the problem of local public services.

Last but not least, political and administrative élites in East Germany initiated the simplification of numerous administrative acts in order to speed up the provision of infrastructure in East Germany. For example, the *Land* Sachsen shortened the administrative planning procedure (*Planfeststellungsverfahren*) in order to accelerate the building of highways.

Looking at what has been achieved and what still has to be done, the question remains open whether the public administration in East Germany would not have been more innovative if approved models of the West German public administration had not simply been transferred to the East. As far as macroeconomics is concerned there is already a discussion in Germany about exogenous factors, i.e. imported structural deficits from the West increasing the costs and duration of the transformation process (Klinger, 1994, p. 5). It seems that the administrative sciences should look to the East and perceive German reunification as a chance for a double modernization process in the East and the West.

Making the second step after the first?

By the fourth year after the reunification it became obvious to the Germans in the East and the West that the cost, duration and depth of the problems have been underestimated. The transformation of a socialist state into a classical European administration has proved to be a difficult task. But is there still such a thing as a 'classical administration', in the Weberian sense, in the West? At least in the northern part of the EC, including West

Table 6.1. Social-cultural behavioural patterns in West and East Germany

Dimension of reality	West	East
Political system and society	market-oriented towards negotiations, conflictory	hierachical, oriented towards commands, integrative
Daily life and personal relations	competitive, expressive-open, extroverted, individualistic	oriented to persons, introspective-closed up, conformist
Steering media	capability to take initiatives, strategy competence, know-how, money, clientelism	capability to improvise, muddling through competence, clientelism

Source: Klinger (1994, p. 6).

Germany, we can observe a break with the bureaucratic model. As described above there is a shift of paradigm taking place in most Western countries. For practitioners in East Germany as well as for other East European administrations in the state of transition, the question arises as to which model to copy – the Weberian model or the new public management administration? As far as East Germany is concerned there was no need for East Germans to find answers to this question since the equivalent partner (each East German *Land* has a so-called sponsor in West Germany sending advice, financial aid and civil servants to the East) decided by themselves which model to use. In most cases, the old well-proven administrative structures from the West were directly imported to the East. Sometimes motivated people, seeing no opportunity for experiments in the West, went to the East to try something new, like for example the district administration of Cottbus-Land which also was among the prize winners of the first Speyer Quality Award in 1992.

Nevertheless, at least for administrative scientists there is a need to ask whether after an arbitrary administrative system we should have a rule-oriented classical administration or an 'entrepreneurial administration' (Osborne and Gaebler, 1992, p. XIX) defining its own economic rules. From the social point of view, East German citizens need an administration embodying the principles of the *Rechtsstaat* giving them security and stability in an unstable environment. On the other hand, the scarce economic resources available to administrative organizations in East Germany force them to find new ways to do their job. However, there is one variable that hinders the full functioning of New Public Management in East Germany and that cannot be changed in the short term: the social-cultural patterns of East Germans are distinct from the behavioural patterns of their West German counterparts. The survey shown in Table 6.1 points out the characteristics of social patterns in the West and the East which have been imprinted by different system-specific variables. The steering instruments describe resources and capabilities which are used to put across personal interests.

This different social-behavioural repertoire shows that people who have grown up in the East have less chance of dealing successfully with the new market environment. With respect to New Public Management this means it is unlikely that East Germans will be able (and wish) to adopt the private economy-oriented management practices. Nevertheless, at least in the version of New Public Management as described in 'Reinventing Government' (Osborne and Gaebler, 1992) there is also the element of empowerment and the participation of citizens. This aspect of New Public Management fits well with the East German mentality and could become an important element for municipal self-government. Having been an extension of the SED in socialist times, the municipalities now have to become 'schools of democracy' (Schneider, 1993, p. 26) if they want to regain the confidence of the population and help them create a political identity. We are anxious to see if this theoretical assumption is empirically verified by the application for the present Second Speyer Quality Award coming from East Germany.

A 'TYPICAL' GERMAN STRATEGY?

In light of this internal German perspective, the described state of the administrative modernization process in Germany has to be seen in relation to the modernization of public administration in other (OECD) countries (OECD Public Management Survey, 1993). From a comparative perspective the logical question that an administrative scientist might ask is whether there are strategies of modernizing public administration that are specific to certain 'types' of countries.

With regard to the present landscape of modern public administration in Germany the authors want to propose the hypothesis that the question of a typical German strategy only makes sense if the macro-strategic level is taken into account. As a result of the bottom-up process of modernization in Germany the micro-strategic level has an infinite variety which is due to random variables (Klages and Haubner, 1994).

As far as the macro-strategic level is concerned, different classes of variables can be distinguished such as basic decisions taken by the administrative leaders/politicians with respect to the scope and role of administrative modernization in the political system; procedural decisions regarding the implementation of modernization in the public administration; and conceptual decisions defining the focus of the modernization program. Table 6.2 shows the choices which administrators/politicians can make within these classes of macro-strategic variables, the strategies chosen in Germany and careful hypotheses about the strategic trends until the year 2000.

The modernization strategies of German public administration are analyzed horizontally with regard to three dimensions: one dimension includes the theoretical choices possible, the second dimension describes current developments in Germany and the third dimension gives a prediction on the development of the variable by the year 2000. Vertically, there are three analytical

Table 6.2. Modernization strategies of the public administration in Germany – Variables, current developments and predictions for the year 2000

Analytical Level	Variables	Current Developments	Predictions for the year 2000
Strategic political-administrative decisions (where to go)	(a) reduction of state activities vs. modernization of state activities	(a) modernization predominant	(a) constant
	(b) state as provider vs. state as enabler	(b) state as provider concepts for the role as enabler: Federal Plan for the Elderly 1993	(b) stronger role as enabler
	(c) maintenance of the civil service status vs. abolishment of the special status	(c) constitutionally guaranteed status of civil servants still valid, yet perceived more and more as obstacle to the modernization of the public administration	(c) tendency to partial reforms but basic structure unchanged
	(d) imposing a specific modernization concept to the whole administrative body vs. allowing for local/sectoral initiatives	(d) German administrative system by tradition 'structurally open', *de jure* and *de facto* impossible to impose centralized reform program	(d) constant
Tactical decisions (how to do administrative modernization)	(e) deductive, model-oriented procedure vs. ad-hoc pragmatic approach	(e) certain models very influential, but administrative practitioners sceptical to science as adviser	(e) constant
	(f) support of experts vs. hand-made internal concepts	(f) mixed situation: boom of private consulting firms; at the same time hand-made concepts because of fiscal restraints/scepticism with regard to consulting firms	(f) hand-made reform programs; external experts only for specific tasks
	(g) holistic strategy vs. step-by-step approach vs. muddling through	(g) start with partial reforms limited to certain business fields	(g) partial solutions remain important for the initial phase of reforms; by the year 2000 successive total coverage of administrations
Operational decisions (what to do)	(h) structural vs. cultural modernization	(h) dominance of structural modernization	(h) structural bias will remain but increasing emphasis on personnel management systems
	(i) internal decentralization vs. agency concept	(i) internal decentralization in the state administration, heterogenous disengagement of administrative units on local level	(i) dualism of modernized core administration with an unleashed periphery of private agencies
	(j) built-in flexibility in structures vs. reforms once in a while	(j) concept of discrete reforms dominant; creation of mobile task forces fall on deaf ears	(j) constant
	(l) flattening of hierarchies vs. functional redefinition of hierarchies	(l) functional redefinition of hierarchies	(l) constant
	(m) citizen vs. customer orientation	(m) actual situation unclear: much rhetoric about customer orientation	(m) constant
	(n) customer/citizen oriented result-orientation vs. internal modernization vs. direct contacts with customers	(n) internal modernization predominant	(n) customer/citizen surveys will be standard repertoire of local governments, also more efforts to find out about the desires and grievances of the citizens

levels: the level of strategic political-administrative decisions which determine the framework for administrative modernization; the level of tactical decisions made by administrative 'leaders' when preparing administrative moderniza-tion in public agencies; and the level of operational decisions telling the ad-ministrative staff what to do in concrete modernization projects.

Strategic level

The most important question on this level is whether to reduce the size of the public sector by handing over non-public tasks (those lacking the char-acteristics of common goods) to the private sector, or whether to keep a large public sector and to modernize the public sector from within. For Germany, privatization is an undesirable option – only 'hard-liners' such as the city of Offenbach dare to pursue rigorous privatization policies. With the strong social welfare state tradition, this tendency is likely to remain in the future. When the state is obliged to guarantee the provision of certain public goods and services, the question is whether public goods and services are to be produced by the public sector itself or whether 'rowing' is transferred to the private sector and 'steering' is the primary task of the state (Osborne and Gaebler, 1992, p. 25). At present, the perspective of the state as a provider is predominant in Germany. How-ever, the Federal Plan for the Elderly of 1993 is a first indication that the German state will increasingly act as enabler. The civil service status has always been a political issue of administrative reforms. The constitutionally guaranteed status of civil servants is still untouched and is unlikely to change fundamentally because of a lock-in situation in the German Parlia-ment (the majority of MPs are civil servants). The question whether to im-pose a national administrative reform program from above or whether to leave freedom for local and sectoral initiatives is only a theoretical one in the Federal Republic of Germany where federal structure and tradition by nature forbid a centralized approach to administrative reforms.

Tactical level

Before running into reform activism, the management of administrative agencies has to consider a number of issues. One important question to be discussed by public managers is whether to apply a specific administrative reform model or whether to use a pragmatic 'trial-and-error' approach. For Germany, it can be stated that certain models (e.g. the Tilburg model) have been very influential in the initial stage of administrative modernization in Germany, but meanwhile practitioners are seeking their own way to mod-ernize their municipality. This issue is connected with the decision to be made to hire experts or to rely on 'handmade' concepts. In fact, private consulting firms currently get their share of administrative modernization projects, but fiscal restraints force many German municipalities to use their own resources for the planning and realization of modernization projects. Another tactical decision to be made by public managers is whether to follow a holistic strategy or a step-by-step approach. If this issue is not considered, a 'muddling through' will be the consequence. In the initital reform phase, partial reforms have been predominant, but by the year 2000 there will be enough experience to use holistic approaches.

Operational level

Here decisions have to be made concerning more specific aspects of administrative modernization activities. One issue to consider is whether to pursue only structural reforms or whether to include the cultural component as well. Most practitioners only focus on structural modernization and leave aside the longer-term cultural change. An exception here is the city of Saarbrücken with its TQM-program. Structural modernization again includes coordinated decentralization (of budget and personnel policies) and the agency model. Here the picture is very heterogeneous at the moment since the extent of decentralization efforts at the state and at the local level varies enormously. However, at the local level in Germany, the picture of a core administration with a periphery of private agencies (for facilities) starts to emerge. A more fundamental question is whether functions should be restructured every once in a while or whether they should have a built-in flexibility. The concept of mobile taskforces has had no success in the German administration where discrete reforms are likely to remain the predominant approach. The German administration also takes a careful approach when it comes to the question of flattening hierarchies. Instead of making administrative agencies leaner, existing hierarchies are redefined with respect to functions. When it comes to terminological issues with respect to the usage of the term 'citizen' and 'client', the situation is not clear in Germany. Both terms are used even though innovative municipalities prefer the term 'customer'. Last but not least, the question for public managers and the staff in administrative agencies is how customer orientation should be realized. One possibility is to define citizen/customer-oriented performance targets and to publish the results. Another possibility is to rely on modernization processes from within which automatically bring about more customer orientation. The third possibility is to invest in direct communication with citizens/customers. In Germany internal modernization is still the prevailing strategy of citizen/customer orientation, but by the year 2000 citizen surveys will be a common practice of local governments in Germany.

OUTLOOK

After making a trend extrapolation for the values of the strategy variables in Germany by the year 2000 it seems useful to see the trends described for Germany in an international context.

First of all we can hypothesize that by the year 2000 there will still exist differences in administrative cultures and traditions but they will be much weaker than today. As a result, research on differences in modernization strategies on the macro-level will be much less productive.

From the first hypothesis it follows that the research into different micro-level strategies of modernization which was omitted here will gain importance. In terms of methodology, the second hypothesis implies that overall comparative country studies will become irrelevant. Instead it will be more profitable to limit the analysis of micro-level strategies to one (part) of a political system that can be studied in detail.

Concerning the selection of countries for the analysis of micro-level strategies, Germany could become a profitable case study. The third hypothesis to put forward in this context says that the volume and significance of micro-strategic differences will be greater in Germany than in other countries. Because of the structural openness (cf. point (e) in Table 6.2) and constitutionally guaranteed freedom of action (see Introduction) it seems reasonable to assume that Germany will become an experimental field of modernization strategies. In other words, the present flow of knowledge – in which Germany learns from abroad – could reverse by the year 2000.

Part II: New models of guidance and steering in the public administration

Christian Pracher

Christian Pracher

THE ADMINISTRATIVE STRUCTURE OF THE FEDERAL REPUBLIC OF GERMANY

The dominant principles of the administrative structure in Germany are federalism, local self-government and division of powers.

The principle of federalism considers the *Länder* (states – at present sixteen including three city-states) as part of the federal government with their own national sovereignty; local government guarantees self-determined administration of communes and districts as far as local affairs are concerned. The horizontal division of powers assigns authorities to the legislative, the executive and the judiciary bodies.

Vertically the administration is divided into five levels. Only the three main levels, the federal government, the *Länder* and the local authorities, however, are developed exhaustively.

Level 1   the federation
Level 2   the *Länder* (states)
Level 3   the government districts
Level 4   the rural counties and county boroughs
Level 5   the communes and the commune associations

The federation, the rural counties and the county boroughs have been exhaustively established. They possess their own legal status and elected authorities. Being subdivisions of the *Länder* without their own legal status and without elected authorities, government districts have not been set up in all *Länder*.

On the level of the *Länder* and the local authorities, the federal government, as a rule, makes use of the administrative institutions of the *Länder* and the communes. Only in exceptional cases does the federal government have its own institutions (e.g. customs, foreign service, military administration).

The *Länder* are irregularly organized according to their size (larger non-city states, smaller non-city states, city-states). The ministries of the *Länder* (in the city-states the senates) stand at the top of the *Länder* administrations, below them are the intermediate and local authorities of the *Länder*. As in the federal administration the higher authorities of the *Länder* fulfil special administrative tasks (the *Land* Statistical Office, the *Land* Criminal Police Offices). As an intermediate authority the government districts (in the larger *Länder*) face general administrative tasks. In essence, they fulfil tasks of supervision, coordination and administration.

The local authorities are the main institution of the communal administration. They fulfil both their own tasks as well as tasks under specialist supervision in respect of a subject. Concerning their own tasks the local authorities are basically responsible for all the local affairs provided that their implementation is not particularly entrusted to superior authorities (principle of last resort).

The rural districts and county boroughs fulfil *Länder* tasks under special supervision in respect of a subject and their own tasks of self-administration which cannot be taken over by the local authorities of the respective districts.

THE ADMINISTRATIVE STRUCTURE OF BERLIN

Apart from Hamburg and Bremen, Berlin belongs to the so-called city-states (as opposed to the non-city states). Thus, Berlin is considered a German *Land* as well as a city at the same time.[1] This means that *Land* and local activities are not separated from each other.[2]

The institutions of direct administration of Berlin is the *Land* of Berlin, the institutions of indirect administration of Berlin are public corporations, institutions and foundations.

Direct administration   *Land* of Berlin
Indirect administration   corporations, institutions and foundations

The administrative structure of the *Land* of Berlin basically consists of two levels:

Higher level   main administrations
Lower level   district administrations

The ministries (*Senatsverwaltungen*) (at present sixteen at the most) and the authorities subordinated to them and the non-incorporated institutions as well as the *Land*-owned (municipal) enterprises belong to the main administrations. They are subdivided according to departmental principles. The supervision of the individual departments falls to a political functionary (monocratic principle). The senate affairs are run by the governing mayor who is not, however, the only one responsible for the general policy guidelines as the federal chancellor is. The governing mayor can only determine the guidelines in accordance with the senate and with the approval of the House of Deputies (the Berlin Parliament). The governing mayor and the senators are elected by the House of Deputies.

The district administrations (at present twenty-three) consist of the district deputies' assembly, the district office and the (non-incorporated) institutions, respectively.

The districts contribute to the administration 'on the principles' of self-government. 'On the principles' means that it is not genuine self-government. The districts have no own legal status, the district administration bodies have no legislative competence and they have no sovereignty of budgets and finances. The latter means that the district budgets are part of the overall Berlin budget and that the revenue of the district administrations flows to the *Land* cash office. In staff affairs, however, the districts have a far-reaching sovereignty.

The district deputies' assembly, being more or less a parliament, fulfils a controlling function towards the district administration. The assembly is entitled to submit budget proposals, have a say in the development plan, make recommendations and requests to the district office and form commissions.

The district office represents the *Land* of Berlin whenever district affairs are concerned and is entrusted with tasks the district deputies' assembly is not responsible for. The district office is currently organized into eight departments (Personnel and Administration, Building and Housing, Youth and Sport, Social Affairs, Education, Health, Economy, Finances). These departments are directed by the municipal councillors. The district mayors and the district municipal councillors are elected by the district deputies' assembly. The district mayor has no authority towards the district municipal councillors to issue directives in departmental affairs. Thus, the district office is considered a collegial office.

When fulfilling the tasks a distinction is made between 'general administrative tasks' and 'regulating tasks' (see Table 6.3). Basically the tasks of the Berlin administration are implemented by the senate and by district administrations.[3]

Table 6.3. Main and district administration

	General administrative tasks	Regulating tasks
Main administration	Reserved tasks, e.g., motorway construction	Public security and order, e.g. police, fire brigade, forestry and fishery
District administration	District tasks under specialist supervision in respect to a subject, e.g. the implementation of the housing subsidy act, tax cards	
	District affairs, e.g. organization of adult education programmes	

Table 6.4. Leading and executing level

	Main administration	*District administration*
Leading level	senator	district mayor/district municipal councillor
Executing level	departments divisions subject areas	departments offices subject areas

The organizational structure of the authorities is based on the principles of the hierarchic-bureaucratic one-line organization. The head of each unit is the respective senator (see Table 6.4).

MAIN FEATURES OF THE NEW MODEL OF GUIDANCE AND STEERING

Basic ideas of steering

When comparing the different ideas of steering, the following elements can be differentiated. In the first instance there is something that does the actual steering. These 'steerers' may be individuals or groups of people.

The objects of this steering may be, for example, the administration, which is steered by political bodies. At the same time the administration, for its part, also acts as a 'steerer', directing administrative units.

The classical instrument for steering the administration is – according to the constitution – steering by law. In principle, other instruments of steering are also possible and quite recently the so-called 'new models of guidance and steering' have been under discussion.

The next question concerns the direction of steering, or the conditions that the steering activities aim to achieve.

In order better to assess and judge the 'new features' of the New Steering Model, two basic alternatives for steering the administration are explained, i.e. control by law and control by target setting.

The steering alternatives mentioned refer to steering the administration by policy, steering the administration itself as well as steering society by administration. Steering within the administration will be dealt with in the section on management concepts which in the final analysis is about steering organizations (in the concrete case of administration). From the different types of steering, two essential groups are chosen: 'steering by law' and 'steering by target setting'. The first type refers to the classical instrument for steering administration, the latter is the type of steering which has been under intensive discussion in theory and practice during recent years and which has been introduced with some success, particularly at the local level.

Table 6.5. Possibilities of steering

Steering type	Description	Examples
Regulating steering	This is the traditional steering by commands and prohibitions and supervision. The compliance with the norms is supervised and pushed through by the bodies of law protection or by administrative bodies of execution. However, part of this type is also the duties of announcement as well as permits and licences	penal law, epidemic law, announcement duty of certain diseases, licence to drive a car, building permits
Personnel steering	The steering of the personnel does not mean excesses such as patronage, nepotism, etc., but general steering of the administrative personnel by law	duty to obey, prohibition of strikes, the public official status importing the concepts of reciprocal trust and service, rejection of so-called radicals from public service, etc.
Procedure steering	This means steering by procedures especially the procedures of decision-making and consent-forming	appointment procedure regulations for university professors
Structure steering	This refers to the connection between administrative organization and administrative activity	administration of universities as academic self-administrative organizations, administration of armies
Financial steering	By this, steering by financial incentives as well as by budget law and budget supervision are understood	housing subsidy, other subsidies, promotions
Performance steering	For the control by services no financial but material means are used. The administration offers certain services which it provides or purchases by itself	provision of flats, offer of education
Informal steering	This is rather a 'soft' form of control by information, recommendations, declarations of intent, etc, but by symbolic rewards too	information of the prospects to attain a job with a certain training; speed recommendations; decorations/ medals, titles

STEERING BY LAW

As mentioned above, the law is considered to be the classical steering instrument. By means of legal norms (law, decrees), certain conditions are to be achieved. As a rule legal norms are characterized by statements like 'if . . . so . . .'. Conditions are defined regarding the existence of which certain modes of behaviour are expected, certain services are rendered, etc.

As a whole steering by law offers a wide range of alternatives to achieve certain conditions (see Table 6.5).

Steering by law generally means an input steering. Financial, material and personnel resources are allotted, procedures are stipulated, structures are realized, conditional prerequisites are fixed ('if . . . then . . .').

Today this form of administrative steering is not regarded as being very efficient. In particular it is criticized because steering is done via the allocation of resources and the intended result is not specified. There are, however, vague target descriptions, e.g. 'increasing security', 'improving traffic flow', 'promoting certain sections of the population'. Although this kind of target description shows the direction for administrative activity, an exact and operational target setting according to its content, extent and time is out of the question. Hence no measurement of target achievement is possible. Another criticism is that the importance placed on regulations paves the way for bureaucracy (in the negative sense).

Output-oriented steering is marked here by steering according to precise target settings, by the formulation of the result aimed at. The executing authorities are free, within certain limits, to act to achieve these targets. The executing authorities are answerable to the target-setting authorities with regard to achieving their target.

The new model of guidance and steering

The discussion is not about one new model of guidance and steering but about several such models. Certainly all the above-mentioned steering systems are based upon the same ideas and elements, but they have to be adapted to the respective special features. The initial stimulus for the concept and development of the new model of guidance and steering was a financial crisis. In addition, criticism of the working methods and the efficiency of the administration arose both from inside (the head of the administration and by policy) and from outside (media, citizens and science). Furthermore, the administration increasingly loses its attraction to capable employees, and political bodies deal too much with operative details instead of taking fundamental decisions. Altogether the administration deals too much with itself.

The starting point of the new movement of guidance and steering was the Dutch city of Tilburg. At the end of the 1970s and the beginning of the 1980s Tilburg and several other Dutch communities were suffering from striking financial problems. This and the increasingly expressed demand for more quality, efficiency and effectiveness prepared the ground for new ways of guidance.

Tilburg is a city with approximately 164,000 inhabitants and approximately 2,000 public civil servants. The project for the 'New Model of Guidance and Steering in Tilburg' has proved its success in all aspects. For some years

Tilburg has achieved a balanced budget; in 1991 and 1992 a surplus was even achieved. According to the opinion of the citizens the quality of the services has increased fundamentally. Irrespective of its success, the model has not yet been fully completed. Without doubt it still needs further development.

First of all the new model of guidance and steering can be outlined by some catchwords such as: 'group (*Konzern*) community', 'contract management', 'output-oriented management', 'management at arm's length', 'thinking in products', 'decentralized responsibility for resources and results', 'stronger orientation towards citizens'.

A comparison of the administration with a group (*Konzern*) shows that independent units of the administration, the specialized sections (*Fachämter*), also team up to make one united overall system, i.e. a commune.

The political-administrative level (group management) has to determine the targets and guidelines. The specialized administration (*Fachverwaltung*) has to implement the set targets within the given constraints.

'Contract management' describes the process of agreeing and coordinating the targets between the head of administration and the *Fachverwaltungen*. This means that binding arrangements are met between the senior and junior authorities about annual performance to be achieved (quantitatively and qualitatively), the means made available for this purpose and the mode of reporting the results.

The *Fachverwaltungen* work independently. They bear full responsibility for the achievement of the set targets. This independence also involves the personnel, budget and organization departments. Thus, the specialized administrations receive clearly defined targets and tasks, the resources necessary as well as the competences needed and the responsibility in order to prepare the products and the services.

An adequate organizational foundation permitting independent activity on one's own authority is considered the prerequisite for a functioning contract management. The specialized departments (*Fachabteilungen*) have to report on performance as compared to goals (three to five times a year) to the management level.

Contract management does not only apply vertically between the hierarchy levels but also horizontally between the particular specialized sections (*Fachämter*). Services which are exchanged between them will always be offset against each other. However, a particular *Fachämter* does not have to buy services from another *Fachämter* but is free to purchase from the free market provided that they are better or cheaper there. On the other hand the specialized departments (*Fachabteilungen*) may offer their services on the free market as long as they are marketable.

The political-administrative head sets targets which are implemented by the *Fachabteilungen*. The head has to keep him/herself strictly out of everyday activity (guidance from distance). Political *ad hoc* interventions are no longer permitted according to the new model of guidance and steering.

In the new model of guidance and steering the allocation or refusal of resources will no longer be the means of steering as has been the case up to now, but steering will be realized by setting goals that have to be achieved. The very core of guidance by output is thinking in terms of products.

A product is something that is delivered by a production centre to an organizational unit outside the production centre in order to meet the demand of another person, irrespective of whether the need emerges voluntarily or is the result of a law or another regulation for which the consumer actually should not pay anything regardless of whether or not this does happen in reality (definition according to Tilburg).

For the specific definition of products, the following procedure is applied in Tilburg: the employees of each particular specialized department participate in the description of the products within a frame set by the administrative head. It is important, then, that the products' descriptions contain all the relevant information necessary to characterize comprehensively the product with regard to the steering and in a convincing way to all those concerned.

In the beginning a list has to be made including all the activities of the respective *Fachverwaltung*. Subsequently on the basis of the catalog of activities the external final products and afterwards the internal products have to be described. External products come into being outside the specialized department (*Fachabteilung*); internal products stem from inside the specialized department (e.g. management activities, personnel and financial administrative activities, organizational tasks). Basically, the product description has to differentiate between the target, the activities and the real product (= output). For the next step the costs are assigned to these products, and this is considered the basis for budgeting.

The following example shows a part of the Tilburg group budget. In the new model of guidance and steering the so-called guidance service, which has the function of a controlling department, plays a central role. Here this guidance service faces – among others – the following tasks: definition of the targets and tasks, setting of a model, strategic planning, 'market' research, organization of the accountancy, internal and external supply of information, budget and resources' planning, calculation of products, reporting, budgeting, internal control and deviation analyses.

In addition, personnel management gains a decisive importance. Without adequately trained employees who are highly motivated and prepared to take over responsibility and who are also able to open new horizons, the new model of guidance and steering will not be destined to succeed.

The KGST describes the following prerequisites for a successful implementation. First of all, it has to be guaranteed that the people acting really do wish a change of the administrative structures in the direction of the new model of guidance and steering. Politicians, heads of administration, staff members, staff representatives all have to recognize that new steering structures will also serve their interests. To begin with, however, there will be fear and resistance to the new model. This situation can only be overcome by an early and broad information campaign for all the participants in order to develop an atmosphere of reform that is as broad as possible.

Here, the heads of policy and of administration play an essential part. Both have to elaborate their targets and jointly agree on them as well as promoting the process of change.

In addition, professional project management is needed including the precise targets, defined steps of work and fixed structures for the time and costs.

With the decentralization of responsibility for results and resources, a central steering service has to be set up, the tasks of which have been fulfilled up to now – at least partially – by the cross-section departments (personnel, finances). These departments often oppose such decentralization because they are afraid of losing responsibilities and hence power and status. Although this cannot be ruled out, the present cross-section departments (*Querschnittsabteilungen*) undoubtedly have to become leaner according to the new model of guidance and steering to enable them to concentrate on the essentials and to keep themselves out of the operative day-to-day working routine.

Frequently adequate investment in personnel is neglected. During the process of change all staff members have to work together, learning and changing in close cooperation. The administration must become a learning organization. The process of change should be connected with adequate provision for staff to gain new qualifications in order to develop operational/management thinking and acting and to promote leadership abilities. In principle a new culture of training and further training has to be developed.

According to the new model of guidance and steering, the ideal employee should be independent, initiatory, responsible, prepared to take risks, enterprising, oriented towards citizens, conscious of the quality as well as of the costs, flexible, communicative, committed, willing to commit and to admit mistakes for the sake of progress, able and ready to learn, full of confidence and self-assurance, willing to achieve something and able to cooperate with his or her colleagues and superiors.

Where are the real advantages of the New Steering Model?

The decisive advantage for political leaders is that they will take their political decisions on the basis of well-founded information on costs and performances and therefore be able to steer and control the administration in a better way. In this way the value of certain administrative services becomes transparent, and economic efficiency can be guaranteed by information on cost and performances.

For the administrative leaders new possibilities will be opened up that will enable them to do their work in a qualified way without the need to interfere with policy in single decisions and without unnecessary steering of operational details. The administrative leaders will fix the way in which to achieve the politically set targets. They will be able to concentrate increasingly on their strategic and coordinating tasks.

The specialized departments (*Fachabteilungen*), which are now responsible for their results and resources, will – like the administrative leaders – be freed from unnecessary and troublesome interferences and can take decisions on the use of resources and completion of works independently.

Staff members have a wider latitude for creativity and will become more independent and responsible in fulfilling their tasks. In this way, by new forms of payment according to performance and by new ways of guidance, motivation and job satisfaction will increase. The better administrative services will also improve the present negative image that the public hold of administration.

Citizens will get information about what is achieved with their tax money, what the different administrational services really cost, and they can confidently expect as efficient a performance as possible. Due to the increased orientation of administration towards the citizens they can rely on the administration to take their wishes and needs into account in a better way than they did before.

Where is the new system of guidance and steering applied already?

In the Federal Republic of Germany the new steering model has mainly been tried, or at least its introduction discussed, in the communes – in a fifth of them as experiments. However, some *Länder* are also thinking about new possibilities for steering.

In Baden-Württemberg a control-oriented steering concept has been discussed within the 'Administration 2000' project.

The 'think tank' of the *Land* chancellery of Schleswig-Holstein has produced some models that deal with, among others, the new steering model. At a communal level, product-relevant information (amounts, cost, quality) has been added to the budgets in some cities, e.g. Osnabrück, München and Nürnberg.

Reform measures in the field of budgeting are successfully practised in Offenbach and Gotha. Due to severe financial difficulties the main emphasis is on budget stabilization by separating out and by increasing the independence of some of its parts. However, thoughts on new steering possibilities play only a secondary role here.

Pilot projects on house and estate management (*Haus- und Grundstücksverwaltung*) in the Schöneberg district and the citizens' office (*Bürgeramt*) of Weißensee are examples that have already achieved some success.

Interim assessment

The testing period is still too short for a final assessment. Real success has only been noticed at the communal level. Apart from that it has to be pointed out that nowhere has an overall introduction taken place up to now. Even within a commune – as in Berlin for instance – only islands of reform have been created, while the compatibility of these partial projects seems not yet guaranteed. The necessary accompanying measures are still waiting to be realized. Most importantly, measures in the field of personnel management still have to be implemented. Organizational changes have been realized only 'half-heartedly'. New controlling organizations are not newly formed but only imposed on already existing structures. Furthermore, the orientation towards the market and competition is still practically non-existent. Finally, the politicians could not be convinced of the realistic advantages of a new steering model. Some of them expect wonders, especially in budget stabilization, whereas others prefer the old structures to remain. Both directions are unsuitable to the implementation of the 'new model of guidance and steering'.

THE BERLIN MODEL OF GUIDANCE AND STEERING

A report of 1984 showed that the Berlin administration had already considered decentralized organizational and cost responsibilities within a financial framework and had target and result oriented management. These reform ideas that already contained essential elements of the present model of guidance and steering were, however, never implemented. Only after the Tilburg model became known in Germany in the revised and adapted KGST version in August 1993 did the Berlin Senate take the decision to introduce a new model of guidance and steering on the basis of the KGST model.

In the beginning it was planned to introduce this new steering model in four district administrations and two ministries (*Senatsverwaltungen*) (for interior and social affairs) on a trial basis. Then, after having gained sufficient practical experience the model was to be transferred to the whole Berlin administration in 1995.

In April and in May 1994 the decision was taken on the exhaustive introduction of the new model of guidance and steering in all district administrations and four *Senatsverwaltungen*. Its target is a far-reaching decentralization of the responsibility for resources and the creation of fields of responsibility.

Systems of cost accounting including appropriate information technology back-up as the basis of the new steering systems have to be developed as early as possible with the help of external consultants. In the beginning cost accounting at the departmental level (*Kostenstellenrechnung*) has to be introduced in

Table 6.6. Organizational developments at the district level

Group management (Konzernleitung)	Group staff (Konzernstab)	Specialized departments
		service/office/department
District deputies' assembly	district office	service/office/department
	central steering service	service/office/department

all districts. The basis for the following cost accounting of the products (*Kostenträgerrechnung*) is the definition of the services as products.

From the financial year of 1997 onwards the global budgets will be continued on the basis of the system of cost accounting.

In principle the planned Berlin steering model is very similar to the 'new model of guidance and steering' of the KGST and of the Dutch contract management.

The survey in Table 6.5 shows the planned timescale for the implementation of the new steering model in Berlin.

From the organizational aspect the new model of guidance and steering on the district level requires the assignment of functions shown in Table 6.6.

The central element of the new steering model is the description of the products according to their quality, quantity, efficiency and success. These catalogs of products will form the prerequisites for the contracts between policy and administration, for cost and service accounting and for the transparency of the administration towards the citizens.

The general Berlin catalog will contain approximately the following

- 100 fields of products
- 400–500 groups of products
- 2000–3000 products

Figure 6.1 shows the Schöneberg house and estate management (*Haus- und Grundstücksverwaltung*). In the product field 'real estate management' the product group 'daily-care facilities' was defined with the products 'nursery schools', 'youth centres', 'retirement centres', 'youth art school' and 'youth school of road safety education'.

A new feature of the new steering system is the definition of the quality of the products too. The quality management in the field of the *Länder* Statistical Office is an example of quality steering. Here the quality of the products is defined by the target of quality, the level of measurement, the measuring point and the procedure of measurement (see Table 6.7).

The target setting of budgeting is the allotment of financial means to administrative units (specialized administrations, *Fachverwaltungen*) on the basis of the product amounts (global budgets). The budget results from the product of the product amount (according to the contract) and the level of the return per product unit:

Product field	Product groups
Real estate administration	residential buildings and homes educational and cultural institutes greens, cemeteries sports grounds office buildings other real estates day-care facilities

Product groups	Products
Day-care facilities	youth school of road safety education youth centres retirement centres youth art school nursery schools

Product

Management of nursery schools

Product description

Management of the buildings and free areas for the pedagogical care of children aged 8 weeks–12 years

Target group

Users of the buildings and the free areas

Targets

Determination and optimization of the operating costs for each nursery school; creation and preservation of an optimum building condition

Scope of services

- Planning, preparation, implementation and supervision of measures for the building maintenance and repairing
- Realization of measures of public health, security and fire prevention
- Management of the projects
- Procurement of devices, equipment and fittings that are firmly connected with the building
- Accounting of operating costs and rents
- Provision of infrastructural services

Figure 6.1.

Budget = planned amount of products × height of the return per product unit

In current budgetary law, certain principles have had to be rethought, including definition of accuracy, clarity, recording of gross expenditure, having to use up the whole budget within the year.

The process of implementation is accompanied by extensive measures of training and information. About 220 people are participating in training courses in the field of information processing, and 27 in the field of controlling; 2100 managers, top executives and 30 other people also participate.

Table 6.7. Examples of product qualities

Target of quality	Target level (%)	Measuring point	Measurement procedure
1. Production of statistics according to the needs	in reality		
1.1 Good quality of the result	in reality	feedback share missing information (questionnaire) mistakes in the plausibility test	public relations amendments in the questionnaires explanations of the questions
1.2 Need-oriented contents	in reality	demand for additional data materials for the assessment or for certain main fields	permanent contact with the clients, market analyses
1.3 Need-oriented structure	in reality	published products asked for	permanent contact with clients, market analyses
1.4 Presentation and publication of the figure material according to the users	in reality	further inquiry and comments of the consumers on the quality of the tables and graphics	guidelines on the design of statistic tables and graphics, advice for supports, etc.
1.5 Observance of the delivery dates, topicality of the dates	100	dates of delivery	supervision of the dates comparison of the estimated and actual dates elimination of the causes for the delay of dates
2 Optimum structure of information and decision-taking			
3 Optimum of the interior organization and the procedures implemented			
4 Good personnel management			
5 Development of the infrastructure of data processing according to the special demands			

Basically all the staff members should receive the information on a regular and comprehensive basis by leaflets, reform papers etc. Individual questions should be answered in a short and not hierarchical way.

In the field of personnel management the following are planned – talks with the staff members, a new method of efficiency reports, qualificational programs according to the target groups, incentives for good performances, a modern selection procedure, planning of the supplies, needs and procurement, promotion, displacement and succession planning, dismissal planning, further education planning, respective management concepts as well as changes of the public service law (flexible times of work, flexible payment, flexible career alternatives and flexible access of new staff members).

Case Study: Implementing Public Management Concepts in Local Authorities

Christoph Reichard

INTRODUCTION

Since about 1990 a widespread and increasing wave of reforms and innovations has been flowing over German local authorities: the so-called 'new steering models'. Under this label many local authorities are discussing and testing different elements of a general concept for the modernization of local government.[4]

The movement of administrative reforms follows the general patterns of 'new public management' (NPM), including among others (Hood, 1991, p. 4):

- Clear-cut accountability.
- Output and performance orientation.
- Decentralized structures with semi-autonomous units.
- Private sector-based management instruments (e.g. cost accounting, controlling)
- Market-type mechanisms to improve competition.

The NPM movement reached the Federal Republic of Germany only about ten years after its start in countries like the United Kingdom or the United States. One reason for the delay in introducing NPM-oriented reforms in the German public sector may be that financial pressure caused by severe cut-back measures in public finances occurred in Germany some years later than in other states. Furthermore, Germans generally seem to believe in a 'strong state' and seldom revolt against severe tax levies. Consequently, the pre-conditions for an administrative change in Germany were weaker than in other countries.

With the costly process of German reunification the financial problems in the German public sector accelerated. Financial pressure particularly at local level became a reform-initiating factor from 1990 onwards. Thus, it is not surprising that local authorities started to redesign their organizational structures and to search for efficiency-oriented and cost-cutting measures in order to guarantee the delivery of local services to their citizens. However, reforms towards NPM have taken place in an increasing number of local authorities since about 1990.

At the state (*Land*) and the federal (*Bund*) level, NPM-type reforms can only be found to a small extent, probably due to a smaller degree of financial pressure. Up to now there are no significant signs at all for implementing reforms of the steering/management concept at the level of federal government. Although present-day policy declarations of the federal government include some general aspects of introducing a 'lean state', effective measures for reforming the federal administrative body in this direction are still missing.

At the *Land* level the situation is diverse. The three so-called 'city-states' (Berlin, Bremen, Hamburg) are busy designing and implementing new steering concepts.[5] A few of the other *Länder* governments are also showing some progress in reforming their managerial systems. The government of Baden-Württemberg has become particularly famous for its innovations in the field of personnel management. The government of Schleswig-Holstein is performing a series of pilot studies in the field of budgeting and controlling, following the guidelines of a general reform strategy. The other *Länder* governments have not produced significant proposals for administrative reforms.

THE PROCESS OF MANAGERIAL CHANGE

In the German local government the process of managerial change took the following sequence.

Phase of conceptual design

In the field of managerial reforms German local authorities rely to a great extent on recommendations of the KGST.[6] From 1988 to 1991 the KGST elaborated some initial recommendations for new management concepts (KGST, 1991). In 1993/1994 a series of detailed reports, dealing with conceptual questions followed (KGST, 1993). The KGST recommendations were distributed under the label 'new steering model' (*Neues Steuerungsmodell*). The interesting thing about these recommendations is that they were based to a large extent on the experiences of the Dutch city of Tilburg. In the 1980s Tilburg introduced a professional management model which was largely influenced by private sector enterprise concepts. This so-called 'Tilburg model' had considerable influence on the development of steering models in German local authorities. The KGST elaborated its recommendations for steering models similar to the Tilburg model, and a larger number of authorities copied some structures and instruments according to the KGST recommendations. However, it may be summarized that local government reforms in Germany have been greatly influenced by managerial reforms in the Netherlands.

Phase of the first pilot communes

Immediately after the publication of the first KGST recommendations some (large) German cities introduced the first elements of this 'new steering model'. As we will see later, the pilot communes concentrated on one or two of the main elements of the model. Well-known pilot cities at the first phase were, among others, Hanover, Nürnberg and Köln (Cologne).

Bushfire of widespread experiments

The power of dissemination of the main ideas of this steering model was unpredictable. Only one or two years after the first KGST impulse about forty local authorities – predominantly large cities – were busy with experiments on certain elements of the steering model. Regionally, most of the steering innovations have been initiated in the *Land* of North Rhine-Westphalia. On the one hand this is a consequence of the extremely severe financial pressure on most of the cities of this highly industrialized state. On the other hand the pressure for reforms was particularly strong in this state because of a difficult municipal and county charter (the so-called 'North German dual system' which experts judged to be less effective and more conflict-generating than the charters of other states).

To a certain extent it became a fashion for German city managers to announce that their city was also working with steering models. Thus, it was not easy to distinguish between real managerial reforms and pure PR declarations from outside. Slowly, the NPM-oriented reforms trickled down from the large cities to smaller ones and to county administrations (*Kreisverwaltungen*). Without any doubt managerial reforms were more important for large cities because of their greater financial problems and their higher complexity.

Not surprisingly, the introduction of the 'new steering model' took place almost exclusively in the 'old' parts of the federal republic, and nearly nowhere in the eastern part of Germany, the former GDR. The main reason for such a 'Western bias' is that East German administration has transformed itself into the Western structures according to a blueprint approach. Transformations occurred at the same time when Western communes were starting their managerial reforms. The introduction of these West German structures and regulations in East German authorities required much time and energy. It did not motivate the administrators to reflect on time-consuming experiments with modern management concepts. However, the process of transformation and of rebuilding the administration absorbed a great deal of reform energy. Consequently, there are remarkable differences between Western and Eastern local authorities regarding their present readiness and capacity to implement 'new steering models'. However, recently there have been the first signs that East German authorities have begun to experiment with steering models.

Phase of consolidation

After about five years more than a hundred communes in Germany have started experiments in the context of the new steering model'. While most of the pilot communes are still in the initial phase of such experiments, a few authorities have gained considerable experience with steering concepts over several years. Some empirical observations (end of 1994) give evidence that around one-third of the cities in the Western part of Germany are undertaking real experiments with steering models. Smaller communes are interested to a lesser extent in introducing formalized steering models, probably because they are able to handle their day-to-day problems without utilizing sophisticated management instruments. Additionally the county administrations in Germany have become increasingly interested in implementing steering concepts in the last two years.

Local authorities in Germany with broad experience in the field of managerial reforms are Bochum, Detmold, Dortmund, Duisburg, Gütersloh, Hanover, Heidelberg, Herten, Cologne, Soest (county), Munich, Nuremberg, Offenbach, Osnabrück (city and county) and Saarbrücken.

MAJOR ELEMENTS OF THE PILOT PROJECTS

Accountability

One of the first elements of the 'new steering model' which has been introduced in several German local authorities was the concept of decentralized resource responsibility. The reason for starting with this element is the following. For decades the German administration practised a pattern of highly centralized responsibility for resource allocation. Responsibility for finances as well as for personnel was concentrated in specialized central service departments (treasurer, organization and personnel department). Consequently, nobody really felt responsible for the overall result, for tasks and for the resources. The incongruity of tasks and responsibilities led to a system of 'organized irresponsibility' (Banner, 1991, p. 6). Therefore, decentralization of resource responsibility, i.e. transferring responsibility from the central service departments to the sectoral units (e.g. social services, housing, construction services) played a dominant role from the outset and became an essential part of the 'new steering model'. This process of re-arranging responsibilities within a local authority finally leads to semi-autonomous result centres which are fully accountable for their tasks. It can be assumed that such a process will be full of conflicts and will require much time for training because the service departments will have to find their new role and are forced to accept a reduction of their powers.

Global budgets

With the increasing cutback of finances some local authorities changed their internal budgetary system. Instead of the traditional detailed central planning of revenues and expenditures for each department by the treasurer, a new flexible system was introduced. The treasurer now only plans global budget figures and prescribes these figures as lump sums within a limited margin to the different departments. The local council no longer decides on the details of a department's budget, but concentrates on the political implications of the budgetary framework. The different sectoral departments are free to allocate their funds – as long as they respect the budgetary framework – according to their respective needs. They are allowed to exchange expenditures among different budget items and to transfer unspent parts of the budget to the following fiscal year. However, the departments are forced to report regularly to top management on their activities and their goal achievements on the basis of previously defined output/performance indicators.

Additionally, a number of communes are implementing methods of internal cost accounting. The traditional public accounting system in Germany, the so-called cameralist bookkeeping (*Kameralistik*), is a pure cash-based system, ignoring all aspects of accrual accounting. As long as this general accounting system cannot be replaced by a new system comprising cost and performance accounting as well as accrual-based financial accounting and reporting, local authorities tend to introduce – as a first step towards 'management accounting' – cost accounting methods to identify costs of certain public services and to allow the internal clearing of overhead costs among service and sector units (Buschor and Schedler, 1994, p. VII).

Several large cities in Germany – e.g. Cologne, Munich, Nuremberg – have been practising this new budgetary system for some years. They have experienced a more cost-efficient attitude by their heads of units, leading to remarkable cutbacks of expenditures without endangering the quality of services. It may be interesting to note that the budgetary reform on the local level took place with only minor corrections of the local government's budgetary laws. However, in the meantime several state governments have introduced certain experimental clauses (*Experimentierklauseln*) into the local government acts in order to enlarge the freedom of pilot communes to experiment with new budgetary methods.

Product orientation

Following the logic of the 'new steering model', managerial emphasis has to be placed from the traditional input to an output orientation. Consequently, several pilot communes began to identify and to measure their outputs, i.e. their products.[7] Reformers try to convince public managers that they should put the product at the centre of their steering activities, asking for the costs and the benefits of a produced service. Local authorities undertake great efforts to exactly formulate their products, their product groups, etc. The KGST is supporting the active communes in exchanging experiences with product catalogs for certain policy fields such as youth services. The aim is to develop product descriptions which are compatible in order to allow intercommunal performance comparisons among German authorities.

Besides these three main elements at the centre of managerial reforms in the context of the 'new steering model', local authorities are also experimenting with some other aspects and instruments. Among them are the following:

- Quality management (e.g. regular surveys of citizens' needs, redesigning procedures for cutting waiting times, etc.; the city of Saarbrücken is an example for implementing TQM).

- The introduction of 'one-stop offices' (*Bürgerämter*: all day-to-day services for citizens will be offered under the same roof, organized in a central citizen office or in several subordinate offices in the different city districts).

- 'Corporatization' of authority units: an increasing number of organizational units of local authorities, particularly public enterprises, are hivingoff into (semi) autonomy. They transform their legal status, mostly from public law into private commercial law, and become legally independent corporations. The respective local government remains the proprietor but usually lacks political influence.

Most of the pilot communes try to integrate several aspects and elements of the 'new steering model' into a comprehensive concept. On the basis of defined products they are implementing a steering cycle in which performance objectives and budgetary targets will be formulated by the council and the top management, and in which the different units are specifying their targets and are transforming them into verifiable performance indicators. The units report to a central controlling unit in a quarterly feedback system. The reports will be evaluated following a comprehensive controlling concept. At least some elements of this internal management cycle do already function in a few local authorities.

THE FIRST EXPERIENCES WITH THE 'NEW STEERING MODEL'

Every two years the Postgraduate School of Administrative Sciences in Speyer hosts a competition to search for the public authorities in Germany which are performing well. The 'best' administrations will be honoured with the 'Speyer Award'. The 1994 experience with this competition shows that we find a large number of administrations – particularly at local level – which are delivering their services to the citizens with a high level of performance and efficiency. Most of them are experimenting with some variants of the 'new steering model'. It is interesting to note that the 'leading' local authorities in Germany have some common patterns in their modernization strategies and have very similar overall performances.

Most local authorities in Germany started their experiments with the 'new steering model' by introducing one of the above-mentioned elements in a carefully selected pilot area. At the beginning of the modernization movement, most administrations started with decentralizing authorities or with elaborating controlling systems. Later on, due to increasing financial pressure, authorities started with budgeting reforms, expecting that they could cut down expenditures to some extent. Nowadays we can observe some convergence: communes try to start from the beginning with a more integrated comprehensive steering concept.

A frequently discussed question is whether to opt for an 'area-wide' or 'pilot' implementation. Nearly all communes decided for pilot studies as the first step of innovation. They feared the high risk and preferred the learning and the corrective opportunities offered by a pilot. On the other hand there is evidence that a commune may be overstretched to manage its organization in two completely different ways, following in some units the 'new' and in others the 'old' steering concept.

The units in local authorities which were chosen for the first experiments were generally small, straightforward departments. Authorities decided to select small units which often were not at the centre of political struggle (theatre, museum, parks and gardens department, school of music, swimming pools, etc.). To date, there has been little experience with implementation in large and conflict-ridden departments like social services, housing or education. Although such a small and 'exotic' pilot unit may be adequate for gaining initial experience, it must be argued that the battle will not be won as long as managerial reforms do not reach the core departments where struggles and conflicts are concentrated and the biggest problems need to be solved.

Implementation strategies of local authorities differ considerably in the degree of participation of their employees. Some authorities tried to introduce steering elements in a rather autocratic, top-down way. It can be assumed that these authorities were not highly successful with this strategy. Other authorities selected a careful participative approach, investing much time and energy to inform and convince their own employees. One German city (Krefeld) started with a large quality circle process which motivated the members to identify with the reform issues. Some cities at the initial phase of the process agreed with the representatives of the workforce (union and employees council) upon an arrangement which commits both sides to the modernization targets and to some social preconditions of the process (no dismissals during the process, participation of representatives within the project teams, etc.).

Another difference in the implementation strategies is the degree to which politicians (primarily members of the respective councils and committees) have been included in the process. In a number of cities the 'new steering model' has been introduced in a rather technocratic way, almost excluding the political sphere. It was an attempt to install managerial reforms in the administrative body of an agency without involving the politicians. Some first lessons have shown us that such attempts were not very successful. Public management includes the political sphere. Politicians have to play a new and active role in the 'new steering model'; they have to formulate the strategic and overall goals of the commune, and they have to control its activities with regard to these strategic issues.

Experience with implementation of 'new steering models' in local authorities shows us the following lessons. The following failures and mistakes are frequent and common:

- Politicians as well as top management are not committed to the goals of the change project and do not support the process over the whole period.
- Politicians do not formulate clear-cut goals for the whole reform project.
- Conflicts among politicians, managers and the workforce (employees council and union).
- Lack of careful and comprehensive project planning (i.e. a project budget, a time schedule, a project organization with steering groups, etc.).
- Time pressure (overcharging of employees, too high expectations within a limited timeframe).
- Contradictions between the reform project and necessary cutback measures (can demotivate the participating employees).
- Lack of qualification measures for those employees who have to practise new steering instruments.

If we compare German experiences with NPM experiences in foreign countries we can observe certain specific features. Managerial reforms in Germany concentrate to a great extent on internal structural changes. German reforms are dealing predominantly with restructuring authorities ('decentralized resource responsibility'), with implementing output- and product-oriented steering cycles and controlling systems, and with innovations to the internal accounting system. They seem to have a structural bias. In some other countries, particularly in Scandinavia, reform efforts are much more externally oriented. Reforms in these countries deal to a larger extent with improvements in the administration/citizen relations, with strengthening market-type mechanisms and (quasi) competition, and with decisions about contracting out and competitive tendering (Banner and Reichard, 1993, p. 75). Contracting out of public services under competitive conditions in Germany is still a rather untouched topic.

Another underdeveloped topic is the field of personnel management. Most reform concepts underestimate the necessity of personnel development and of leadership behaviour. There is evidence that even excellent management concepts will not function in practice if the 'new' knowledge and behaviour related to such concepts are not transferred to the bosses of the employees. Therefore, immense efforts must be undertaken to recruit the right management staff, to qualify the existing staff, to set attractive incentives for change, to improve leadership behaviour of superiors, and generally to develop the human resources of the authority. Until now personnel management in the German civil service has been oriented towards the traditional values and principles of the Prussian servant (*Beamter*). The energy to implement modern personnel management concepts and instruments is limited (however, a few cities like Duisburg are experimenting in a progressive way with such concepts). Unfortunately, managerial reforms in Germany suffer from legal restrictions, particularly in the field of civil service laws. These laws, which are centrally regulated by the federal government, do not allow performance-related pay; they impede opportunities to motivate employees with other incentives, and to take flexible personnel decisions. In 1994 and 1995 the first move to reform the rigid civil service system of Germany could be observed.

In summary, German local authorities are comparatively strong in reforming their internal organization structures and their steering and controlling systems, but they are relatively weak in redesigning their external relations, in opening themselves to market incentives, and furthermore in managing and developing their human resources.

Open questions, existing problems and limitations

The legal framework of public sector laws and regulations is a severe restriction for managerial reforms in the German public sector. The following three legal areas are causing severe problems in the implementation process of the 'new steering models':

- Civil service laws because of their restrictions on performance orientation.
- Public budgetary laws and regulations because of their rigid rules for planning, performing, and accounting the budget, which conflict with managerial flexibility.

- Local government acts and charters which do not provide clear rules for separating the political and the administrative spheres.

Some German states are beginning to increase the freedom of local authorities. As already mentioned they passed certain experimental clauses (*Experimentierklauseln*) in the local government acts which allow communes to perform pilot studies to test new steering models without being bound to all legal norms. This approach has been influenced by the Scandinavian movement of the 'free commune experiments'. It is expected that the responsible ministries will extend these experimental clauses to cover also the fields of budgetary law and of civil service law.

Although the scientific community in Germany up to now has not dealt deeply with analytical and empirical questions concerning the 'new steering concept' (Reichard and Wollmann, 1995), the following questions on possible effects and frictions of this management concept are under discussion:

- Will this concept be compatible with the existing administrative culture? Can it be expected that the traditional bureaucratic values can be transformed in a managerial culture? Isn't administrative culture resistant to change?

- Will the concept be compatible with the existing political rationale and behaviour? Will politicians be ready to behave according to a rather economic rationale, to govern by means of political, strategic targets, and to avoid isolated detailed interventions in the apparatus?

- Is a clear-cut division between the political and the administrative spheres feasible, and is such separation of roles desirable at all?

- Isn't there a danger of a greater political patronage within the fragmented decision-making structure of a local authority? Do we have to expect an increased separation of sectoral-oriented policy networks?

- Can we expect the managers of the central services departments to accept their new roles and to renounce interference in detailed resource decisions? Can we on the other hand expect the managers of the sector units to decide in an autonomous and self-responsible way, and to manage and effectively control their own units?

- Don't we have to handle massive problems with performance measurement if we intend to quantify all outputs (products) in quantitative terms? Do we expect goal deviations because of a preference of quantifiable goals?

- Is the reduction of a citizen to a role as 'consumer' of public services too narrow a view? Do we exclude other roles for citizens (e.g. the elector, the participator, the civic problem solver)?

- Is the belief in the universal power of the 'market' realistic after years of experience with 'market failures'? Can we expect a sustainable public management system if we continue to transfer private sector-based corporate management concepts into public management? Is the 'managerialistic view' of public management the right perspective or does it need to broaden the perspective towards a concept of 'public governance'?

Such questions do not play a significant role in the daily struggles of German local authorities when they are experimenting with 'new steering concepts'. Nevertheless it will be necessary to discuss these questions and to elaborate the existing concepts of public management further to make them feasible and sustainable in the long run.

NOTES

1. Article 1/I, Die Verfassung von Berlin (Constitution of Berlin).
2. § 1AZG Allgemeines Zuständigkeitsgesetz (General Act of Jurisdiction).
3. Ibid. § 2/I AZG.
4. For the design of these elements also see Germany/Part II.
5. See also Germany/Part II for the case of Berlin (The Berlin model of guidance and steering).
6. KGST is the association for managerial reforms in local government, situated in Cologne. Nearly all German local authorities are members of this association. The KGST is elaborating recommendations for its members in the field of public management, organization, budgeting, cost accounting, data processing etc. KGST is distributing about 20–30 reports on specific topics to its members.
7. For details of the product orientation see Germany/Part II (The new model of guidance and steering).

REFERENCES

Banner, G. (1991) Von der Behörde zum Dienstleistungsunternehmen. In *Verwaltungsführung-Organisation-Personalwesen*. Vol. 13, no. 1, January-February, pp. 6–11.

Banner, G. and Reichard, C. (eds) (1993) *Kommunale Managementkonzepte in Europa*, Deutscher Gemeindeverlag/Verlag W. Kohlhammer, Köln.

Bernet, W. (1992) *Die Verwaltungs- und Gebietsreformen in den Gemeinden und Landkreisen der Länder Mecklenburg-Vorpommern, Brandenburg, Sachsen-Anhalt, Sachsen und Thüringen*, Expertise im Auftrag und mit Unterstützung der KSPW, Speyer, Jena.

Blume, M. (1993) Tilburg: Modernes betriebswirtschaftliches Verwaltungsmanagement. In Banner, G. and Reichard, C. (eds) *Kommunale Managementkonzepte in Europa*, Deutscher Gemeinderverlag/Verlag W. Kohlhammer, Köln.

Budäus, D. (1994) *Public Management-Konzepte und Verfahren effizienter Verwaltungssteuerung*, Sigma Rainer Bohm Verlag, Berlin.

Buschor, E. and Schedler, K. (eds) (1994) *Perspectives on Performance Measurement and Public Sector Accounting*, Paul Haupt, Bern/Stuttgart/Vienna.

Commissariat Général du Plan (1988) *Le Pari de la Responsabilité*, Rapport de la Commission Efficacité de l'Etat presidée par M. François de Closets, Documentation Française, Paris.

Die Zeit, no. 24, 10/07/1994, p. 24.

Haubner, O. (1993) Zur Organisation des 1. Speyerer Qualitätswettbewerbs. Von der Idee zum 'Ideenmarkt'. In Hill, H. and Klages, H. (eds), *Spitzenverwaltungen im Wettbewerb*, Eine Dokumentation des 1. Speyerer Qualitätswettbewerbs 1992, Nomos Verlag, Baden-Baden.

Hausschild, Ch. (1991) DDR. Vom sozialistischen Einheitsstaat in die föderale und kommunale Demokratie. In Bernhard, B. (ed.), *Staat und Stadt* PVS Sonderheft 22/1991, Westdeutscher Verlag, Opladen.

Hoffmann, H. and Dill, G. (eds) (1993) *Berlin 2000*, Beiträge zum Umbau der Verwaltung, Interne Studien und Berichte Nr. 53/93 der Konrad-Adenauer Stiftung, Bereich Kommunalwissenschaften, Bonn.

Hogwood, B. W. (1993) Restructuring central government: The Next Steps' initiative in Britain. In Kjell Elisassen, A. and Kooiman, J. (eds), *Managing Public Organizations: Lessons from Contemporary European Experience*, Sage, London.

Hood, C. (1991) A public management for all seasons? *Public Administration*, vol. 69, pp. 3–16.

KGST (1991) *Dezentrale Ressourcenverantwortung: Überlegungen zu einem neuen Steuerungsmodell*, 12.

KGST (1993) *Das Neue Steuerungsmodell* (The New Steering Model), 5, Köln.

KGST-Berichte (reports) 19/1992, 6/1993, 5/1993, 10/1993.

Klages, H. and the Speyer Award Team of the City of Duisburg (1994) Quality improvement in the German local government. In Bouckaert, G. and Pollitt, C. (eds), *Quality Improvement in European Public Services: Concepts, Cases and Commentary*, Sage, London.

Klages, H. and Haubner, O. (1994) Strategies of public sector modernization: three alternative perspectives. In Bouckaert, G. and Halachmi, A. (eds), *Challenge of Management in a Changing World*, Jossey Bass, San Francisco.

Klinger, F. (1994) Aufbau und Erneuerung. Über die institutionellen Bedingungen der Standortentwicklung in Deutschland. In *Aus Politik und Zeitgeschichte*, B17/94, 29/04/1994.

König, K. (1991a) Verwaltung im Übergang – Vom zentralen Verwaltungsstaat in die dezentrale Demokratie in *DÖV*, Vol. 44, Issue 5, p. 177–84.

König, K. (1991b) Zum Verwaltungssystem der DDR. In König, K. (ed.), *Verwaltungsstrukturen in der DDR*, Baden-Baden, p. 16.

Ministerpräsidentin des Landes Schleswig-Holstein (1994) *Modernisierung des öffentlichen Sektors in Schleswig-Holstein*, Statusbericht, 3.

OECD (1993) *Public Management Developments Survey 1993*, OECD, Paris.

Osborne, D. and Gaebler, T. (1992) *Reinventing Government: How the Entrepreneurial Spirit is Transforming the Public Sector*, Prentice Hall, New York.

Reichard, C. (1994) *Umdenken im Rathaus: Neue Steuerungsmodelle in der deutschen Kommunalverwaltung*, Sigma Rainer Bohm Verlag, Berlin.

Reichard, C. and Wollmann, H. (eds) (1995, in preparation) *Kommunalverwaltung im Modernisierungsschub*.

Schmidt-Eichstaedt, G. (1993) Kommunale Gebietsreform in den neuen Bundesländern. In *Aus Politik und Zeitgeschichte*, B36/93, 03/09/1993.

Schneider, H. (1993) Der Aufbau der Kommunalverwaltung und der kommunalen Selbstverwaltung in den neuen Bundesländern. In *Aus Politik und Zeitgeschichte*, B36/93, 03/09/1993.

Staatsministerium Baden-Württemberg (ed.) (1993) *Verwaltungsreform in Baden-Württemberg: Erster Bericht der Regierungskommission Verwaltungsreform*, Stuttgart.

7

Austria

Franz Strehl and Ulrike Hugl

Overview

The Austrian constitution regulates the foundations of the organization of the state functions of 'legislature' and 'executive' (separated into 'jurisdiction' and 'administration'). Legislative institutions are the Federal Assembly, the Federal Council, the state assemblies and assisting bodies. Jurisdiction is strictly separated from all other authorities. Therefore the functions of legislature and administration are defined according to the requirements of independence and the principle of legality.

The organization of the state function 'administration' is regulated by constitutional laws in very great detail. The division of responsibilities and tasks between federal and state level is based on the federal state principle: in Austria the federal administration (direct and indirect) is highly structured (nine *Länder* = states, and approximately 2300 municipalities). This background focuses on federal and state administrative organizations.

The federal president, the federal government (committee of federal ministers), the vice-chancellor and the chancellor are the most important bodies and institutions of the federal administration.

At the state level the top administrative bodies are the state governments, consisting of the state governor and some state councillors (their number and responsibilities are defined by the state constitution). The state government (acting as a committee) is responsible to the state parliament.

Austrian municipalities act as self-governing bodies and are autonomous within their domain.

As far as administrative control is concerned, high-level administrative action is controlled by the Administrative Court of Appeal and the Constitutional Court. In addition, independent Administrative Tribunals of Appeal are installed at the state level.

The National Accounting Office is a constitutionally regulated institution for financial and formal control of public administration (also including public enterprises, subsidies, state shares in enterprises, etc.).

The parties represented in the Austrian government agreed on the development and implementation of a management control system ('controlling') as a more holistic orientation of important management functions in all ministries providing strategic and operational steering possibilities based on the principles of a cybernetic feedback loop. 'Controlling' and 'cost accounting' are put into effect as central management instruments in the ministries through small-scale pilot projects, in a slow and incremental way.

The legal and organizational conditions at federal, state and municipal levels are reflected in the design and organization of the public budget administration of territorial bodies. Budget data, revenues and expenditures are systematically organized by the Federal Accounting Centre (within the Ministry of Finance). Selected data are the starting-point for the above-mentioned management instruments – controlling, cost accounting and budget management.

Concerning personnel, specific characteristic aspects of personnel and personnel management – e.g. the Austrian pay system, performance appraisal, career conversation, training system of civil servants and components of personnel and organizational development – are relevant to understanding the Austrian system.

Civil service regulation policy is strongly determined by the construction of the Austrian Social Partnership and the influence of political parties. Any change in civil service regulation policy is a highly sensitive issue, increasingly observed by taxpayers and media. Reform of the Austrian pay system is currently a matter of some controversy and a much-discussed issue. The reform became effective in January 1995 and concerns about one-third of all federal civil servants (80,000) under public law and from 1996 on all civil servants under private law. The central point of the pay system reform is a performance-related pay component which is not based on length of service.

Management and personnel issues are part of one of the most complex and prominent reform projects of recent years, known as 'Public Administration Management' (*Verwaltungsmanagement*, 1988–1994). The focus of the project is on increasing productivity, reorganization of task and management structures, reducing costs of administrative procedures and improving service functions for citizens.

The case study at the end of this chapter focuses on the reform of Austrian universities as centrally run federal institutions. Necessary reform activities are based on the University Organization Law of 1993: a new management-oriented structure was intended to transform all universities into autonomous units acting on their own authority. This case is an example of a current very important and controversial reform project encompassing the complete university system.

BASIC STRUCTURES

The constitution regulates the organization of the various federal functions ('distribution power') and thus forms the legal foundation of execution, jurisdiction and public administration.

The constitutional foundations of the organization of state functions (at all levels) are not restricted to general and global principles but regulate the functions in great detail (also at state and municipal levels).

The legislative institutions are the federal assembly, the federal council and the state assemblies (nine states/'provinces'), as well as assisting bodies like the National Accounting Office and the ombudsmen.

According to the federal state principle the Austrian structure is based on a vertical division of power between federal level, state level and municipalities. Functions and tasks which are not explicitly given to the federal level by the constitution remain the responsibility of the states. In the field of 'sovereign administration' the execution of federal tasks in the states is carried out by the state administration (indirect federal administration).

Jurisdiction is strictly separated from all other authorities.[1] In this way the functions of legislature and administration are defined according to the requirements of independence and rule dependence of the bodies:

- Legislature as the execution of legal norms is the responsibility of judges and their assisting bodies and has to be performed according to the principle of independence. This guarantees independence from orders, and the impossibility of transfer and removal.[2]
- Within the administration order depending bodies execute the tasks.[3]

Derived from the requirements of predictability of administrative activities for the citizens concerned (democratic administrative behaviour), all activities are based exclusively on legal norms (legality principle). One exception, however, is the so-called margin of discretion which is regulated in the form of authorization rules: from the point of view of legislative bodies it remains open how detailed decisions are taken in a specific case – the administration interprets the case according to the intention of the respective legal norm.[4] This indicates that the legality principle can never be realized completely but only approximately despite the enormous and increasing flood of norms. The discussions and interpretation of these principles indicate that there is a sensitive field of tension between dangerous administrative arbitrary acts, overly soft legal norms and overregulation.

The principles of the 'classic administration' (even considering the differences between theoretical compliance to norms and reality) are realized in the constitution and are part of the tradition of Austrian bureaucracy: parliament as the legislative body steers the administration based on the legality principle and various parliamentary controls (e.g. National Accounting Office). In this respect the 'parliamentary principle of public attention (openness)' contradicts the 'bureaucratic principle of official secrecy'. According to the principle of the division of power, the administration is independent from legislature and executes legal norms under the responsibility of government; the respective minister has the instrument of directives at his/her disposal. The opposition between civil servants and politicians can be seen as a constant dimension of political and bureaucratic business which is, however, rarely taken as a theme (Gerlich, 1992, p. 264). The overall involvement of today's bureaucracy in political networks is very explicit in the area of high federal bureaucracy, in which, to some observers, top executives seem to be powerful mandarins of politics (Gerlich, 1992, p. 267, adapted from Pelinka and Welan, 1971, p. 178). Political parties and associations also exert considerable influence on the administration. This tends to be neglected since it is in contradiction to the classical formal bureaucratic model. Political parties tend not only to exert their influence on the administration in legitimate ways through senior political represen- tatives but also through intensive activity on the personnel policy of the administration (Gerlich, 1992, p. 268). An increasing 'politicization of the administration' and simultaneously an increasing 'bureaucratization of poli- tics' is taking place (Gerlich, 1992, p. 270).

Administrative organization

The organization of the state function of 'administration' is regulated by the constitution in very great detail. The federal state principle regulates the division of responsibilities and tasks between federal and state level. The federal administration is highly structured: there are nine state administra- tions and more than 2300 municipalities.

The federal state principle focuses on the separation into the respective administrative organizations. The federal and state authorities create their own organization. Matters that are 'not expressly assigned by the Federal Constitution to the Legislature, or even to the executive power of Federa- tion', remain within a state's independent domain (Brandtner, 1992, p. 115–48).

FEDERAL ADMINISTRATIVE ORGANIZATION

The most important top-level bodies (and institutions) of the federal admin- istration are the federal president and the federal government acting as a committee consisting of the federal ministers, vice-chancellor and chancel- lor. All activities are carried out by thirteen ministries of equal status, each headed by a minister. The minister is in charge of and has responsibilities for strategic planning and overall coordination. The ministries are organized according to divisions in several hierarchical levels by sections, depart- ments, subdepartments and various staff positions for support functions. The complex (and problematic) interministerial coordination mechanisms are subject to constant reform discussions. In the states (*Länder*) there are a number of functions under the direct control of the ministries, e.g. labour market services, tax administration, security and federal police.

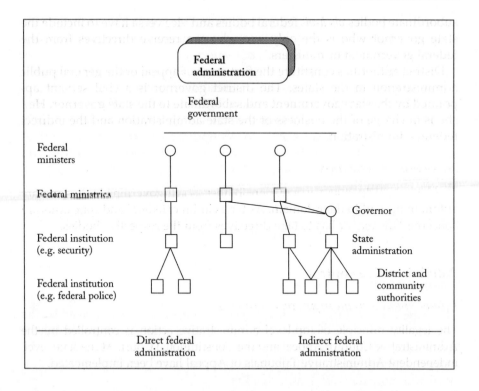

Figure 7.1. Federal administration. (Adapted from Raschauer and Kazda, 1983, p. 146.)

Figure 7.1 illustrates the direct and indirect federal administration and the basic organization between federal and state level.

STATE ADMINISTRATIVE ORGANIZATION

The top administrative bodies at the state level are the state governments, which consist of the state governor and a number of state counsellors. Their number and responsibilities are defined by the state constitution. The members of the state government carry overall responsibility to the state parliament. As a body they act as a committee. In addition there exists the possibility of organizing government according to a division principle: each member carries independent responsibility for his/her division combined with the opportunity to exert greater political influence. The state administration, headed by the administrative director of the state, executes the tasks. Subordinate units are district authorities and municipal authorities. The district authorities play a central role as they have responsibilities in many areas of federal and state administration.

The state governor is responsible for the indirect federal administration and plays a central role: the stages of appeal and the reporting system of subordinate bodies *vis-à-vis* federal bodies and vice versa have to include the state governor who is the only one who can receive directives from the federal government or ministers.

District authorities constitute the first stage of appeal of the general public administration in the states. The district governor is a civil servant appointed by the state government and subordinate to the state governor. He/she is in charge of the business of the state administration and the indirect federal administration.

MUNICIPAL ORGANIZATION

The 2300 municipalities carry responsibilities or self-governing bodies and are autonomous within their domain. As far as indirect federal and state tasks are concerned the mayor has to take directives from the respective bodies.

Administrative control

INDEPENDENT AND HIGHEST COURT CONTROL

The legality principle of top-level administrative action is controlled by the Administrative Court of Appeal and the Constitutional Court. At the state level, independent Administrative Tribunals of Appeal have been implemented.

NATIONAL ACCOUNTING OFFICE

Financial control of public administration[5] is embodied in the constitution and falls under the remit of the National Accounting Office (NAO), which supports the legislative bodies. Its domain covers the whole range of public administration, public enterprises, subsidies and state stakes in enterprises, and there are no such areas outwith its control. The NAO is organized monocratically, and the president alone bears the responsibility for audits and audit reports. Independence is the most important feature: members of the NAO have to be independent from the audited organization (no functions in government administration and enterprises). Audited organizations have the right to comment on audit results. Audit reports have to be published after their approval by parliament, state council or municipal council. A specific situation can be found at the state level in this field: states dispose of their own audit institutions; the NAO does not have a monopoly there.

Duties of administrative bodies

The duty of 'official secrecy' is laid down by constitutional law.[6] This refers to all bodies charged with public administrative duties. Such bodies are obliged to keep secret all facts concerning the interests of maintaining public law and order, national defence, foreign relations, the economic interests of public bodies or predominant interests of parties. All bodies have a duty to provide information concerning their domain if this is not in conflict with office secrecy.[7] Federal and state bodies have a mutual obligation to support and assist each other within their domains.[8] This obligation is a central dimension in order to avoid or reduce cooperation deficits and hindrances resulting from the high degree of division of work and specialization within the overall bureaucratic machinery (Funk, 1989, p. 137).

MANAGEMENT PROCESSES

Public budget administration

BACKGROUND

The Austrian public sector is represented at the federal, state and municipal level by many institutions. The legal and organizational conditions are reflected in the design and organization of the public budget administration of the territorial bodies. The most important legal basis is the Fiscal Constitutional Law on which federal and state laws are enacted regulating the budget, and the distribution of revenues and expenditures between the bodies (Lödl and Matzinger, 1992, p. 303).

The central element in this respect is the tax equalization (Tax Equalization Law)[9] covering the following areas:

- Active tax equalization distributes revenues; passive tax equalization distributes expenditures.
- Primary tax equalization allocates resources to the territorial bodies that can dispose of them on their own; secondary tax equalization allocates resources for specific purposes.
- Vertical tax equalization regulates the financial interdependencies between federal, state and local levels; horizontal tax equalization regulates interdependencies within one level (Lödl and Matzinger, 1992, p. 305).

FEDERAL BUDGET[10]

New legal foundations of the federal budget were developed in 1986 in order to adapt it to the requirements of modern budget systems. The main issues of the reform are as follows (Lödl and Matzinger, 1992, p. 313):

- Enlargement of constitutional definitions relating to the main matters of budget administration.
- Increase in the overall responsibility of the minister of finance.

- Introduction of new budget instruments (budget forecast, investment programs, calculation of financial consequences of legal norms, cost–benefit estimates, control of success of programs).
- Statement of goals for the budget.
- Adaptation of parliamentary participation in the budget administration.

Several important reasons for this reform can be identified (Csoka, 1993, p. 51):

- Insufficent vertical structure of the federal budget: the information content on resource use was felt to be unsatisfactory.
- Too low transparency concerning the quantitative registration and proof of budget execution.
- Too long duration of drawing up annual and monthly budgetary results: the results were frequently out of date by the time they were issued.

Goals of public budgeting

The main goals of public budgeting are as follows (Lödl and Matzinger, 1992, p. 314):

- Calculation and provision of resources for federal tasks.
- Economies, efficiency and effectiveness.
- Economic-political goals, balance of employment, growth, monetary stability, balanced foreign trade and investment.

From a management perspective the notions of economies, efficiency and effectiveness are of special interest. Efficiency of administrative action means optimizing the relation between resources (input) and performance (output), to do things economically right. Effectiveness means to produce benefits (satisfy needs) for the various target groups, i.e. to define and attain the right goals and fulfil the relevant tasks. These two dimensions can only be specified and evaluated if the appropriate instruments are developed and implemented (e.g. ratios and indicators, cost accounting, management by objectives, strategic and operational planning, portfolio analyses).[11]

In the Austrian context the emphasis and implementation of concepts of efficiency and effectiveness as a complement to the legality principle will have to be intensified and improved, and are only realized adequately in very few areas.

Organization of the federal budget

The differentiation between directive and executive bodies (authorities) is a basic principle.

DIRECTIVE BODIES

On top is the minister of finance, who is responsible for the planning and execution of the overall budget. On the next level are the directive bodies of the chancellor, all federal ministers, the federal president, the presidents of parliament, the federal council, the NAO, the ombudsmen and the managing bodies of national enterprises.

These bodies have planning, directive and decision-making competencies in the areas of revenues, expenditures, assets and debts. The ministries are fully directive bodies, whereas the subordinate offices are only partially directive bodies with limited competencies.

EXECUTIVE BODIES

Bookkeeping departments
At the level of fully directive bodies the bookkeeping departments are budget clearing units with the following functions:

- Accounting (bookkeeping).
- Control of budget plan realization.
- Budget transactions.
- Control of credits and debits.
- Data transfer to the Federal Accounting Centre.[12]

All bookkeeping departments of the federal public administration are linked to the Federal Accounting Office via regional computer centres.

Cashier's offices
These are subordinate to the bookkeeping departments and, principally, have the same functions:

Business offices
These document and account federal assets.

The Federal Accounting Office/Federal Accounting Centre is organized within the Ministry of Finance and has service functions for the bodies mentioned above and the NAO with respect to the budget calculation and accounts closure.

Throughout Austria there is a clear organization structure headed by the Ministry of Finance. This structure is illustrated by the organization chart shown in Figure 7.2.[13]

Budget planning

The Federal Finance Law provides for annual budget planning and regulates the following areas (Lödl and Matzinger, 1992, p. 317):

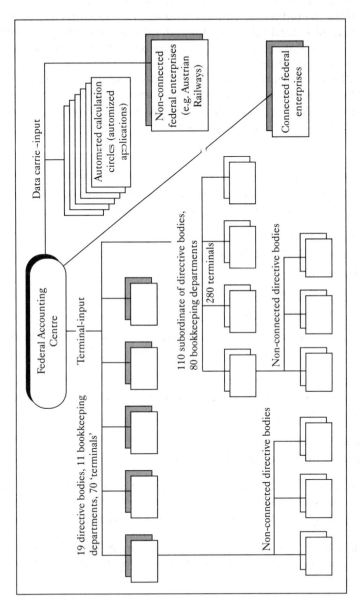

Figure 7.2 Federal accounting centre. (Adapted from: Csoka and Promberger, 1993, p. 54)

- Approval of the Federal Budget Plan.
- Rules concerning overrun and restructuring.
- Takeover of liabilities.
- Power over federal assets.
- Use of savings.

The Federal Budget Plan submitted by the government is the most important appendix to the Federal Finance Law. It shows the revenues and expenditures of the next fiscal year structured according to organizational and financial criteria. The organizational criteria refer to the competencies and tasks of the institutions. The financial criteria refer to personnel expenditures and material expenditures structured according to the purpose of expenditure and the sources of revenues. These positions are organized in accordance with a unified accounts system which is closely related to the system of the private sector (Csoka and Promberger, 1993, p. 56).

The construction of the annual budget occurs incrementally, i.e. based on last year's budget, some percentage plus or minus is estimated and applied for. A management-oriented linking with goals and objectives, tasks and performance can be found only in very few cases; the concept of zero-based budgeting, however, is not found.

The federal budget submitted by the government is binding in three ways:

- Resources may be used only according to the defined purpose.
- The indicated maximum may not be overrun.
- The time period for budget use is one year.

The restriction of the annual budget results in the phenomenon of the so-called 'December panic' (of expenditures)[14] since the balance of unused budget positions is transferred back to the Ministry of Finance and the respective institution no longer has these resources at its disposal. Therefore, there is a tendency to use resources come what may, even if not required. Failure to do so could indicate that they are not needed to the planned extent and this might have the consequence of decreasing the respective budget positions in the next period (hence economies do not always pay off).

Of course, pluriannual forward estimates concerning the budget and investment development (four-year overview) have to be drawn up as well.

These estimates must be characterized as not very meaningful mainly because they are oriented at inputs (resource use) and are not linked to output or performance. They are based on the assumption that institutions have to apply for as much as possible in order to receive the necessary resources. The system of pluriannual budgets was not implemented, as it was argued that in other European countries the expected advantages did not materialize.

Budget execution

It is a principle that the responsible bodies have to use the allocated resources according to the planned and fixed purpose and overall revenues have to be used to cover expenditures. Expenditures not planned, i.e. not fixed in the Federal Finance Law in terms of kind and amount, may only be realized upon approval by the Federal Finance Law.

Projects and programs must be coordinated between the applying (planning) ministry and the Ministry of Finance. Large projects need a cost–benefit assessment and must be submitted to an *a posteriori* evaluation. Both cost–benefit assessment and *a posteriori* evaluation are rather problematical because data are not always available to the extent required and the planning, steering and control instruments in many areas are only rudimentary and do not (yet) live up to expectations from a management perspective.

FINAL STATEMENT OF ACCOUNTS (OF THE FEDERAL GOVERNMENT)

For each fiscal year the offices have to draw up annual statements of account. The consolidated overall balances of each ministry have to be submitted to the Ministry of Finance and the NAO which aggregates the data to the federal overall balance and has to submit it to parliament eight weeks before the end of the following fiscal year.

States and municipalities are responsible for their own budgets and the annual statements of account within the margins provided by the Federal Budget Law. Municipalities are under the supervision of the states.

Cost and performance accounting in the system of the federal electronic budget calculation

The new design of the federal budget calculation is aimed at cost and performance calculation and an integrated electronic data transfer between all federal offices and the Federal Accounting Office. The federal accounting system has been developed into a fully integrated and complete system characterized by the following features:

- 'Calculation circles' are an integration of accounts of the same kind serving the systematic representation of each business activity.
- Entries occur simultaneously: one single entry triggers the respective changes in the relevant calculation circles. In this way completeness and transparency are achieved.

BUDGET EXECUTION STATUS

Representation, documentation and control of the overall budget execution status.

The areas are: approval by Parliament, budget allocation to the ministries, distribution within the ministries to the offices, order system, claims and debts, payments.

For each budget position there is a debit (d)/credit (c) account representing the legally and economically relevant activities and their interrelations in a consistent way.

The most important phases are:

1. Approval – the approved budget positions are related to the organizational units.

2. Disposal – the resources are put at the disposal of the organizational units.

3. Obligation/entitlement – at the point in time of an order the financial obligation is registered. Entitlements (claims) stem from payable activities.

4. Debt/claim – when the order is not paid for immediately a debt is registered. Claims are registered upon payable activities.

5. Payment – the payment of debts results in a reduction of financial means; incoming payments result in an increase of financial means.

ASSET AND DEBT CALCULATION SYSTEM

The asset and debt calculation represents the status quo and the changes during the fiscal year. The cases registered in the phases 4 and 5 of the budget execution status are simultaneously transmitted into the asset and debt calculation system and change the amount and structure of the respective positions.

COST AND PERFORMANCE ACCOUNTING SYSTEM

The principles, structure and implementation of the EDP (Electronic Data Processing) of the federal budget system provide favourable points of departure and conditions for an automatic transfer of all accounting entries into a management-oriented cost and performance accounting system representing resource use and its relationship with output/performance of the organizational units.

The system encompasses three main perspectives:

Cost type calculation

This type of calculation asks the question: what types of costs are incurred for different levels of the organizations?

The starting point for calculation are the expenditure accounts of the budget system (account classes: material, personnel, other). These are differentiated according to the criteria of time, kind, value (amount) through the transfer of the budget positions into the calculation system.

Since personnel costs are the major cost type within the federal administration (except, of course, transfer payments) and their structure is very
detailed, a complex and comprehensive federal personnel information system was developed representing all relevant personnel cost information
(and other data) for each civil servant.[15]

Cost centre calculation
The cost centre calculation provides a further differentiation of cost types
and asks the question: in which organizations (organizational units) and at
what level are costs incurred?

The organizations are charged directly if the entry documents make this
possible. Other costs are charged indirectly according to specific keys (e.g.
volume, time, persons, assets).[16]

Cost unit calculation
The cost unit calculation permits the attribution of costs to the concrete
output and tasks of an organizational unit. It is the basis for performance-
oriented ratios used to guide the efficiency of 'production' and organizational units and the calculation of fees.

The federal budget calculation system offers important information opportunities for management. However, in practice, they are developed and
used to a rather small extent. Above all, cost accounting systems are in their
infancy and their development is still at an early phase in several ministries.

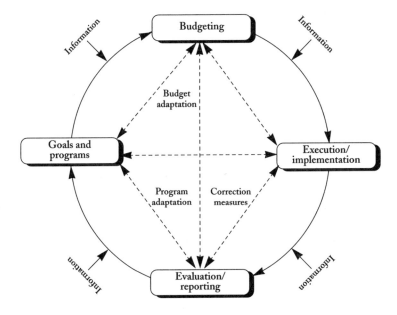

Figure 7.3. Basic model of a management control loop. (Adapted from Promberger, 1991a, p. 54.)

'CONTROLLING'[17]

In the system of federal public administration the Ministry of Finance and the Federal Chancellery as central coordination institutions have wide-ranging decision-making competencies and power with respect to financial and personnel matters. Because of the task overload of the system the resulting complex decision-making and problem-solving processes have become increasingly difficult and expensive. One (reform) tendency is to reduce these competencies even if they contribute – despite their weaknesses – to efficiency and effectiveness. However, this can be done only if there are alternative instruments which can provide these effects.

The cooperation agreement of the parties represented in government establishes the development and implementation of 'controlling' in all ministries providing strategic and operational steering possibilities based on the principles of a cybernetic feedback loop and offering a more holistic orientation of important management functions (see Fig. 7.3).

GOALS AND PROGRAMS

Goals and programs means the development of planning systems, goals and work programs. Decisions are made as to which programs are to be used to attain the goals of the administration. Activities and outputs are identified.

BUDGETING

Budgeting means the development of guidelines for budget construction, the identification of budget needs, and budget distribution to organizations. A major issue is the output and performance orientation of budget construction. It encompasses resource decisions concerning the execution of tasks and programs and clarifies responsibilities. Programs and tasks are transferred into monetary values and preset for the organizations. One goal is to construct direct relations between goals and programs and respective monetary values.

EXECUTION/IMPLEMENTATION

In the execution/implementation phase the instrument should enable the management to steer and 'control' the activities based on ongoing information about resource use and the related output (performance). One major precondition is a functioning cost accounting system.

EVALUATION/REPORTING

In order to monitor the performance of organizations, quantitative and qualitative information about programs and tasks is needed: planned criteria are compared with realized results on the basis of ratios and/or qualitative indicators.

An important issue is the relationship between political goals and priority setting and their execution by the administration. The dominant philosophy is that these two dimensions should be treated separately and that the political goals define the framework for administrative action. However, this reflects rather more the model than the day-to-day practice; one consequence of the implementation of this kind of instrument is the information improvement for decision making on the political level. In this way new criteria (emphasizing efficiency and effectiveness) may become (more) important: 'Controlling' should – and hopefully will – result in changes and amendments of laws and ordinances.

The strategic dimension of 'controlling' on the one hand refers to the formulation of political goals and programs by government and the National Council, on the other hand to their transformation into feasible measures and projects for the senior administration within the ministries. The focus is on effectiveness. The main question is to what extent political and administrative decision-makers are able (and willing) to formulate complex issues at all as goals and tasks and to increase transparency and decision-making discretion.

The operational dimension of 'controlling' refers to concrete, detailed planning and operationalization of goals/tasks in subordinate organizational units (offices) in order to guarantee the systematic operational execution. This dimension also concentrates on efficiency. Various major advantages of the implementation of 'controlling' are expected:

- The development of programs and measures can be managed in a better way by government and ministries.
- Better management quality will bring about better results.
- The possibility of reducing organizational complexity and obstacles for decision-making processes between the Ministry of Finance, the Federal Chancellery and other ministries.
- Increased performance orientation and an emphasis not only on resource (input) orientation.

The concept and approach of 'controlling' are closely connected with other reform issues, especially in the field of planning, the federal budgeting system and personnel. Training is given central importance.

The implementation of 'cost accounting' and 'controlling' in the ministries is put into effect by small-scale pilot projects, in a slow and incremental way. As a general conclusion it should be stated that both approaches will have to be developed much further, and a broad realization of success will only be established in the long run.

The responsibility for the implementation is to a large extent with the ministries themselves and more or less developed projects exist here and there. However, a tendency to accept the innovations only with reservations and reluctance can be observed. Factual and conceptual problems play a role; however, diverse resistance strategies at the political and organizational level (micropolitics) of the interest groups concerned also account for the slow progress: traditional, habitual tasks are being reduced, and new tasks requiring new qualifications developed; beloved habits must be given up; areas of influence and power change; vital interests of the decision-makers involved are endangered; a higher degree of (economic) transparency results which may not be appreciated. All these and more may be good reasons not to support innovation.

ADMINISTRATIVE COSTS OF LEGAL NORMS

In the context of cost accounting and 'controlling' the concept of calculation of costs of legal norms was developed as one important topic.

The increasing number of laws and amendments creates major factual and personnel capacity problems for the administration. In order to be able to assess more precisely these internal consequences for the administration, the obligation to calculate the costs of legal norms as early as possible in their planning phase was introduced by the Federal Budget Law of 1986.

The law states that a commentary on the financial consequences has to be developed for each federal norm draft. This includes the following aspects:

- Additional expenditures for the execution.
- Amount per year.
- Reasons for expenditure and benefit assessment.
- Proposals on how to meet the expenditures.

Thus, transparency concerning the following issues should be increased:

- What are the costs caused by the implementation of the legal norm?
- What portion of the costs directly affects the budget?
- To what extent can the administration be asked to put up with the additional tasks?
- How should fees be calculated for payable services?

PERSONNEL MANAGEMENT

In order to provide a basic understanding of Austrian management reform endeavours some characteristic aspects of personnel and personnel management are outlined and linked to specific reforms in the personnel area.

Background

Civil servants are categorized into two groups by service regulations: lifetime civil servants (by public law) and civil servants under contract (by private law).[18]

Lifetime civil servants enjoy special dismissal protection: they can only be dismissed for disciplinary matters, (extremely) low performance or a criminal offence. In all three cases evidence is very difficult to provide.

There is a complicated and complex pay system which traditionally is oriented at different classes and groups of civil servants based on equal positions and at different service grades within each group. From the beginning of 1995 new regulations including and formally emphasizing a performance component aim at a higher degree of performance orientation.

'Private law' civil servants work under contracts: there is a formally lower level of job security and different regulations concerning pension entitlement.[19]

The federal and state levels have their own respective legislature and practices concerning 'their' civil servants.

There is uncertainty about whether the constitution guarantees 'the institution of a permanent civil service'. There are clear rules only in the area of jurisdiction which is reserved for the civil service group of judges. Besides this exception there are no formal reservations whatsoever for specific positions for public law civil servants.

The authority of the top-level bodies (chief executives) to issue directives is determined by law. Directives stemming from other state functions (legislature, jurisdiction) or political parties are legally unfounded. The top-level bodies are legally and politically accountable for enacted and unenacted directives. Directives are only binding when they are enacted by the formally competent body and do not infringe criminal law regulations. In all other cases directives, even unlawful directives, have to be executed. The executing civil servant is obliged to draw the attention of the supervisor to the fact that a directive is unlawful. Based on the principle of liability the employer is accountable for damage caused by unlawful decisions to a third party. Employees are accountable for damage caused by unlawful behaviour to the employer.

Service regulations are extremely complex and detailed; from a management perspective there are three topics of interest:

- *Vocational training* At federal level the 'Federal Academy' is responsible for the basic training and training for promotion, management training and so forth.

- *Transfer and change of functions of civil servants* There is an extensive protection laid down by law against transfer and change of functions. Transfer against the free will of a civil servant used to be practically impossible.

However, changes in these respects are being realized in the reform of the pay system and will be effective until the end of 1995.

- *Performance appraisal* Performance appraisal has been formally introduced, but is rarely applied in the way it is used in the private sector and its effectiveness is rather low. It is expected that through pay system reform some higher degree of performance orientation can be implemented and high performance rewarded adequately. (It should be mentioned that the notion of performance is not well defined and there is the problem of confusion with the notion of function.)

Civil service regulation policy is strongly determined by the construction of the Austrian social partnership and the influence of political parties. Any change is a highly sensitive issue and increasingly observed by media and taxpayers.

Situation and scenario: personnel development model for the federal public administration

The topics of management and personnel are integrated into the reform project *'Verwaltungsmanagement'*. Nineteen per cent of all proposals concern personnel; in particular topics like leadership, leadership style, motivation, pay and training are identified as being of primary importance for a positive long-term development and performance improvement for the federal public administration (Dearing, 1992, p. 301).

In project phase 2 an international project expert group 'Management and Personnel' was installed in order to conduct interministerial in-depth studies. In cooperation with a consulting firm the project group developed a comprehensive model of personnel development. Based on internal analyses and experiences from international reforms in the areas of personnel and organization development, three factors fundamental to success were identified (Trigon Entwicklungsberatung, 1990, pp. 18, 23).

PERSONNEL DEVELOPMENT AND STRATEGIC ORIENTATION

In the long run personnel development can only be successful if it is adapted to actual demands on performance and change of the administration. A balance between organizational demands (derived from strategic models, planning and program requirements) and the development possibilities and needs of those concerned have to be developed.

The field of personnel development must be seen – with few exceptions e.g. in training – to have room for improvement. Measures of personnel development are not related to a sufficient degree to concrete goals and objectives of the organization, and there is no comprehensive and integrated approach to relating personnel and organization development.

In the long run administrative reform can only be successful if sufficient resources for integrating personnel and organization development are provided. On a strategic level the definition of the ministries' mid- and long-term performance goals constitutes the starting point for the goal definition of personnel development: specifically the question has to be asked what are the key qualifications of the civil servants concerned in order to enable them to attain performance goals. These qualifications form an important foundation to measure personnel development, and can only be used fruitfully if they can be derived from the strategic overall goals of the ministries. However, as in most public administrative organizations, there are difficulties (and also reservations) concerning the formulation of strategic and operational goals and objectives. Another important task for personnel development is to reduce organizational obstacles to efficient and effective administrative behaviour and to find ways and means to maintain and increase the motivation and satisfaction of civil servants. The supervisors as promoters and sponsors of successful measures must look for continuing coordination and integration with internal personnel experts (and, of course, must be supported by them).

Figure 7.4 illustrates a strategic goal-finding process and its implementation. It includes some plans which have been discussed and sometimes implemented.

INSTITUTIONALIZATION OF PERSONNEL AND ORGANIZATION DEVELOPMENT

The perspective of 'personnel as the most important factor of success for every organization' influences orientations and approaches. To what extent institutions live up to the realization is primarily shown in concrete implementation and in providing the required organizational capacity and resources.

In order to realize a structural integration of personnel and organization development in the Austrian federal administration various measures will have to be introduced:

- Increasing the personnel capacity of the reform unit in the Federal Chancellery in order to carry out interministerial personnel and organization development tasks.
- Installation of respective units in each ministry to fulfil consulting and service tasks.

These measures are expected to bring about positive effects such as the following:

- Support of various reform projects.
- Analysis of tasks and organization structures.
- Development of proposals concerning productivity.
- Attainment of higher degrees of client orientation.
- Development and support of self-renewal within ministries.

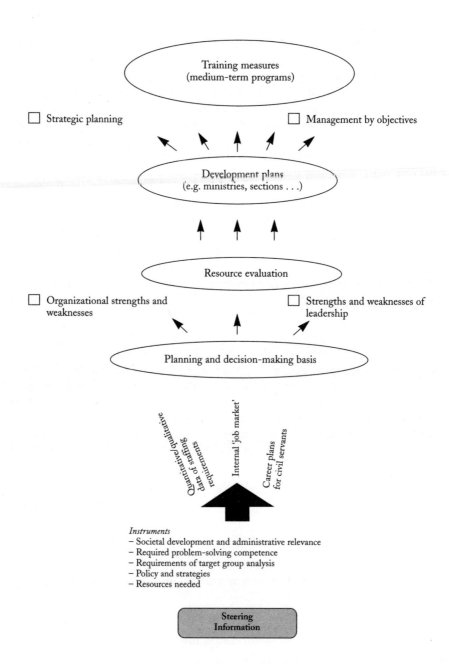

Figure 7.4. Strategic goal identification process.

It should be emphasized that – at the end of 1994 – these reflections were only at the stage of planning and discussion in some ministries, and had not yet been widely realized and implemented.

Future societal situations require a reorientation – away from short-term, day-to-day reaction policy – towards the development of long-term, all-embracing programs with a corresponding management. In order to realize a 'proactive' policy (as opposite to reactive) and programs, appropriate management of the administration is necessary: politicians determine the basic orientation, the administration has to manage an efficient and effective strategic and operational execution.

A necessary condition is training concerning program development, project management, instruments of strategic planning, team work and new forms of cooperation between politicians and top civil servants.

The reform project group developed important proposals that are fruitful and necessary for the implementation of the personnel development approach in the ministries:

- Ministerial strategic models covering the next one or two legislative periods (4–8 years).
- Linking personnel planning with strategic goals.
- Development of a recruitment procedure that is flexible and labour market specific.
- Top civil servants should take on responsibility for the development of their subordinates. (There is an increasing interest in evaluation and career conversation and instruments of career planning.)
- Overall job description and profiles and position assessment (this has already been realized in many organizations).
- Combination of on-the-job training and theoretical 'classroom' training.
- A systematically planned management training and development model based on the development of management principles.
- Implementation of 'management by objectives' as a basis for performance appraisal.
- Promotion of mobility and transfer of civil servants between organizations.

Pay system reform

The reform of the pay system is one of the more controversial and discussed issues in Austria. In June 1994 a new federal consitutional law was passed by the parliament.

The central point is a performance-oriented pay component which is not based on length of service. It became effective in January 1995 and concerns about one-third of all federal civil servants (80,000) under public law and from 1996 on all civil servants under private law.

The new law applies to new civil servants. All other civil servants have the option to choose between the old and the new system. The main features are as follows:

- *Relaxation of transfer and dismissal protection* There is the possibility of dismissing a civil servant after two negative performance appraisals. Transfers can be carried out because of 'important official interests' even without the consent of the civil servant concerned. An important official interest exists especially if there is an urgent need for a qualified civil servant in another office, if tasks and organization structures are changed, or if there is low performance or a disciplinary proceeding of a minor nature. Naturally, there is a committee of appeal that deals with objections within three months. On the other hand, if a civil servant wants to transfer he/she must be released within six weeks.

- *Performance rewards* One of the main criticisms of the former system was the rigid grade structure and the linking of promotions with long waiting times which often led to incompatibilities between duties (responsibilities) and pay with young and capable civil servants. The reform aims – within the budget framework – actively to relate career progress to performance. The new system (see Fig. 7.5) focuses on a regrouping of classes and grades and a combination of a guaranteed basic income and a performance-based bonus in case of exceptional responsibilities. The system does not only apply to management functions but also to specialized and demanding positions. The performance-based bonus takes the quality and importance of the position and the performance appraisal of the position holder into account.

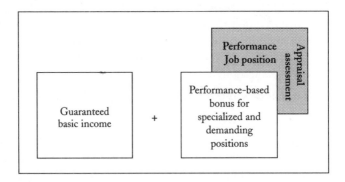

Figure 7.5. New pay structure.

- *Temporary management functions* The pay reform also provides instruments to increase the mobility of civil servants. Instead of lifetime employment, top positions will be filled for a five-year period; renewal for another period depends on performance. There are no flexible pay components.

- *Career conversation* Career conversations are obligatory and intended to serve as an instrument of performance appraisal, and a survey of training needs, as well as to improve communication and motivation and shape the career of the civil servant. Career conversation as a basic element of a future appraisal sheme should be institutionalized by 1998.

- *Lifetime employment* The trial period is extended from four to six years and lifetime employment is only possible after this period

- *Official titles* There is a minor change of an old Austrian tradition which concerns the abolishment of some (low-ranking) categories.

- *Costs of the pay reform* If all 80,000 civil servants change to the new system it is estimated that the cost will amount to the order of AS 1.3 billion per year (which is much more than expected).

COMMENTARY ON PAY SYSTEM REFORM

Compared to the former system, the new one focuses on the 'performance-related pay component' (additional functional allowance). The concept is obviously based on the implicit assumption that money can be used as motivator. However, the notion of performance is interpreted and used in terms of 'function' and the 'extent of responsibility' of a position. A precondition for the amount of this component is the assessment of the position and the degree of responsibility linked to it. There are critical views that capabilities, knowledge and experience of the position holder may not be taken into account and that even the performance principle cannot be realized: a mediocre civil servant in a high position would earn considerably more because of the additional functional allowance than an excellent civil servant whose position is classified in a lower category. Since every new assessment must be approved by government and be fixed in the federal position plan (Federal Fiscal Law), the flexibility and discretion of the ministries could be further reduced.

The linking of functional allowances to performance appraisal may increase tensions between the administration and politics because of the increased dependence of civil servants. As long as there is no overall objective and operational performance appraisal system, critics who predict – depending on the interpersonal conflict handling competence – a 'non-evaluation of performance' because of the lack of instruments and appropriate interpersonal behaviour seem to be right.

There are about 400 temporary top positions with appropriate fixed income which should promote the mobility of top civil servants. Also in this area the aim is a performance orientation by contract renewal and a functional allowance based on performance appraisal. Critics see the problem in an automatic positive perception of future performance after one or two positive evaluations because of the lack of an evaluation instrument and the so-called 'habituation effect'.

The new approach is not likely to cause a new fundamental personnel flexibility within the administrative system or between the public and private sector. The approach will not change the traditional micropolitical and power networks which function according to very different rules.

One of the strengths of the pay reform can be seen in the implementation of social and career conversation in combination with performance appraisal. In particular an improvement in supervisor–subordinate communication is to be expected. However, there is considerable resistance against this procedure since it increases the exposure of those involved and the transparency of work relationships. The major weaknesses are the lack of training and the underdeveloped performance appraisal system. The overall impression is that implementation of the reform for day-to-day use shows room for improvement.[20] But progress is being made.

ADMINISTRATIVE REFORMS: PUBLIC ADMINISTRATION MANAGEMENT

The most complex and prominent reform project of recent years is the so-called *'Verwaltungsmanagement'* project. The notion indicates that the focus of the reform on a management orientation is both necessary and fashionable.

In 1986 a special department was installed in the Federal Chancellery and given responsibilities in the areas of federalism and reform. This represented a considerable change compared to former reform endeavours: no isolated, independent projects within the ministries could be undertaken, but rather one large, complex, integrated and interministerial project planned. This means the integration of a variety of subprojects based on the same method, aiming at the same overall goals and covering basically the same contents.

The development of the project approach is based on the experiences of some ministries, and on Swiss, German and British reform projects. The specific – and strongly critized – feature of the project is that all fourteen ministries are involved in the project simultaneously, that organizational analyses are conducted in each of them, and that rationalization and change proposals are developed within an overall strategic framework. Those proposals with high priority are then implemented in a coordinated way. Based on a resolution of the ministerial council (end of 1989) the project was started in all ministries for a planned period of five years.

The formal framework and guidelines are laid down in an official project manual. In the following the main features of the project will be described.

Project goals

- Reorganization of task and management structures, concentration on core tasks – adjustment of competencies and responsibilities, contracting out, abolishment and reduction of tasks.
- Increasing productivity by 20 per cent within four years – critical evaluation of core tasks, improving efficiency and effectiveness.
- Reducing costs of administrative procedures – development of cost and performance ratios and indicators as management instruments.
- Concentration of management tasks – relieving top executives of day-to-day overload and thus creating capacities for strategic tasks.
- Improving service functions for the citizens.

One major (planned) feature of the project is that the focus should be on a stronger emphasis on results and output rather than on a management by mere resource allocation (input orientation): performance and performance responsibility are the key words. However, an important precondition is the setting of goals and objectives by the politicians and chief executives in the administration. (This, being a complex and difficult task, could not be reached on a broad basis until 1994/95 and will need considerable further efforts in order to be realized at least partially.)

Strategic project principles

- Emphasis not on a 'test-office' but on 'office-tests'.
- Demonstration by the federal government that there is a serious attempt to improve the performance of public administration.
- Improving close relationships with citizens – 'the citizen as client'.
- Reforms implemented in cooperation, rather than in conflict, with civil servants.
- High degree of involvement and participation of civil servants.
- Creating synergies and a general positive 'reform climate' in the long run.
- Maintenance of ministerial autonomy: the project management in the Federal Chancellery is only responsible for project methods, organization, results analysis and coordination.
- Organization of the project according to the principles of project management concerning the planning, steering and monitoring of performance, time and costs, and the definition and allocation of competencies and responsibilities among the participating institutions.

One of the crucial issues of the administrative reform is the way in which increased efficiency and effectiveness can be realized: should the central functions and competencies for the federal budget administration (Ministry of Finance) and job positions (Federal Chancellery) be strengthened within these organizations? *Or* should these functions and competencies go along with a simultaneous development and implementation of increased autonomy in the other ministries?

The department of the Minister for Federalism and Administrative Reform is organized within the Federal Chancellery and its main reform responsibility is the coordination of the relevant activities within the federal administration. Based on the constitutional law the implementation of any project lies exclusively within the responsibility of the ministries.

The reform project is oriented towards two directions. The first direction refers to an adaptation to changing challenges and requirements which are necessary in the long term and the resulting concepts of development. The second stresses short-term restoration with respect to economies and efficiency.

The short-term dimension is rather seen as a 'therapy of symptoms' through which small-scale successes can be achieved quickly. The long-term concept emphasizes the analysis and removal of the fundamental causes of the deficiencies and in this respect is a slow and laborious learning process which has to overcome many obstacles in an incremental way.

The emphasis is primarily on 'development' and long-term orientation in the areas of personnel and finance.

The project course is divided into three phases:

Phase 1 basic administration analysis (1989).
Phase 2 in-depth and interministerial studies (1990–1993/94).
Phase 3 autonomous implementation of subprojects (1994 ongoing).

In phase 1 a general analysis of the strengths and weaknesses of the ministries was conducted. The primary purpose was the identification of the main areas with high potential for improvement.

The main issue is to ensure consistency of the project philosophy and goal orientation in all ministries and with all external consulting firms (laid down in two project manuals).

The project directly covers fourteen ministries with about 8700 civil servants. Indirectly – in all decentralized organizations – some 150,000 people will be affected by the project in the long term.

Project organization (Fig. 7.6)

COORDINATING COMMITTEE

The chairman is the Federal Minister of Federalism and Administrative Reform. The Coordinating Committee includes representatives from all ministries and civil service unions.

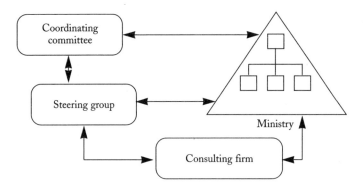

Figure 7.6. Project organization phase 1.

Roles

- A central organizational/political institution that decides on project matters and provides the basis for governmental decisions.
- Provides the organizational and financial basis for the entire project.
- Monitors the project.
- Applies for tendering and contracting the consulting firms and for budget allocation.
- Assesses and comments on the consulting firms' reports on the ministries.
- Prepares and resolves reports to the government.
- Decides on motions and proposals of the steering group.

STEERING GROUP

Roles

- Coordinates the overall project and the subprojects at the operational level in respect to deadlines, costs and goals in close cooperation with the respective ministry.
- Prepares the business of the coordinating committee.
- Transforms the project reports about the ministries into condensed information for the government via the coordinating committee.
- Coordinates all activities concerning interministerial issues.

INTRAMINISTERIAL ORGANIZATION

Project coordinator
The intraministerial project organization follows the principles of a matrix organization (see Fig. 7.7); the project coordinator has competencies and responsibilities which put him/her into a position to control the project.

The project coordinator has the following roles:

- Directly supports the ministerial top management regarding the project.
- Directly reports to the ministerial top management (section chief and/or minister).
- Is in direct contact with the steering group.
- Is the representative of the ministry in the coordinating committee.
- Is the 'turntable' between the project manager of the consulting firm, the ministerial project group (civil servants on different levels of hierarchy) within the organizational units in the ministry and the steering group.

Ministerial project group

This group is appointed by the minister; for the duration of the project the group members are exempted from other duties according to project workload and priorities (approximately 25 per cent of regular working time).

Group members have sound professional knowledge of the ministry, and are responsible for supporting the implementation of the subtasks and for the deadlines and performance of these tasks.

They remain in their organizational units and work part-time on the project as required.

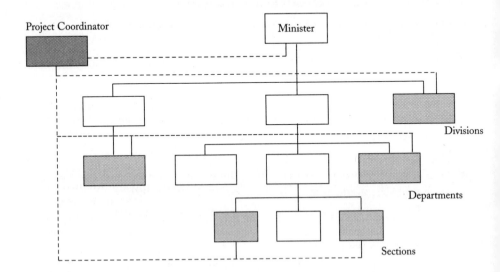

Figure 7.7. Intraministerial matrix organization.

Union representatives are involved in all decisions on important project steps and in the assessment of measures and recommendations.

EXTERNAL CONSULTING FIRM

The consulting firm is selected by the ministry concerned and the steering group in a joint decision-making process based on criteria specified in advance. A detailed differentiating profile is developed against which the firms' proposals are measured.

In general, the firm must fulfil the following conditions:

- Be professionally and methodologically equipped to fulfil the contract.
- Possess sufficient expertise and experience in the relevant fields.
- Inform the project coordinator and the steering committee on all matters.
- Problems should be solved at the lowest possible hierarchical level and should only be taken to the next level if they cannot be solved and if the topic is relevant to more than one ministry.

Reform project phase 1

Analysis areas of phase 1 are as follows:

- Organization (goals, structure, distribution of competencies, strengths and weaknesses, relationships between central and subordinate organizations, work process analyses, interministerial issues).
- Basic resource/performance relations.
- Costs.
- Personnel and financial capacities.
- Savings potentials.

These topics are worked on by the external firms and ministries using methodologically and conceptually different approaches and – not surprisingly – the results are many and diverse. The major results are a structured representation of the organizations and tasks, and the identification of those areas in which a high potential for rationalization is to be expected. Important problem areas concerning the interfaces between ministries and between the centre and the decentralized (subordinate) organizations can be defined in detail. In particular, civil servants on all hierarchical levels are invited to develop proposals and suggestions which are systematized as a basis for the in-depth studies in phase 2.

The following major rationalization/reorganization potentials are identified: reduction of the participation rights and approval duties of ministries

(Ministry of Finance, Federal Chancellery) concerning matters within other ministries, decentralization, organizational improvements within ministries (structure, process, technology), privatization.

In total about 3700 suggestions from all ministries are structured systematically. Two-thirds of these suggestions can be realized within the ministries themselves. The rest are structured according to specific themes and formed the basis for in-depth studies concerning complex and encompassing problem areas which were thought to offer a high potential for rationalization. They are pursued as major projects in phase 2.

The most important issues resulting from phase 1 are as follows (Bundeskanzleramt, 1994, p. 11):

- More than one-third of the suggestions concerned volume, effectiveness and efficiency of task fulfilment.
- About 40 per cent concerned improvements to organizational structures and processes.
- Twenty per cent show room for improvements in information technology and the workplace.
- Twenty per cent concern leadership, motivation, pay and training.
- Ten per cent concern legal matters (change of laws).

Reform project phase 2

The analysis of phase 1 resulted in nine interministerial in-depth studies, seven of which were started in 1990/91. The most important subprojects are described in brief below.

REDUCTION OF COMPETENCE/RESPONSIBILITY OVERLAP

Overlapping of competencies/responsibilities between ministries results in considerable problems regarding efficiency and effectiveness. The main task of this in-depth study was the analysis of existing multiple responsibilities in the top federal administration and the development of proposals for change. In particular, the following areas were identified: task-related non-overlapping structures, optimization of areas of control, positioning of staff units, abolition of overlap in the areas of budget and personnel, environmental protection, agenda of the European Union and international organizations, economic and cultural development, financial share management, issues of youth and family, traffic, statistics.

LEADERSHIP AND PERSONNEL

Leadership and personnel are being given increasing attention. Modern approaches to human resource management will have to be emphasized in future projects: leadership profiles, leadership guidelines, motivation issues, personnel requirements and personnel development, growing mobility of civil servants, delegation of decision making, performance orientation.

BUDGETING AND 'CONTROLLING'

Main issues are an increase in the transparency of budget planning and execution, the development of 'controlling' (i.e. management control system) and cost accounting systems.

STRATEGIC ELECTRONIC DATA MODEL

The ministries provided numerous proposals for an improvement in information technology. This subproject focuses on the development of an integrated strategic electronic data model with three major areas:

- Societal conditions for the implementation of information technology (citizens' expectations, information management in law-making processes).
- Management aspects of technology (organization, resources, internal service fee calculation).
- Technical infrastructure and international standards.

BUILDINGS AND OFFICES

A problematical feature of the federal administration is the permanent shortage of office space and the fact that organizational units are scattered in many buildings, resulting in logistic and work process inefficiencies: by Austrian standards there is a high degree of scattering of ministerial units across 86 sites.

This subproject aims at the following:

- Maintenance of value and usability of federal buildings.
- Efficient office allocation.
- Office maintenance and logistics.
- Setting of priorities based on transparent and objective requirements.

OFFICE MANAGEMENT, TECHNICAL COMMUNICATION, DOCUMENTATION

One issue is the technical state of the art in different ministries that varies to a high degree; another issue is the long duration of file work processes (transport and inactive time is almost 80 per cent of the total file processing time).

The project focuses on the efficient completion of files under the given legal and organizational conditions which is considered to be an important element of the legality principle and openness to scrutiny of administrative action.

In order to improve the situation the emphasis is on office information sytems (electronic filing), rationalization and technical workplace design.

PROCUREMENT

Federal procurement shows a high potential for rationalization, decentralization and standardization.

CIVIL SERVANTS' BUSINESS TRIPS

It is interesting to note that the costs of federal business trips have developed in a way which makes it necessary to analyze the respective legal norms, organization (application, approval, financial clearing) and management aspects as internal dimensions, and to take the advantage of the size of the federal administration as a contract partner for services like airlines, travel agencies, railways, hotels, cars, etc., as an external dimension.

The overall organization is assessed as being too complicated and expensive and does not use (to a satisfactory degree) modern possibilities of travel management because of obsolete technology and legal norms.

Reform project phase 3

The main issue of this phase is the implementation of intra- and interministerial projects with respect to methods, interministerial coordination, and financial and personnel support from the Federal Chancellery. One strategic idea is to initiate learning processes between organizational units working on the same topics and thus to foster project development.

Critical assessment of the reform project Verwaltungsmanagement

ROLE OF THE FEDERAL CHANCELLERY

Due to the legal, historical and organizational situation the Federal Chancellery is in a rather difficult position regarding reform responsibilities. In fact, it does not have formal competencies *vis-à-vis* the autonomy of ministries. Several functions are not clear. Concerning the reform agenda, the Federal Chancellery on the one hand is in a 'staff position' (coordination, recommendation without direct possibilities of intervention), but on the other carries responsibilities and competencies for the overall federal administration concerning decisions on personnel positions. Because of this the Chancellery is identified by the ministries as very powerful and many conflicts concerning personnel development issues result. The permanent issue is the centralization or decentralization of personnel-related competencies. The perception is one of 'Big Brother' and traditionally there is strong reluctance to accept the Federal Chancellery's influence and control.

POLITICAL PRIORITIES

Political interests and changing priorities at the highest levels tend to reduce the status and importance of management-oriented reforms and to retard the respective projects. Accordingly, reform projects are allocated relatively low financial and personnel resources and, therefore, the desirable momentum is lacking. In addition, traditionally, the need and interest to really work on efficiency and effectiveness cannot be said to be highly prominent and there are no well-developed incentives to do so.

Some believe that success of the reform could be improved if the allocation of certain budget positions and personnel positions could be linked to the successful realization of reform projects.

In phase 1 the overall success is rather limited compared to the expectations. One very positive effect is that many organizational units have developed a high degree of problem awareness and various projects promise further developments (in the long term).

PHASE 1 FROM AN ORGANIZATIONAL-POLITICAL PERSPECTIVE

- Open and/or hidden resistance exists in many organizations (organizational units).
- 'Politicalization' of project and project results: use/misuse of data for other than project interests.
- Different procedures and methods used by the external consulting firms and also, depending on these, more or less resistance and better or worse results of their work in phase 1.
- Most external consulting firms lack in some respect specific knowledge of administrative norms, regulations and procedures, and therefore are not in a position to ask the right questions or to assess reported situations correctly. As a consequence many of the stated results are being contended by the organizational units concerned, and not accepted as 'correct facts'.
- One basic critique from insiders is that firms use the ministries as a paid opportunity to learn and only give feedback on issues that are known anyway. However, an external view and integration of details without wearing organizational blinkers are of great value and add to the momentum for change. In particular, the top decision-makers are informed and involved in the decision-making processes.

COMMENTARY ON PHASE 2

In 1993 the reform project was closed formally, but the subprojects continued. The project has nevertheless provided many opportunities to initiate an encompassing change in the federal administration.[21]

The strengths and weaknesses of the project with respect to the stated project goals can be summarized as follows:

- *Reorganization of task and management structures, concentration on core tasks* The main problems are the finding of now obsolete tasks and the self-definition of responsibilities and tasks by managers. In this highly sensitive area political and organizational-political strategies of resistance (micro-politics) play a particular role. The official project evaluation arrives at the conclusion that this goal has been attained in only a very limited way (Bundeskanzleramt, 1994, p. 127).

- *Increasing productivity by 20 per cent within four years* It is interesting to observe that on an official as well as an informal level (whether intentionally or nor) the term 'increasing productivity' is equated with 'personnel reduction'. This leads to serious arguments and resistance from civil servants. However, this goal has precisely directed awareness towards thinking in terms of efficiency and effectiveness and has promoted the reform climate. In some organizations modest successes have been attained.

- *Reducing costs of administrative procedures* At the beginning of the project, cost consciousness within the administration was practically zero (Bundeskanzleramt, 1994, p. 125). The project contributed to the development (and implementation) of cost accounting approaches in several organizations and to a growing interest in the topic. As an overall result there has been an increase in cost accounting projects.[22]

- *Concentration on management tasks* In connection with other project goals a very important approach to leadership and personnel has developed which contributed to a climate favourable for a new way of perceiving management and leadership tasks, leading away from the mere administration of organizations and personnel by top civil servants. However, concerning this goal too – as holds true for most of the reform details – it must be said that change has occurred slowly and incrementally.

- *Improving service functions for citizens* The idea that citizens (taxpayers) are not only 'addressees of legal norms' but 'clients' having a right to receive services has been accepted and realized to an increasing degree. This is reflected on the one hand by a more intensive call for transparency of administrative costs, and on the other hand by an increasing focus on behavioural issues of civil servants (leadership, motivation, personnel development, performance).

The projects in phase 2 can be classified as rather promising. The most important topics – 'leadership and personnel development' and 'controlling/cost accounting' – are emphasized in principle and promoted officially. However, only little progress can be registered. A major problem in the area of 'controlling' is the semantic closeness to *Kontrolle* (the traditional audit and *a posteriori* control): it is interpreted as a modern (fashionable) and very subtle instrument of *a posteriori* control combined with *a priori* elements.

There is no systematic and effective promotion and marketing of successful subprojects in diverse organizations. However, projects contribute to an improved climate and topics can be discussed now which could not be approached before.

The Minister of Federalism and Administrative Reform has only limited possibilities in demanding the realization of resolutions taken in the Council of Ministers. He has competencies of coordination, but no right of order whatsoever in the ministries and mainly has to rely on the goodwill and cooperation of the other ministers. On the one hand a reform of this dimension can only be undertaken and realized in the long run, on the other hand politicians tend to formulate their criteria of success on a short-term election-to-re-election basis.

Concerning the standpoint of the unions, it can be said that their overt behaviour is generally constructive, though naturally they want to score points concerning pay. One of the issues of the reforms concerning leadership and personnel development is the representatives' fear of a weakening of their traditional position and influence because of improving relationships between supervisors and subordinates and the possibilities of direct and individual participation and codetermination.

Prospects for reform success should mainly exist at the level of interpersonal relationships between those actively and passively involved, the increasing build-up of direct contacts, incremental approaches and 'snowball effects' as individuals accumulate skills and confidence. Frequently the view is held that cutting back resources represents the only strategy possible to foster reforms, and resource allocation should be undertaken on zero-based budgeting. However, this type of concept presupposes specific attitudes and ways of thinking, which are assumed to be initiated and intensified by reform endeavours. In this respect the reforms somehow create a vicious circle.

Another basic reform problem is the view that innovations imply that former approaches were wrong and faults would have to be admitted. The traditional roles and structures of the civil service stand in the way of a discussion about and a reorientation of goals and performance. Legal norms are argued to be reasons for non-alterable situations, though, of course, there should be sufficient room for manoeuvre. As always, the administration is dominated by a strong internal orientation; planning and fulfilment of tasks, performance and service benefits for the clients will have to be focused on much more strongly.

There are also certain discrepancies between the resolutions of the Council of Ministers and their realization within the ministries and their organizations.

Another problem concerns the low quantitative and qualitative personnel capacities and the budget shortage in the organization of the Minister of Federalism and Administrative Reform as well as in the ministries themselves. One is inclined to raise the difficult question as to what extent this situation results from strategically oriented intentions – which sound very reasonable in the light of budget restrictions – which can be interpreted as standing against reforms.

In principle it is accepted that if reform endeavours are not strongly supported by top politicians and the administrative top executives who would have to actively foster them, the prospect of success tends to be zero.

These issues mentioned above show much room for improvement and the *Verwaltungsmanagement* project has not been very successful at making the reform a broadly accepted political topic (Bundeskanzleramt, 1994, p. 136).

The project teams in the ministries have not been relieved of day-to-day business which results in an incompatibility of tasks and responsibilities and a considerable overload, which can only be compensated by high personal committment. In this context the problem of low (non-existent) incentives for innovative managers and civil servants has not been solved at all.

Performance orientation must be seen as a goal that is very difficult to attain, and is likely to be achieved, if at all, only in the long term. The traditional principle of 'resource use' (input orientation) still predominates administrative processes and the issues of efficiency and effectiveness have by no means been fully treated.

However, the project has various merits (Bundeskanzleramt, 1994, p. 13):

- Encompassing and integrated high-quality collection of proposals forming a very valuable basis for further projects.
- Establishment and advancement of project management methods.
- Topics that had been taboo several years ago are now broadly discussed issues, building an important basis for ongoing work in the ministries.
- Increasing awareness of the necessities of implementing management know-how and promotion of an organizational culture.[23]

Case Study: Reform of Austrian Universities

Cäcilia Innreiter-Moser

Original Condition

All Austrian universities and art colleges (hereafter both are referred to as universities) are centrally run, federal institutions. According to a working agreement concluded by the governing parties in 1990, all Austrian universities had to be reformed over the next four years in a way that would enable them to work more efficiently.

The last comprehensive reform of University Organization Law (UOL) in 1975 aimed at opening the universities to all classes of society and at a democratization of decision-making structures within universities. The basic organizational principle was to create committees (composed of professors, assistant professors and students) with fundamental democratic elements in order to achieve greater transparency of and identification with internal decisions. The extremely dynamic changes in Austrian universities (steady increase of student numbers) caused considerable difficulties in practical organization and decision-making.

Defects in the existing university system can be assessed by their 'products' (research and teaching) on the one hand, and the internationally compared high share of research expenditures and the simultaneous lack of room, staff and equipment on the other hand. This paradoxical situation indicates an inefficient use of resources in the whole system as well as an inadequate distribution of competence between the Federal Ministry of Science and Research (FMSRA) and among the ministries (Beirat für Wirtschafts- und Sozialfragen, 1991 p. 7).

Specific criticisms are as follows (Hochschulbericht, 1993, p. 21):

- Centralization of competence at the top (FMSRA).
- Lack of clear decision-making structures within the universities as well as among them, between universities and the FMSRA, and among different governmental bodies involved.
- Lack of unity between decision-making committees and other responsible authorities.
- Too many regulations in general.

- Lack of competence of universities concerning the execution of budget and staff administration.
- Overly rigid regulations for employment and remuneration.

All these items cause problems, such as inefficient administrative channels, lack of readiness for commitment and innovation among the members of university bodies and a general lack of motivation.

NEW ORGANIZATIONAL STRUCTURE

The UOL intends to eliminate the defects mentioned above by creating new decision-making structures and by changing the distribution of competence. In this way it continues to promote the transformation of universities into enterprise-like institutions (Fig. 7.8).

All universities remain federal institutions; they will have to fulfil their tasks within the existing laws, though without being subject to instructions. Fewer regulations in favour of the university statutes which are elaborated by the universities themselves and the delegation of competences in decision-making should bring more flexibility to the universities' internal organization. By means of creating independent profiles, universities should be able to compete on a national as well as an international level. Nevertheless financing and controlling of all universities have to remain the responsibility of the state.

Apart from collegial committees responsible for the establishment of standards and holding a control function, the new organizational model mainly consists of strong monocratic bodies which will be endowed with detailed decision-making competence. The latter carry out managerial tasks.

Deregulation and decentralization are the leading principles of the new structure.

Deregulation

At present universities are strictly bound by laws, regulations, implementing ordinances, etc., which are an impediment to their flexibility and economic actions. Deregulation has to take place with regard to qualitative (more autonomy in decision-making) as well as quantitative (clearing out of existing legal standards) aspects (Ruegg, 1987, p. 74).

Decentralization

The decentralization and shift of essential decision-making responsibilities from the central body (FMSRA) to the universities should improve the

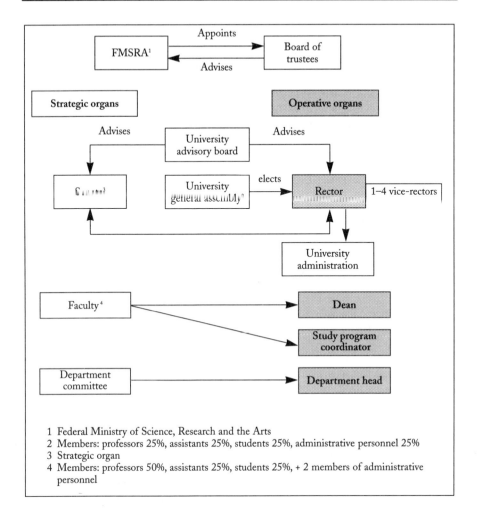

1 Federal Ministry of Science, Research and the Arts
2 Members: professors 25%, assistants 25%, students 25%, administrative personnel 25%
3 Strategic organ
4 Members: professors 50%, assistants 25%, students 25%, + 2 members of administrative personnel

Figure 7.8. Strategic and operative organs. (UOL, 1993)

quality of decisions and result in an increased identification with decisions taken.

The central structures in Austrian universities in general can guarantee neither an efficient nor effective decision-making process or results thereof. Too many offices and departments are responsible for university administration but none has managerial competence. Apart from university bodies a range of federal bodies – even several federal ministries up to the Austrian president – take part in the decision process of significant issues.

By means of redistributing essential competence in decision-making responsibilities and rights are shifted to an institutional controlling level.

Inevitably, this has to bring about a redefinition of both the role of the central controlling level (i.e. the FMSRA) and that of the individual institutions (i.e. the universities). In its capacity as supervisory body, the FMSRA will take over the control of subordinate units – which is given by the skeleton legislation – and the observation of university progress by means of benchmark data which are to be set up (of considerable importance in this respect will be the elaboration of meaningful key numbers and their integration in a controlling scheme).

FIELDS OF AUTONOMY

In order to provide a sort of operational management of universities, the UOL 1993 plans to change the actual existing autonomy of implementation-making into a real autonomy of decision-making, particularly in the fields of staff, budget and internal organization.

Staff autonomy

In future universities will be able to decide on recruitment of new staff. This applies also to the appointment of university professors. In addition, conditions of employment may be subject either to civil or public law.

Financial autonomy

Each university will obtain a budget which is structured according to salaries and expenses for investments and expenditures which it may dispose of as it likes. Legally established possibilities of redistribution guarantee a higher flexibility in budgeting, i.e. the budget can be used in a flexible way according to the needs of each individual university. The control of and the responsibility for an economic use of resources are also tasks for the universities (Smekal, 1991, p. 113).

Organizational autonomy

By having the right to create their own statutes, universities will be able to pass proper ordinances within the framework of existing legal provisions which are necessary to fulfil their tasks. The right to determine their internal structure will give every university the possibility to develop its own profile, thus increasing adaptability to changing conditions.

REDEFINED TASKS AND COMMITTEES

At all levels of the Austrian university system the following tasks and committees were reconsidered and redefined.

Supra-university level

BOARD OF TRUSTEES

Advisory body to the Federal Ministry of Science and Research (FMSRA); creates a link between universities on the one hand, and the economy and society on the other. It is composed of four experts from within and outside the universities. It is responsible for giving expert opinions to the FMSRA on comprehensive development planning, the establishment of courses of studies, the assignment of posts, etc.[24]

University level

UNIVERSITY ADVISORY BOARD

Consultative body for rector (president) and senate which is responsible for issues of development planning, distribution of staff, budgeting and long-term calculations on future requirements.[25] It is a link between the university and the economy on the one hand, and the university and society on the other.

RECTOR (PRESIDENT)

The rector's role has gained considerably in importance. He/she is the manager (monocratic decision-making body) of the university who after an open advertisement of the position is elected from the senate's election proposal for four years by the university general assembly. In fulfilling his/her tasks the rector is supported by a maximum of 4 vice-rectors.[26]

SENATE

In its capacity as a board (collegial body) it enacts the statutes and is responsible for the creation of ordinances and the control of the rector's activities. The rector participates with a consultative vote in the senatorial sessions.[27]

UNIVERSITY ADMINISTRATION (CENTRAL ADMINISTRATION, CENTRAL INFORMATION SERVICES, UNIVERSITY LIBRARY)

In future these functions will all be subordinated to the rector.[28] Cost accounting and controlling will be the main pillars to be created in this sector for the proper management of universities.

Faculty level

DEAN

The dean embodies the monocratic decision-making body and is elected by the faculty from the rector's election proposal for four years. The dean is responsible for the managerial tasks at the faculty level.[29]

FACULTY

Faculty is responsible for the creation of regulations for the dean and the study program coordinator as well as the control of their activities. The number of the members is to be defined in the statutes, to a maximum of forty-two.[30] The democratically composed commission of budgetary affairs and position planning as well as the personnel commission will be eliminated. Their tasks will be taken over by the monocratic bodies (rector, dean).

STUDY PROGRAM COORDINATOR

More attention will be dedicated to university teaching by establishing the position of a study program coordinator who will be elected by the faculty from the group of university professors. He/she will be responsible for ensuring that teaching and examinations are coordinated and guaranteed in accordance with the courses of studies. He/she decides in all matters of organization and evaluation concerning the areas of studies offered and the exams administered.[31]

Departmental level

At the level of the departments the system remains unchanged in that the department head remains the monocratic decision-maker and the department committee the collegial organ.

COST ACCOUNTING AND CONTROLLING

The implementation of operational tools – especially those of cost accounting and controlling – is necessary to guarantee a university management based on entrepreneurial thinking in compliance with the demand established by law to provide an economic and suitable fulfilment of its tasks.

The first question to be put in this context refers to the effectivity of university work. What kind of qualitative and quantitative output do universities have to produce in order to meet social demands? In this respect it has to be taken into consideration that this will require long-term financial means, i.e. how to finance university performances? In addition the principle of economic viability forces universities to work at the lowest possible cost (efficiency). If budgetary planning is output-oriented, i.e. if there is a link between performance and the need for resources, it is immediately possible to urge economic thinking. In order to reach this goal, the university output has to be defined and recorded (elaboration of output statistics) and linked with the budgetary calculation. The benefit for universities of such a cost accounting and performance calculation is to be seen in three areas (BMWF, 1992):

- Control of economic viability.
- Provision of information for budgetary planning (budgeting, consequential cuts on the budget caused by investments and legal standards)
- Provision of information for the calculation of fees, claims for reimbursement of costs and of remuneration according to civil law.

As neither the universities nor the FMSRA have established proceedings for the cost accounting of diverse measures (e.g. the introduction of a new course of studies) at their disposal, the basics for long-term budget planning and the consideration of the costs resulting from such measures are lacking. To fulfil this task, the FMSRA has engaged a study group to develop a cost accounting and control system for universities. The following shows how this team elaborated the present plan.

Since the decisions taken at different university levels directly influence the economical viability of university bodies and their efficiency, the question arises: for which university decisions is this information on cost and efficiency needed? In this respect the following areas of decision, which, however, are not to be seen independently of each other (BMWF, 1992, p. 16), must be highlighted:

- Decisions on the offer of courses.
- Decisions on research work.
- Decisions on events taking place at the university.
- Decisions regarding the establishment and abolition of university institutions.
- Decisions regarding the number of staff.
- Decisions on room facilities.
- Decisions on general equipment.
- Decisions on current expenditures.
- Decisions on structures and scheduling.

Cost and efficiency accounting show the effects of existing alternatives in decision-making on the economic viability in a quantitative way, giving at the same time rational arguments in the process of decision-making.

There are two possible applications of cost and efficiency accounting at universities:

- Application outside the system of automated budget accounting.
- Application within the system of automated budget accounting.

Universities are institutions subordinated to the FMSRA, and are therefore integrated into the budgetary system of the state. Through federal accountancy it is possible to control quantities such as liquidity, success and economic viability. Only after evaluating the advantages and disadvantages is it useful and more economic to implement cost and efficiency accounting for universities within the system of automated budget accounting. However, the monetary aspect in the budgetary calculation is dominant, while in the field of cost and efficiency accounting consumption of resources comes to the fore. This means that the financial and economic aspects of the budget account 'revenue and expenditure' and 'payments and receipts', respectively, are to be transformed into costs and efficiency, i.e. they have to be limited in time, matter and value.

CONSEQUENTIAL COSTS OF THE UOL REFORM

The responsible minister is obliged by article 14 of the Federal Budgetary Law to state the financial consequences of legal actions in his/her area. For this purpose a project group was set up with the following tasks:

- Analysis of the proposals made by the project team 'Reform of the UOL' with regard to the financial impact on the budget (surplus expenses).
- Calculation or evaluation of the amount of the financial consequences.
- Evaluation of the benefit from the business management standpoint.

First of all the project team had to analyze the planned changes. The question was: which and how many functions, bodies and jobs in the whole university system are to be redefined or adapted from a qualitative point of view and which ones are to be eliminated or relieved?

In order to be able to evaluate the jobs that were to be redefined or newly created, the necessary qualifications according to category of employee had to be classified.

The fundamental data (estimates of needed workplaces, salary expectations for positions at the top level) derive from interviews with key persons in the FMSRA.

The calculation of the financial impact caused by the reform of the UOL was based upon the 'costs of a job', composed of staff cost, material cost and general administrative cost.

The calculation of staff costs was abstracted from individual employees and based on the average annual salary.

For material costs, which comprise capital cost for furniture and office material and their maintenance, cost for rooms, office supplies (stationery), telephone charges, etc., a figure drawn from past experience (AS 100,000) of a comparable department was used.

For the general administrative cost (cost of general administrative departments like staff administration, wages and salaries, office administration) an amount of AS 60,000 per workplace was used.

Benefits of the UOL reform

In order to assess the benefits of the reform of the UOL from the business management standpoint at the university level, the relief caused by the elimination of bodies or the reduction of committee members was expressed in years per employee and compared to the corresponding staff cost.

Moreover, the competencies of the rector, the dean and their deputies were redefined by the UOL 1993, which eliminated the corresponding additional payments/benefits.

The planned delegation and decentralization of essential responsibilities and decisions to the universities mean a great relief for the FMSRA. Presumably 20 percent of all university posts could be transformed into new activities. Hence the annual costs of the reform of the UOL are reduced by the cost rates of these posts. Apart from the benefits of the UOL reform calculated in these ways, the non-quantifiable part also has to be pointed out, which from a business management point of view is related to the following areas:

- Promotion of a professional management of the universities.
- More stress on management orientation by means of organization (elaboration of development plans), budgeting, cost accounting, controlling and evaluation.
- More stress on the efficiency and effectivity of university work by means of cost accounting and evaluation.
- Creation of more transparency.
- Improvement of university management by decentralization.
- More responsibility for results.
- Creation of clearly defined responsibilities.

In the course of this project it was interesting to see the effect of cost information on the UOL reform project team. The great financial impact of first proposals made the team reconsider the purpose of the planned actions and stimulated the elaboration of alternatives.

CHANCES AND RISKS RESULTING FROM THE UOL REFORM

Since people concerned by or interested in the UOL reform by no means represent a homogeneous group, it is important to identify the diverse interest groups and their aims in order to be able to evaluate the chances and risks of an UOL reform. In the following, the internal and external groupings of a system are listed:

- Federal Ministry of Science and Research.
- Political university associations.
- Students.
- University administration.
- Suppliers of resources.
- Market area (e.g. economy).
- Society.
- Politicians.

These groupings represent different types of shortcomings in the university system. They try to explain the reasons for these shortcomings and present proposals for the changes resulting from the latter (Titscher, 1992, p. 5). The only existing agreement so far concerns the demand for greater autonomy of the universities, which was also granted by the legislator in the UOL 1993.

Within the universities the *de facto* abolition of co-determination by UOL 1993 is an obstacle to the students' and assistants' interests. Strong monocratic bodies (rector, dean, study program coordinator) are 'controlled' by much weaker collegial committees. Only decisions regarding general directives can be taken, but not decisions concerning specific staff issues, the allocation of resources or teaching assignments. But the group of professors, too, finds itself confronted with a loss of influence because of the future composition of the few collegial committees (this refers also to the maximum size of faculty boards). It is feared that there will be an increase of bureaucracy which would simply be shifted from ministry level to university level, i.e. the expected further rise in efficiency is not going to happen.

NOTES

1. Bundesverfassungs-Gesetz (= B-VG = Austrian Constitutional Law), Art. 94.
2. Ibid., Art. 87, Abs. 1 and Art. 88.
3. Ibid., Art. 30 (except for administrative authorities which due to special constitutional rules are not bound by directives).
4. Ibid., Art. 18; in practice legality principle refers to 'sovereign administration'. According to private sector economy (*Privatwirtschaftsverwaltung*) its observance is based on many open questions. See also Funk (1989, p. 131), Novak (1992, p. 80).

5. For more details see Schwab (1992, pp. 215–36) and Funk (1989, pp. 165–8).
6. Art. 20, Abs. 3, B-VG (Austrian Constitutional Law).
7. Ibid., Art 20, Abs. 4; There are detailed regulations on federal and state level.
8. Ibid., art.
9. The Fiscal Equalization Law is the most important ordinary law. It regulates the key regulations on the actual financial relationships between the federation (*Bund*), the states (*Länder*), and the municipalities or local government units (*Gemeinden*).
10. For details see Lödl and Matzinger (1992, p. 313–28).
11. In Switzerland there exists a concept of strategic management ('controlling' in the sense of a management control system).
12. Not to be confused with the National Accounting Office below.
13. Further details on the structure (data flows and processes) obtained from the Ministry of Finance, Vienna (Federal Accounting Centre).
14. The financial year runs from January until December.
15. For details see Promberger (1991b, p. 47).
16. For details see Csoka and Promberger (1993, p. 64).
17. In the discussion the term 'controlling' is used in the sense of management control system. The notion of controlling in all German-speaking countries was taken from the Anglo-Saxon term 'to control' with the meaning of guiding, steering, and does not mean *a posteriori* control in the sense of evaluation of conformity of administrative action to rules and legal norms.
18. The number of civil servants is about 600,000 active civil servants and about 280,000 retired civil servants (federal, state and community level). Personnel expenditure amounts to some 25 percent of overall budget (Federal Budget Plan, 1991).
19. For details see Jabloner (1992, p. 284).
20. Recent developments in the decision-making processes between employers and employees representatives tend towards a slow-down of the implementation and several changes of the concept details.
21. For details see Bundeskanzleramt (1994, p. 125).
22. The project presented demonstrates an interesting organizational and cost accounting approach of the Ministry of Science and Research within an overall reform beginning 1994.
23. At the end of 1994 following parliamentary elections the position and functions of the Federal Minister of Federalism and Public Adminstration Reform were 'abolished'. It is to be expected this reduction of formal power will have negative impacts on the reform endeavours at the federal level.
24. § 83 UOG 1993 (Universitäts-Organisationsgesetz = University Organization Law).
25. Ibid., § 56.
26. Ibid., §§ 52–54.
27. Ibid., § 51.
28. Ibid., §§ 75–78.
29. Ibid., § 49.
30. Ibid., § 48.
31. Ibid., § 43.

REFERENCES

Beirat für Wirtschafts- und Sozialfragen (1991) *Vorschläge zur Reform des Hochschulwesens und der Forschungspolitik*, Wien.

Brandtner, W. (1992) The organization of State administration. In Federal Chancellery (ed.), *Public Administration in Austria*, Österreichische Staatsdruckerei, Vienna.

Bundeskanzleramt (Federal Chancellery) (1994) *Verwaltungsmanagement Projektbericht 1994* (project report), Universitäts-Buchdruckerei Styria, Graz.

Bundesminister für Wissenschaft und Forschung (1992) *Kostenrechnung und Controlling an Universitäten und Hochschulen, Hochschulplanungskommission*, Arbeitsgruppe Kostenrechnung, Wien.

Bundesminister für Wissenschaft und Forschung (1993) *Hochschulbericht 1993*, Band 1, Wien.

Csoka, S. (1993) Die Kosten- und Leistungsrechnung im System der automatisierten Haushaltsverrechnung des Bundes. In Promberger, K. and Pracher, C. (eds), *Kosten- und Leistungsrechnung für die öffentliche Verwaltung*, Österreichische Staatsdruckerei, Wien, pp. 93–124.

Csoka, S. and Promberger, K. (1993) Das Rechnungswesen der Bundesverwaltung als Managementinformationssystem. In Strehl, F. (ed.), *Managementkonzepte für die öffentliche Verwaltung*, Österreichische Staatsdruckerei, Wien, pp. 45–88.

Dearing, E. (1992) Das Projekt 'Verwaltungsmanagement' – Chancen einer Verwaltungsreform in Österreich, *Die Öffentliche Verwaltung*, vol. 7, pp. 297–305.

Funk, B.-Ch. (1989) *Einführung in das österreichische Verfassungs- und Verwaltungsrecht*, Leykam Verlag, Graz, pp. 165–8.

Gerlich, P. (1992) Administration and politics. In Federal Chancellery (ed.), *Public Administration in Austria*, Österreichische Staatsdruckerei, Vienna, pp. 257–75.

Hochschulbericht (1993) Bundesminister für Wissenschaft und Forschung, Bund 1, Wien.

Jabloner, C. (1992) Personnel in public administration. In Federal Chancellery (ed.), *Public Administration in Austria*, Österreichische Staatsdruckerei, Vienna, pp. 277–301.

Lödl, M. C. and Matzinger, A. (1992) Public budgeting. In Federal Chancellery (ed.), *Public Administration in Austria*, Österreichische Staatsdruckerei, Vienna, pp. 303–40.

Novak, R. (1992) The constitutional basis of the administration. In Federal Chancellery (ed.), *Public Administration in Austria*, Österreichische Staatsdruckerei, Vienna, pp. 73–94.

Pelinka and Welan (1971) *Demokratie und Verfassung in Österreich*.

Promberger, K. (1991a) Ermittlung der Vollzugskosten von Rechtsnormen. In Promberger, K. and Pracher, C. (eds), *Kosten- und Leistungsrechnung für die öffentliche Verwaltung*, Österreichische Staatsdruckerei, Wien, p. 155. (The Federal Chancellery, Vienna, has published a practical manual to be used by civil servants.)

Promberger, K. (1991b) Grundzüge der Kosten- und Leistungsrechnung für die öffentliche Verwaltung. In Promberger, K. and Pracher, C. (eds), *Kosten- und Leistungsrechnung für die öffentliche Verwaltung*, Österreichische Staatsdruckerei, Wien, pp. 13–91.

Promberger, K. (1995) *Controlling für Politik und öffentliche Verwaltung*, Österreichische Staatsdruckerei, Wien.

Raschauer, B. and Kazda, W. (1983) Organisation der Verwaltung. In Wenger, K., Brünner, C. and Oberndorfer, P. (eds), *Grundriß der Verwaltungslehre*, Hermann Böhlaus Nachf., Wien/Köln, pp. 146, 147.

Ruegg, W. (1987) *Zementierung oder Innovation. Effizienz von Hochschulsystemen*, Österreichische Rektorenkonferenz, Norka-Verlag Dr Norbert Kastelic, Wien.

Schwab, W. (1992) The financial controls placed on public administration. In Federal Chancellery (ed.), *Public Administration in Austria*, Österreichische Staatsdruckerei, Vienna, pp. 215–36.

Smekal, C. (1991) Autonomie und Finanzierung. In Peterlik, M. and Waldhäusl, W. (eds), *Universitätsreform: Ziele, Prioritäten und Vorschläge*, Eine Dokumentation des österreichischen Wissenschaftstages, Wien.

Titscher, St. (1992) *Zusammenhangsanalyse zur Planung und Reformation der Universität*, Ein Forschungsbericht im Auftrag der Österreichischen Rektorenkonferenz.

Trigon Entwicklungsberatung (1990) *Personalentwicklung in der Österreichischen Bundesverwaltung Projektstudie*, Graz.

8

Switzerland

Franz Strehl and Ulrike Hugl

Overview

Federalism, local implementation and subsidiarity are the main principles that characterize the politico-administrative system of Switzerland. The constitution combines two principles: the committee and the ministry principle. The Federal Assembly elects the government consisting of seven ministers and the chancellor as the central staff unit of the Federal Assembly. The committee of the seven equal ministers forms the government. Parliament and government are clearly separated from the point of view of organization and personnel.

Overall, the existing system led to continually increasing expenditure and personnel. The starting point for reform was the realization that the traditional political and administrative structures did not provide the necessary prerequisites to cope satisfactorily with the complexity and dynamics of national and international tasks. The development and implementation of fundamental approaches in the field of management instruments in the financial, personnel and organizational domains became necessary and very clear. Concerning these circumstances, basic reform issues in Switzerland can be interpreted as fundamental and strategic changes to the politico-administrative system and the respective legal foundations.

In October 1993 an organization law was passed on the position and functions of government members as ministry heads: the committee principle was established, which is said to be best for complex management- and decision-making processes and will be further strengthened. The duality of the committee/ministry principle is being maintained as a successful and effective approach; furthermore the function of secretary of state is institutionalized at senior ministerial level. Secretaries of state operate at the level of ministries, groups and offices and have to contribute an efficient and effective ministerial leadership; emphasis is given to flexibility of the administrative structure and a timely and factual internal and external coordination. Other important aspects are the reorganization of the federal administration concerning the organizational design of the ministries, and the contingent and flexible application of management instruments.

The major principles of budget and budget management are conformity to legal norms, urgency, efficiency and economies. Much effort is given to the modernization and systematization of budgeting procedures.

Management control systems ('controlling') are one of the important management instruments in the Swiss administration organized within the Ministry of Finance and offered as a service to all offices (see also Case Study). The notion of 'controlling' has developed from a fashionable slogan to a major management issue and is increasingly seen as a central instrument for the fulfilment of public administration tasks at the strategic policy (program) level as well as at the operational level. The concept of 'controlling' as an instrument for assessment, diagnosis and guidance should enable decision-makers to take into account a long-range overall view of economic, social, political and scientific interrelations and their effects on federal expenditure.

To ensure rule conformity, efficiency and effectiveness of the administration, the Council of Ministers decided in 1990 on the development of a strategic model of personnel and organizational development for the legislative period of 1992–1995. The main goals of the model were personnel qualification, organizational flexibility and responsiveness, and the improvement of leadership. Personnel and organizational development was defined as a primary management task. The personnel management unit as central staff functions as supplier and mediator of internal and external training and consulting, has the roles of developing, initiating and supporting the implementation of respective strategies and concepts, the assessment of their effectiveness and the overall coordination of all strategically important measures.

BASIC STRUCTURES

Federal Assembly (parliament)

The Federal Assembly consists of two chambers with equal rights:

- The National Council consists of 200 members and represents the people.
- The Upper Chamber consists of forty-six members and represents the provinces (cantons).

Parliament is elected for a period of four years. Some specific decisions (elections, reprieves) have to be taken in common.

Several standing commissions are also elected for a period of four years.

- Financial matters.
- Auditing.
- External affairs.
- Science, education, culture.
- Social security, health.
- Environment, regional development, energy.

- Public security.
- Traffic and telecommunications.
- Economy and taxes (fees).
- State policy.
- Legal matters.
- Public buildings.

The Federal Assembly elects the government, consisting of seven ministers and the chancellor. They head the seven ministries and the Federal Chancellery. The ministers are elected for a period of four years. The president is 'first among equals' (*primus inter pares*) and elected by the Federal Assembly for a period of one year. The president chairs the meetings and takes on responsibilities of representation.

The Federal Chancellery is the central staff unit of the Federal Assembly. It coordinates all business and prepares the Federal Assembly's meetings. It supports and assists the president in managing the government's business and is in charge of coordination and interrelations with Parliament.

The seven ministries are the following:

- External Affairs.
- Internal Affairs.
- Justice and Police.
- Defence.
- Finance.
- Economy.
- Traffic and Energy.

In principle, the ministries are organized according to divisions whose tasks are subdivided in federal offices.

The Swiss system

The politico-administrative system of Switzerland can be characterized by the principles of federalism, local implementation and subsidiarity (Horber-Papazian and Thévoz, 1990, p. 133).

The twenty-six cantons possess a high degree of autonomy concerning their own legislation, financial matters, resources, policy and human rights. Government at the canton level operates in a very citizen-oriented way, implements federal laws and is financed to a high degree through federal resources. There are practically no inferior federal offices at the canton or municipal level executing and/or monitoring federal laws.

The principle of subsidiarity implies that the federal government does not take on responsibilities for tasks which can be carried out by the cantons and/or municipalities. The same principle applies to the relationship between cantons and municipalities.

The present governmental system is oriented towards high stability, integration and balance of the political powers. The constitution combines two principles: committee and ministry. The committee of the seven equal ministers forms the government, which can be characterized as an independent unit. At the same time each member of the committee represents the highest monocratic level in one of the seven ministries. Parliament and government are clearly separated from the point of view of organization and personnel. However, functionally they are closely interrelated through institutionalized and informal cooperation and coordination mechanisms.

The origin of the Swiss system of government stems from the first half of the nineteenth century. In recent years the system has been subject to increasing criticism. There is pressure to change both the political and the administrative systems on two fronts: tasks which have to be fulfilled are getting more difficult and complex. On the one hand there are accelerating developments and changes in societal values, economic developments (privatization, deregulation), ecological and technical challenges and demands, and in the field of international relations. On the other hand there is increasing pressure towards change from the resource side: the resources available for the fulfilment of tasks remain constant or even become scarcer. In addition there are growing internal criticisms and requests, especially from junior civil servants who are questioning more critically job contents, hierarchies and incentives.

The development of these demands has increased the internal and external performance pressure over the last fifteen years and the limits of financial and personnel capacities of the various public functions are gradually being reached.

International complexity and internationalization – especially the European agenda – have resulted in a multiplicity of international relations, with each of the ministries requiring a higher degree of political and administrative coordination and integration.

The overall developments led to continually increasing expenditures and personnel. They were also reflected in a rising number of laws and ordinances based on which the administration has to execute its tasks. This unfortunately in itself resulted in new, additional tasks and in consequence in the creation of new positions and organizational units and a highly fragmented and specialized administrative organization.

Special attention has been paid to political and administrative public relations in which the media play a significant role, and in this context the development of internal information systems is also very important.

The requirements and tendencies towards the emphasis on output and outcome orientation, and the efficiency and effectiveness of administrative behaviour become very clear. It is now generally accepted that the existing and future situation can be managed less and less by single measures, and that the development and implementation of fundamental approaches in the field of management instruments (partially adapted from the private sector) in the financial, personnel and organizational domains are necessary.

Criticisms focus especially on the following areas (Botschaft, 1993, p. 18). The overall situation results in an increasing quantitative and qualitative overload of the government as an institution and also of the individual government members. Capacity and speed of decision-making are considered to be insufficient; the traditional structures of the political and the administrative dimension do not provide the necessary prerequisites in order to be able to cope in a satisfactory way with the complexity and dynamics of national and international tasks. Demands range from the modification of the committee principle, an increase in the number of members of the Council of Ministers, to an empowerment of the heads of ministries and to the implementation of a parliamentary government system.

In 1991 a working group 'Federal Management Structures' was constituted; this group developed reform proposals on the basis of which a draft of a new law on government and administrative organization was designed.

In the *Botschaft* (circular) concerning the governmental and administrative law, the following goals and criteria of government reform were listed (Botschaft, 1993, p. 21):

- To ensure efficient and effective management distinguishing
  - the state in general
  - the governing institution (organ)
  - the overall administration and the ministerial administration
  - the parliament
  - the people as the fundamental decision-makers in a referendum democracy.

- To ensure timely decision-making and action ability based on
  - planning concepts
  - rational consultation and decision-making procedures
  - coherent decision-making
  - overall coordination
  - analysis and transfer of experiences.

- To cope with the factual complexity and manage the decision-making procedures in a sound way by
  - sufficient information
  - optimum preparations
  - mutual adjustment of tasks, competencies and responsibilities.

- To increase the innovative capacity of the political and administrative system.

- Ability to deal with the public and the media.

- Organizational flexibility through simple and transparent structures and functions.
- Effective job design and office management by
  - less overload
  - efficient work processes
  - concentration on core tasks.
- Power restriction and control *vis-à-vis* government and by government.
- Concrete and real responsibilities to control institutions and the public.
- Stabilization and security concerning the issues of state and societal dynamics and intrastate integration.

Through these reform criteria the present demands on government and the administration are expressed explicitly, and the principal strategic reform goals concerning political dimensions are derived:

- Unity of government and efficient and effective leadership.
- Securing the government's decision-making capacity and ability to act under conditions of high complexity and dynamics and societal demands.
- Prevention of permanent overload on the government.
- Acceptance of the government through convincing performance and as a consequence the legitimization of its leadership role.

Basic reform issues

The reform plans can be interpreted as fundamental and strategic changes in the politico-administrative system and the respective legal foundations. In addition to the factual content of the approaches, the reform methods are also heavily emphasized in order to gain support and acceptance for the proposals from the administration and the public. Priority is given to establishing leadership and the freedom to act, to perform tasks, overall national coherence and international activities (Botschaft, 1993, pp. 35, 141).

The strategic overall goal of reforms is to strengthen governmental functions and the Council of Ministers, while simultaneously reducing their workload through organizational improvements, a more efficient management of the administrative system and the installation of 'secretaries of state'.

COMMITTEE AND MINISTRY PRINCIPLE

The committee principle of government is interpreted as one of the traditional and deeply embodied models forming the basis and legitimation of the state. It has proved to be best for complex managerial and decision-making processes and will, in any case, be continued and further strengthened. In a legal sense there are only very limited sanctions to make this principle work. It is emphasized that it mainly functions on an informal and personal level, and because of the positive attitudes and the willingness of the members (Botschaft, 1993, p. 37).

The members of the Council of Ministers are moreover ministry heads. This principle is based on the experience that the development of effective political strategies can succeed only if this is undertaken in close interdependence with the operational implementation. Therefore, the duality of the committee and ministry principle is being maintained as a successful and effective approach. The present duties of the ministry heads are divided into two main groups of functions: the responsibilities for the political leadership remain with the ministry heads as members of the Council of Ministers, and their major functions are the political and strategic leadership of their ministries.

Ministry directors are responsible for the management of the ministries; their position is defined as 'chief of staff' and as such they hold line management responsibilities. They may represent the ministry heads in parliamentary committees.

The leadership organization refers to two levels: the cabinet of the Council of Ministers as a committee concentrates on the politico-strategic dimensions of government. Under its management and responsibility the ministries are led by the ministers possessing a large degree of operational autonomy within the guidelines of the Cabinet of the Council of Ministers. The ministers are coordinated in the so-called Administrative Cabinet to which the Council of Ministers may delegate decision-making competencies.

The Federal Chancellery represents the central staff unit of the Council of Ministers and as the linchpin is responsible for information procurement and distribution, coordination and administrative supervision.

Secretaries of state

As the high quality of ministerial management and leadership needs to be maintained the function of a secretary of state is institutionalized at the highest level of the ministry. The main responsibilities of the secretaries of state are to support and relieve the members of the Council of Ministers concerning internal as well as external matters. They have to contribute to an efficient and effective ministerial leadership and operate on the level of ministries, groups and offices. Their functions are not subject to central fixed bureaucratic rules but are defined by the heads of the ministries in a pragmatic and flexible way according to internal and external contingencies and demands.

Flexibility

The flexibility of administrative structures is to be increased and adapted to the changing situation (Botschaft, 1993, pp. 40, 135). First of all a sound job-

and performance-oriented structure and process organization is to be developed; the main objective is to reach an optimum and effective job structure for the organizational units and to optimize the overall interdependencies between government and the administration.

The main principles are as follows:

- Areas with long-term validity should be ruled by law.
- Those functional and organizational areas underlying the requirements of high flexibility are transferred to the decision competencies of the Council of Ministers or the heads of ministries respectively.
- Operational details should be decided at office level.

A major goal is to construct and attain a congruence of tasks, competencies and responsibilities.

COORDINATION

Another major organizational maxim is to guarantee a timely and factual internal and external coordination. This refers mainly to interministerial areas, the federal and canton level and foreign countries. Coordination is labelled as a management responsibility of prime importance and the new law institutionally and in binding norms places high value on coordination (Botschaft, 1993, p. 42).

REORGANIZATION OF THE FEDERAL ADMINISTRATION

The reorganization of the federal administration focuses especially on the organizational design of the ministries and the contingent and flexible application of management instruments.

Concerning the organizational design of the ministries there are three major criteria:

- Homogeneity of tasks, i.e. internal and factual relations of tasks within a ministry.
- Effective management of a ministry based on the optimum spans of control at the individual as well as at the unit level.
- Balance of capacities in respect to political domains and administrative workload in respect of the following dimensions (Botschaft, 1993, p. 45).
  - Number and volume of motions to the Council of Ministers and decisions to be made by the ministry.
  - Number and volume of ministerial tasks and resulting workloads.
  - Degree of internal commitments.
  - Degree of public relation tasks.

In order to realize these principles and to implement the main reform goals with respect to flexibility and increasing the performance capacity of the organizations, management instruments aimed at fostering result responsibility and orientation towards effectiveness have been developed. First in line were the issues of personnel development, organizational development and financial management.

Besides the implementation of these concepts in phase 1 (governmental reform, beginning in 1993), in phase 2 overall structures and processes of the governmental system were dealt with. The main areas are as follows:

- Design of the relationship between parliament and government.
- Procedure of the design of law.
- Legal reforms.
- Renewal of the federal governance.
- Implementation of the governance concepts decided by the Federal Council.

Critical commentaries emphasize the appropriateness of the new law to the organization of government and administration. However, a discrepancy between current political behaviour and previous possibilities is indicated and a certain scepticism is expressed concerning the implementation of the reform plans and concepts especially concerning the themes of phase 2. This conclusion is drawn from the experience of former reform endeavours in which the Council of Ministers has shown a certain reluctance really to change the administration (*Neue Zürcher Zeitung*, 268/18.11.1993, p. 29).

Critical questions refer especially to the role of the secretaries of state model, the goal of which – namely relief of the ministry heads by civil servants – is seen as being unattainable. The nomination of secretaries of state is not approved by parliament, and hence they cannot be seen as politically valuable partners (*Neue Zürcher Zeitung*, 249/27.10.1993, p. 27).

Mäder and Schedler (1994, p. 360) have summarized the main weaknesses of the Swiss system as follows:

- Input instead of output orientation in day-to-day administration work.
- Lack of incentives to managerial thinking in the public sector.
- A culture of mistrust rather than confidence in government and service.
- Central palace organizations instead of decentralized tent structures.
- An unmanageable jungle of state aid cementing obsolete structures.

MANAGEMENT PROCESSES

Budget and budget management

Budget and budget management are regulated by federal laws on finance and budget.[1] The major principles are conformity to legal norms, urgency, efficiency and economies. The law does not only apply to the general federal administration but also to dependent (not self-supporting) public enterprises and institutions. (The Swiss railways and post, telephone and telegraph corporations do not operate under this law; they possess a relatively high degree of autonomy and their budget management is subject to specific regulations.)

In contrast to the cantonal and municipal budgets the federal share in the total performance volume is very low: federal self-investments only account for 2–5 percent of total expenditure.

To a large extent expenditures are tied by law and much more than half are allotted to non-investment areas such as contribution to social security, shares of cantons, research subsidies, development aid, deficit coverage, price subsidies, direct payments to agriculture and more. About two-thirds of the total expenditure are transfer payments. The expenditures and their financing are integrated in the financial accounts, which is the most important basis for financial policy and financial management. The instruments of budget management are oriented both to the past and to the future.

Legislative planning

Every four years after parliamentary elections a new legislative period starts for which the Council of Ministers has to publish the plans. They include operational plans, personnel and financial plans and describe the following topics:

- Execution of the guidelines of the previous legislature.
- Goals of the new legislature.
- Tasks related to goals ranked according to priorities (importance and urgency).

Operational, personnel and financial plans are interrelated according to content and time.

The guiding philosophy is qualitative growth, i.e. to achieve a higher quality of life with decreasing or at least not increasing resources and decreasing or at least not increasing environmental pollution (Eidgenössische Finanzverwaltung, part 1/1989, p. 5).

Pluriannual financial planning

Financial planning covers a period of four years: the budget for the first year and a three-year financial plan. Due to the interrelation concerning timescale and content with the guidelines of government policy it represents a quantification of the government's program. Based on a priority ranking, the future financial requirements are prescribed and their budgetary coverage is shown. Financial bottlenecks are to be identified as soon as possible in order to plan for possible financial steering. The legislative plan is revised simultaneously and in synchronization with the development of the new financial plan including the following year. These so-called 'perspectives' present estimates of demands and revenues and serve as a necessary and binding management basis for the administration; however, at this point in time they have not yet been decided formally by the Council of Ministers.

This four-year period system follows the rhythm of elections to the Council of Ministers and as a consequence several disadvantages can be identified (Eidgenössische Finanzverwaltung, part 2/1989, p. 42):

- The financial plans for the first year are developed without the government making decisions on priorities.
- Important decisions can only be taken every four years.
- The quality and compulsory nature of the revolving planning are reduced by the given periods of decision-making.

Forward budget plan and budget principles
The budget plan can be characterized as an integrated overview of annual expenditures and revenues organized by various criteria; this refers to the binding approval of expenditures and an estimate of revenues.

Budget principles are as follows:

- Completeness – all positions of revenues and expenditures are to be described.
- Unity – revenues and expenditures are presented within a single consistent framework.
- Gross representation – revenues and expenditures are to be separated and to be presented fully; there may not be any mutual offset possibly resulting in a cover up.
- Specification – the budget may only be used for the purposes defined in the forward budget plan. Only upon approval by parliament can there be transfers of unused credits to other accounts.
- Annual presentation – revenues and expenditures have to be presented in the forward budget plan of the fiscal year in which they are expected to be realized.

Federal budget[2]
Concerning structure the federal budget is consistent with the forward budget plan and presents the total of revenues and expenditures, and the composition of and changes to federal assets.

The budget includes information about all revenues/expenditures as a major instrument of management, control and information concerning the setting of financial policy strategies and decision-making as well as budget adminstration (execution) and control. In this respect it is a basis for the evaluation of the effects of the federal budget on the economy.

The budget presents the changes of assets for one fiscal period, i.e. increases and decreases in value are defined according to the period. It presents the total capital values and obligations. The integrated balance sheet provides information on the total of debits and credits.

In addition there are special calculation systems for the dependent public enterprises.

BUDGETING PROCESS AND FINANCIAL PLANNING

Budgeting process
The federal budgeting process consists of the following phases (Eidgenössische Finanzverwaltung, part 1/1989, p. 9 and part 2, p. 78);

- Budget directives/budget goal.
- Budgeting and proposals of ministries.
- Budget adjustments.
- Adaptation and decision on proposal by the Council of Ministers.
- Parliamentary treatment and decision.

Budget directives/budget goal During the months of January and February material budget directives are developed. On the basis of the definition of the financial political position the budgetary goals and the expenditure policy are designed. In order to facilitate enforcement of these directives/goals in the ministries the budget directives are decided by the Council of Ministers and are provided to all federal offices including the necessary survey and analysis forms (beginning of March).

Budgeting and proposals of ministries In March and April the offices estimate the necessary expenditures and expected revenues for each purpose and position. This has to be carried out within the given framework of budgetary directives. The objectively based budget proposals have to be submitted to the Ministry of Finance by mid-May.

Budget adjustments The budget proposals normally exceed the framework. Upon examination of the proposals by the fiscal administration they are analyzed in close cooperation with the offices, and the possible effects and consequences of cuts and corrections are brought into the open. Before the summer recess the Council of Ministers is informed about the status of the budget and if necessary the goals are called into question. Practice shows that the goals are not fully achievable and the framework directives of annual growth rate have to be increased.

The margin for cuts is very limited: about 80 percent of federal expenditures cannot be influenced because of legal or contractual obligations and commitments. The remaining 20 percent present the theoretical cut potential, but in fact do not offer many possibilities for cutting because to a large extent they are functional and operational expenditures needed to maintain the functioning of the office in accordance with regulations.

Adaptation and decision on proposal by the Council of Ministers The Ministry of Finance elaborates a budget proposal on the basis of the pre-decisions of the Council of Ministers (mid-August). This includes an informative commentary concerning the balance sheet and revenue/expenditure development. The budget is decided by the Council of Ministers at the beginning of October.

Parliamentary treatment and decision   At the end of October the parliamentary treatment of the budget proposal begins in the two finance committees and is concluded with the approval by Parliament in December.

FINANCIAL PLANNING PROCESS[3]

The process of financial planning consists of two phases:

- The construction of the legislative financial plan. This plan is interrelated according to content and time with the development of the governmental directives and personnel planning.
- The annual revision and modification during the legislative period (in parallel with budgeting).

Of specific strategic importance is the financial plan of the legislature containing the following elements (phases):

- *Planning guidelines/planning and proposals by ministries* Interministerial working groups develop goals and measures for the parliamentary term and these are related to personnel and budgetary consequences. Of great importance is the critical review of all current positions and their reduction potential.
- *Treatment of proposals* Proposals and measures are coordinated and brought into line on the basis of the proposals of the working groups within the ministries/offices. The Council of Ministers is informed about the planning figures, examines the financial policy goals and entrusts the Department of Finance to cut the personnel and financial requirements as much as necessary.
- *Prescription of task priorities and financial ratios/indicators* The ministries are ordered to set priorities concerning their proposals and the Council of Ministers opens a selection procedure consisting of several steps in order to coordinate and match the planned tasks with the goals of the budgetary policies. In the month of September, tasks, the legislative financial plan and the personnel plan are definitely fixed.
- *Approval* The Council of Ministers approves the planning of the legislature at the beginning of the year.

One main goal is to increase budget flexibility and to install partially global budgets for functional expenditures in several pilot offices (one per ministry). Global budgets exist especially for interorganizational cross-section tasks. At the present time there are about 2000 expenditure positions and the National Council has to take decisions on each position. About 1000 of these positions concern functional expenditures which represent merely 8 percent of the total budget. There are estimates that the positions could be reduced by 300–400 items.

The abandonment of the annual budget and time flexibility is not currently planned. Each supplementary credit has to be approved by parliament. In general, credit approvals are decided in an extremely generous way and cutbacks are sure to come. Budgeting is exclusively input oriented and is an incremental continuation of last year's budget. There are arguments that because of the high proportion of fixed budget positions there are rather narrow margins for an output orientation.

Control mechanism

With respect to the management emphasis of this volume the main focus here is on financial control. Other important control mechanisms, e.g. legal control, federal control of the cantons, political control by the electorate, are not discussed.

One of the important issues is how planned and expected results and effects (outputs and outcomes) can be evaluated and related to the resources required.

PARLIAMENTARY CONTROL OF GOVERNMENT'S ACTIVITIES

Parliament disposes of the following control possibilities:

- Questioning of civil servants.
- Motions that government shall examine if specific measures are to be decided.
- Motions that government undertakes specific steps.
- Installation of parliamentary and management committees.

The main control mechanisms are carried out by the management committees of the National Council and the Upper Chamber. They ensure *a posteriori* control. The central issue is the control of conformity to legal norms and regulation of the activities of the judiciary and the administration.

This delegation of control from parliament to the committees partially results from the fact that parliament is a body of 'non-specialists'. Because of the complexity of topics and constant time pressure parliament does not fulfil control functions. It is possible that this leads to certain control inconsistencies and to control tendencies varying from case to case.

An important basis of the control mechanisms is the rules on budgeting procedures and legislature financial planning as described above.

ADMINISTRATIVE CONTROL

Economies and efficiency are considered to be more important than the strategic control of effectiveness. However, as will be illustrated below (p. 238) the strategic steering and evaluation dimensions of tasks are being paid more and more attention by the political and administrative levels.

FINANCIAL CONTROL

General background

In Switzerland there is no independent national accounting office reporting directly to parliament. Financial control is carried out by a financial control department within the Ministry of Finance. However, this department acts independently within a legal framework and has no instrumental functions for the Ministry of Finance.

Parliamentary financial control is the responsibility of a Financial Committee for each of the two chambers, and of the Standing Finance Delegation consisting of six members of the Financial Committees. The main fields of financial control are accounting for expenditures and formal conformity to the respective legal norms. Financial control occurs both concomitantly and *a posteriori* and is being applied to the following organizations and institutions:

- Ministries with all their reporting offices.
- The Federal Chancellery.
- Public enterprises with financial autonomy.
- Enterprises and institutions fulfilling public tasks and receiving public financial support (subsidies, loans, advances).

Organization of financial control

The basic organizational principle is that the *a priori* control of expenditures and revenues (control of orders of payment before execution) may not be separated from external auditing. *A priori* control represents an important part of the workload and the control areas are organized in such a way that horizontal comparisons of revenue and expenditure positions are possible. External auditing is organized according to the functions of the offices, i.e. either civil or military areas, autonomous public enterprises and enterprises fulfilling public tasks (acting on public order).

Sections (departments/ministries) of financial control

- Special departments: upon the order of the National Council financial audits of specialized institutions of the United Nations, international insititutions and representations in foreign countries are carried out. Furthermore there are special control tasks in other organizations such as radio and television.

- Section of national accounts: its responsibilities are the control of the national accounts and their EDP – dimensions and basic issues of auditing philosophy and techniques.
- Section of ministries of civil affairs: this section is mainly concerned with the external auditing of the organizational units of the civil ministries in the areas of running expenditures on personnel, materials and services. Another important task is the auditing of federal polytechnic schools.
- Section of the Ministry of Defence: this section exercises control over the overall military affairs including arms factories and the military administration on canton level.
- Section for federal support: this section controls compensation payments, subsidies for running expenditures, loans, capital shares and investment subsidies.

Control philosophy

The relevant control criteria are precise bookkeeping, the correct application of legal norms, economy and efficiency of resource use. It is not within the competencies of control to comment on the political dimensions of budgets and goals.

Financial control is not only restricted to carrying out controls on the basis of general orders but also acts to an increasing degree on its own initiative or upon order of the Standing Finance Delegation. Areas are specific controls of complex projects with high financial volumes. Goals, procedures and experiences are also analyzed.

In practice financial control verifies orders of payment before execution. This procedure is aimed mainly at the formal conformity to legal norms but also at economy and some aspects of efficiency. *A posteriori* control occurs in parallel in the offices and other federal institutions according to the same criteria. In this respect the picture of the status quo is incomplete regarding the dimensions of efficiency and effectiveness. In particular, the evaluation of policy formulation and implementation is not given priority (Horber-Papazian and Thévoz, 1990, p. 140).

Financial control cooperates directly with the offices responsible for the financial management. Reports are commented on and passed on to the Standing Finance Delegation.

There are growing pressures on politics to account for its results in more concrete ways, and pressures caused by scarcity of resources which result in rationalization and cost consciousness, project management, strategic planning, strategy and project evaluation. At the same time, managers have to cope with the routine administrative duties. Important goals are flexibility, emphasis on results and orientation towards effectiveness of administrative task fulfilment. In this respect two instruments are being discussed: project management and 'controlling' (management control system).[4]

Project management
Project management is seen as an important management tool for increasing coordination and efficiency, as well as the effectiveness of specific complex tasks.

The strategic model of the Council of Ministers concerning personnel and organizational development project management yielded one of the central and encompassing reform programs and a key management function for solving complex, interdisciplinary, cross-ministerial issues (EPA, 09/1993, pp. 12, 16).

The intended change of rigid hierarchic and highly divided organizational structures towards more flexible temporary concepts of project management is expected to ensure the fulfilment of varying tasks by the exisiting administration under permanently changing conditions without having to establish new organizational units.

The legislative program 'promotion of project management', developed and offered by the personnel department as one of the services for management and organization development, supports office management in respect of the following issues:

- Increasing organizational flexibility.
- Implementation of project management.
- Development of clear and complete projects.
- Efficient and effective project steering.
- Development of personnel and organizational prerequisites for a successful application of project management.

The active participation of the management is part of the personnel and organizational development concept and is based on the willingness to change, and the readiness to share responsibilities and power. The objective is to develop a 'project management culture', team work, motivational foundations and clear role distributions within projects, and between projects and line management.

The practice of project management is supported and fostered by systematized manuals on all aspects of project management and, of course, through training programs that emphasize transfer orientation offered by internal specialists together with external consultants (team teaching) (EPA, 1994, pp. 54, 86, 94).

Controlling (management control system)[5]

In the Swiss public administration the notion of controlling has developed from a fashionable slogan to a major management issue, and is increasingly seen as a central instrument for the fulfilment of tasks at the strategic policy (program) level as well as at the operational level.

The notion of controlling in all German-speaking countries was taken from the Anglo-Saxon term 'to control' with the meaning of guiding, steering, and does not mean '*a posteriori* control' in the sense of an evaluation of the conformity of administrative action to rules and legal norms.

For the discussion in this chapter the notion of controlling can be interpreted as 'management control system', the meaning of which is described as follows.

In principle, controlling involves the systematic provision and processing of quantitative and qualitative key information in a timely manner, an user-oriented presentation and a basis for evaluation. The following areas are concerned:

- Goals and objectives.
- Priorities of goals and objectives.
- Personnel, budget and other resources.
- Contingencies (circumstances).
- Qualitative and quantitative criteria for result evaluation as compared to goals and objectives.

Controlling encompasses the characteristics shown in Fig. 8.1. Controlling is a specific form of management support that develops and prepares information for management and shows the effects of decision alternatives on efficiency and effectiveness and the respective resource requirements. In addition it increases and systematizes the coordination capacity within and between organizations, and contributes to a goal- and result-oriented management. This means that a major function of controlling is the

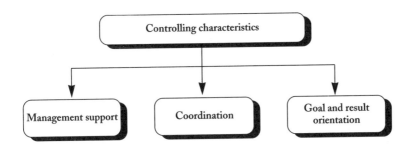

Figure 8.1. Controlling characteristics.

steering and guidance of goal achievement, to relate results to goals and to enable management to take corrective action if appropriate.

The Swiss overall project 'controlling the federal administration' is organized by a department within the Ministry of Finance and offered as a service to all offices. It represents an opportunity to analyze the usefulness of controlling to their own organizational unit in a systematic way and on a voluntary basis, and if desired to develop and implement a tailor-made concept.

At the beginning of the project (1989) certain difficulties resulted from the fact that the traditional control and audit functions as well as this new controlling project were organized within the Ministry of Finance. There were reservations with respect to a mingling of these two concepts to the disadvantage and increased control for the offices concerned.

The project was started with a feasibility study to answer questions as to what extent the concept of controlling is able to

- Support the offices in increasing efficiency and effectiveness?
- Support the Ministry of Finance with the task of evaluating expenditures?
- Analyze strategic policy goals and priorities and offer standards for goal achievements?
- Achieve incrementally better planning, policy-making and financial management?

A major issue concerning the application of controlling is the transformation of political goals and priorities into tasks for the administration. The Swiss concept is based on the assumption that political goals are accepted by the administration as a fixed framework and data.

However, the effects of controlling enhance the possibility of improving the information basis for political decisions and of creating some pressure to take note of 'new' criteria like the necessity of setting goal priorities in the light of scarce resources. It is assumed that controlling makes amendments to law and ordinances feasible. Of course, there are interrelationships between the strategic and the operational level; however, they are broken as a consequence of the division of power.

The strategic level (long-range goals) is mainly determined by political issues and requirements; fundamental and general political goals and the derived main tasks of the administration cannot be changed or adapted in the short term. In this way, the achievement of goals and the performance of the administration are influenced. These relationships have to be taken into account explicitly in the controlling design.

In the basic organizational structure of the Swiss administration all responsibilities and competencies are assigned to the seven ministries.[6] On the next organizational level there are about 120 federal offices and about 150 directly subordinate organizational units (offices).

Cross-ministerial tasks like committees, financial delegation, financial control, administrative control, coordinating and consultative bodies burden the offices at all levels to a large extent. In this respect the issue of the ability to manage and guide the overall organization has become of increasing importance: the implementation and application of controlling should not additionally burden the given structures and capacities and must be integrated without the use of additional resources.

If an office desires to implement controlling this is defined as a formal task that is undertaken with the support of the Ministry of Finance.

PURPOSE AND GOALS[7]

As formulated explicitly in the Swiss discussion, the concept of controlling includes the following main goals:

- Creation of more secure political and financial planning and management on the basis of objective evaluation criteria with respect to giving good reasons and priorities to federal expenditures.

- Creation of optimal information preconditions for strategic and operational decisions at all levels (Council of Ministers, ministries, offices).

- Ensuring a permanent comparison between desired goals and achieved results, especially in the following areas (Witschi, 1994, p. 20):
    - Evaluation of programs with respect to goal achievement and the evaluation of laws with respect to the achievement of political goals.
    - Analysis of the results as to the rational and efficient use of resources.
    - Assessment of the necessity and way of using financial means.

The concept of controlling should enable the decision-makers to take into account a long-range overall view of economic, social, political and scientific interrelations and their effects on federal expenditures. From this basic intention the following goals of controlling are derived:

- Support of the federal offices concerning the development and analysis of goals and decision-making procedures on the tasks to be fulfilled.
- Support of the federal offices concerning an efficient and effective task fulfilment and the best use of available resources.
- Support of the financial administration concerning the tasks prescribed by federal laws on finance and budget, especially budget control.
- Clearly defining the political goals, ensuring that they are achieved by the administration, and assessing the degree of goal achievement.
- Incremental development of an improved political and financial planning and management of the overall system.
- Comparison of planned and achieved goals.

Controlling is, first and foremost, an instrument of assessment, diagnosis and guidance and serves to support the decision-making process of the management of ministries and offices. The existing organization has not been changed but controlling is being integrated into the structure. A change in the ways of thinking and acting (organization culture) is emphasized.

METHODOLOGICAL BACKGROUND[8]

The approach of the Swiss federal administration is based on the 'cybernetic feedback loop' model containing the important elements of management as illustrated in Fig. 8.2. The basic principle is that each 'start/goal-process' can be steered and guided. The cybernetic feedback loop expresses the central idea of a meaningful and continuous linking of goals and objectives, measures and results.

Steering occurs at three levels:

- Overall strategic goals and plans at the federal political level.
- Objectives and performance at the federal office level, i.e. effectiveness.
- Ways and means of task fulfilment, i.e. efficiency, at the federal office level.

Controlling is interpreted as a management philosophy that fosters a fundamental, global and dynamic way of thinking for civil servants. The main issue is the construction of links between goals, required resources, methods and results. This approach integrates administrative internal and external

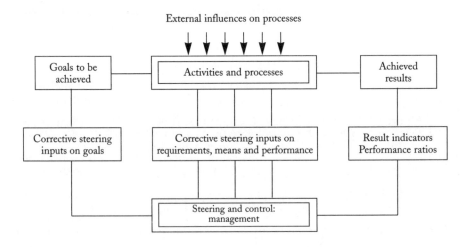

Figure 8.2. Cybernetic feedback loop.

factors and their mutual interdependencies and takes into consideration mid- and long-range developments. A main focus of the controlling project is on the further development and dissemination of the basic approach and the existing instruments, and adapting these to the specific contingencies of the administration and the Council of Ministers.

IMPLEMENTATION STRATEGY

In December 1990 the Council of Ministers decided that federal offices should assess the feasibility of the controlling concept and implement it if useful and required.

In general, a participative approach is followed based on the willingness of the organizational units and on the conviction that the implementation of this instrument would be helpful. The overall strategy encompasses the following aspects (Toriel, 1992, p. 7):

- Support by external consultants.
- Internal project coordinator.
- No development of a generally valid model but office-specific approaches. Controlling is implemented by concrete projects in those offices that decide independently in which areas the concept shall be tested. The needs and priorities of the office are the main criteria.
- Incremental policy: a step-by-step policy with a high degree of participation of the involved offices is pursued. At a time no more than four or five projects are organized. The basic idea is that large-scale and demanding projects are failing easily and overly complex projects quickly provoke resistance from those concerned.
- There is a high degree of project support from the top management in the ministries and offices, and furthermore the politicians are involved in the project.
- Transparency of the overall project and parts of it and an intensive information policy: all offices are informed (in writing) by the project management and asked to formulate their interests and willingness to cooperate. The offices are invited to plan presentations in which the principles, methods and actual experiences are presented and discussed. In addition the project is also presented in the offices.
- A strong emphasis is placed on training. Seminars and workshops are offered for all hierarchical levels. The main philosophy is to 'help the offices to help themselves, and to become independent from external support.
- Snowball effect: through the dissemination of the project through the various offices, the information policy and the training strategy effects of synergy are produced which are expected to lead to a common and widespread 'culture of controlling'.

- Controlling is not delegated to a single external (staff) position. This management instrument must be developed and applied under the responsibility of line management within the organizational units.
- The financial administration has taken on the role of initiating, promoting and accompanying the projects in order to increase know-how and experience and to ensure that these will be disseminated in the federal administration to the highest possible extent.

PROJECT ORGANIZATION (FIG. 8.3)

The 'Expenditures Policy' department with its groups takes on the overall responsibility and has the task of developing the concepts and representing federal interests on the basis of the laws on finance and budget as well as on contributions and subsidies. The 'controller' is responsible for the planning and organization of the various controlling projects and their coordination.

The external experts contribute to the development of the overall concept and methodology, and give guidance to the project groups.

Each project is organized in three phases (Witschi, 1994, p. 34):

- Feasibility study.
- System development.
- Implementation.

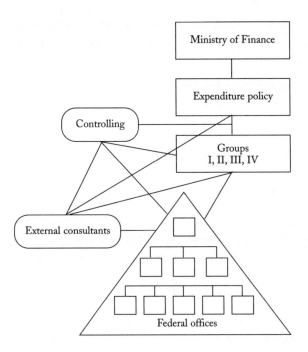

Figure 8.3. Project organization.

FEASIBILITY STUDY

The feasibility study analyzes and assesses the practicability of the controlling approach in an organization. Besides the methodological and technical appropriateness, the willingness to cooperate and the organizational and informational prerequisites are also being assessed.

In order to define the approach in detail, three levels of controlling are analysed:

Strategic controlling
The approach is applied to the overall strategic level of an organization. For example.

- Traffic policy and its improvement by the federation.
- Development and fostering of disadvantaged regions by the federation.
- Science, education and research policy for Switzerland.
- Strategic management of agricultural policy.

Strategic controlling refers to the overall goal and task planning, the assessment of long-range quantitative and qualitative resources and the analysis of the prevailing conditions and contingencies.

Controlling a task area
In a second step the extent to which the controlling approach can be applied to the management of a task area within the superordinate strategic level is assessed. Examples are:

- Traffic policy and its improvement by the federation – investment subsidies within the traffic policy.
- Development and fostering of disadvantaged regions by the federation – granting of federal contributions.
- Science, education and research policy for Switzerland – university promotions and focus programs.
- Strategic management of agricultural policy – grain supply for Switzerland.

Operational controlling
A third step follows the concrete application of the controlling approach to the management of a project or a task within this area:

- Investment subsidies within the traffic policy – project realization within the framework of investment programs.
- Granting of federal contributions – project realization of grants.
- University promotions and focus programs – management and operation of university and research institutes.

- Grain supply for Switzerland – closure of agricultural areas, extensive exploitation of agricultural areas, participation of producers in the costs of utilization.

The detailed definition of tasks, structure and process organization, project goals and resources, analysis and evaluation of the contingencies are important aspects of the feasibility study.

SYSTEM DEVELOPMENT

On the basis of the feasibility study, the controlling approach is precisely adapted specifically to the respective office, developed and implemented. Particular attention is paid to defining the various elements of the cybernetic loop, their process interdependencies and details of data and information required. Furthermore it is established how these elements can be integrated into the existing structure and processes as a management and steering instrument.

Attention is given to the following steps:

- To complete the development of the approach, and demonstrate its functioning.
- To expound the resources required.
- To expound the organizational and informational prerequisites.
- To define the distribution of roles and forms of cooperation between the office concerned and the financial administration.

The implementation of controlling is supported by a precise, detailed and voluminous manual, in which the overall philosophy, the conceptual and practical procedures and the implementation approaches are described in detail. This manual is a very helpful combination of theoretical and practical arguments and examples.

EXPERIENCES[9]

The possibilities and areas of application of controlling are as manifold as the advantages for the user. However, some favourable and less favourable areas of application can be identified (based on the experiences with various controlling projects).

Favourable controlling areas

- Credit administration on the basis of priorities.
- Systematic monitoring.
- Operational execution of administrative tasks.
- Management of projects and programs.

Less favourable controlling areas

- Areas in which managerial discretion is limited by detailed legal norms.
- Areas in which it is difficult to evaluate achieved results.
- Areas in which it is difficult to follow the management process which has brought about the results.
- Areas in which it is not possible to construct clear relationships between goals, measures and results (e.g. because of goal complexity and contradiction between goals).

As an overall picture in all applications of controlling there emerge three issues (Siegenthaler, 1990a, p. 101):

- Definition and description of goals and objectives (and their differentiation from the tasks). This can be seen – also internationally – as one of the more difficult management issues in public administration. In areas where the main tasks consist of formally executing laws it is argued that there is no sense in formulating goals since these are already defined by law.
- Adaptation of measures and resources to goals and objectives.
- Recording and assessment of results.

The developed method and approach are flexible, can be adapted to the specific situation and have been shown to be fruitful at both the strategic and operational levels of the administration.

The benefits of controlling with respect to the output dimension can only be assessed after a period of about two years. However, it is evident that even the discussion about goals, their interrelationship with resources, measures and evaluation is very fruitful for and within the offices. It contributes to a systematization and improvement of work fulfilment. Resistance and anxiety could be reduced by the presentation of functions and benefits and a certain degree of acceptance could be achieved. It is estimated that the implementation is feasible and fruitful only in the long term: the main goal is to increase the effectiveness of the administrative (and ultimately the political) level; a minor goal is the creation of additional information.

However, it is interesting to note that in times of (very) high financial pressure and resource scarcity the rationally planned and strategic controlling projects seem to become of less priority and short-term problem-solving based on other instruments is more urgent and uses the available capacities. (Comment: in periods of affluence this type of management instrument is not seen as necessary and in times of scarcity it takes too long until it is developed and shows the desired results.)

The instrument of cost accounting which plays an important role in controlling approaches in the public administration is being discussed in Switzerland with reference to 'close to market organizations' and the field of personnel. The implementation of cost accounting is expected to form the basis for a cost-based calculation of fees which is mainly aimed at personnel costs. There is a general opinion that in many offices a higher degree of cost transparency would be desirable and necessary.

An important reason for the organizational integration of the controlling project into the Ministry of Finance is the possibility of combining the functions of resource allocation to offices with the creation of transparency, to define priorities and to use resources as efficiently and effectively as possible. Resource allocation can only be effective when the required relevant information is provided by the offices and systematized according to the controlling functions. From the point of view of the Ministry of Finance, the controlling approach is the strategic key to the management of offices.

On the other hand, the mixing of audit and control functions with the controlling approach is regarded as major disadvantage of this approach. This combination results in certain reservations at office level because transparency and output orientation cannot be taken for granted in all offices.

PERSONNEL

Background

As already mentioned, the Swiss administration is under considerable pressure to change: on the one hand the tasks are changing, on the other hand resources change. Administrative tasks become increasingly complex. Societal developments (changing values), economic, ecological and technological developments as well as changing political conditions (impacts of the European Union) make it necessary to focus on an increasing strategic policy orientation, output emphasis and closeness to the customer, including finding an active consensus. Leadership and behavioural competencies of managers are required to cope with new task requirements and constant or decreasing resources. The supply of junior civil servants will probably decline and a change in motivation can be observed: besides tangible needs, intangible ones need to be satisfied by the administration in order to remain competitive with the private sector. The changed conditions require holistic (interlinking) thinking and acting and the active commitment of all concerned. Short-term administration has to be changed to goal-oriented shaping and arranging (EPA, 03/1991, p. 1n).

Strategic model of personnel and organizational development

Based on the legal obligation to ensure rule conformity, and the efficiency and effectiveness of administrative behaviour,[10] the Council of Ministers

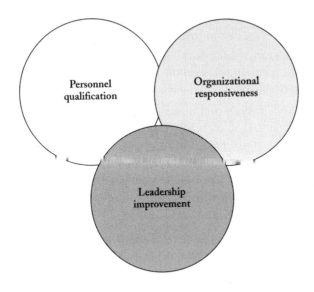

Figure 8.4. Model principles as stated by the Council of Ministers.

decided in 1990 on the development of a strategic model of personnel and organizational development for the legislative period 1992–1995.[11]

The principles of guidelines for change and the allocation of roles have been laid down. Operational objectives and measures have been developed by the EPA (= Eidgenössisches Personalamt = Personnel Management Unit) in cooperation with the ministries and incorporated into the guidelines. The model focuses on the following:

- An integration of training, consulting and support.
- A consideration of centralized and decentralized responsibility levels.
- Standardized and tailor-made results.

The goals of the model (see Fig. 8.4) are personnel qualification, organizational flexibility and responsiveness, and the improvement of leadership (Leitbild des Bundesrates zur Personal- und Organisationsentwicklung in der allgemeinen Bundesverwaltung, 1990, p. 1).

The goals and principles of personnel and organizational development are oriented towards the following aspects (Leitbild des Bundesrates zur Personal- und Organisationsentwicklung in der allgemeinen Bundesverwaltung, 1990, p. 2)

- The overall administrative system – support and implementation of personnel policy, design of a performance-oriented and responsive administration, efficient exchange with cantons and communities, science and research, the private sector and associations.
- Personnel – fostering of holistic, goal-oriented thinking and acting, social and technical competence, responsibility, and citizen-oriented behaviour.
- Management – development and retention of managers.
- Organization – orientation towards performance, effectiveness, transparency, best practice, learning, innovation, cooperative leadership and delegation, meaningfulness and development.
- Personnel and organizational development as permanent common tasks of line managers as well as civil servants at all hierarchical levels.
- Maintaining and improvement of personnel and organizational resources through training, consulting and support.
- Definition of goals of personnel and organizational development in the respective legislative planning.

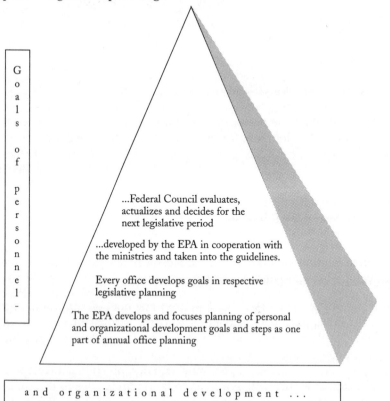

Figure 8.5. Goal-setting process and goal integration of personal and organizational development.

- Fostering equality of opportunity of male and female civil servants and multilingualism – which is of particular importance in trilingual Switzerland – through personnel development.

Personnel and organizational development is defined as a primary management task and the EPA as a central staff function has the roles of developing, initiating and supporting the implementation of respective strategies and concepts, the assessment of their effectiveness and the overall coordination of all strategically important measures. One focus of activities is on professionalization through training and consulting. The EPA functions as supplier and mediator of internal and external training and consultancy. Independent and neutral consultancy in management and organizational issues should be offered in closest cooperation with the offices that formulate their specific requirements based on internal concepts on personnel and organization design. The respective office has to define and initiate the training and support requirements and evaluate their effectiveness (see Fig. 8.5).

Based on the strategic model of personnel and organizational development for the legislature period of 1992 (decision of the Council of Ministers) the following explanations examine the derived stategic goals of the EPA and the actual steps of realization.

Strategic goals of the EPA

IMPROVEMENT OF COMPETITIVENESS IN THE LABOUR MARKET AND REINFORCEMENT OF CORPORATE IDENTITY

One of the primary goals of the Swiss administration is to develop and maintain personnel resources of sufficient quality and quantity. In order to improve the attractiveness of the public administration in the labour market several measures have to be taken. It seems to be necessary to develop an incentive system in order to reward performance and to take into account the labour market situation. In order to increase the attractiveness of jobs in the public administration, the possibilities of flexible working times should be developed. Taking into account the increasing scarcity of qualified junior management, the promotion of women and language minorities should improve the chances of future recruitment. On the other hand a profound change of societal values seems to take place: attitudes like a sense of duty, diligence and commitment have decreased. Instead there is an increasing search for independence, self-steering and self-development. People are looking for positive relationships with their work and results, supervisors and employers. They request participation in decision-making, to live in an interactive social job environment and object to strong power and hierarchical barriers (EPA, 1991, p. 2 and interview results).

The EPA develops and focuses its goals and measures based on these assumptions. The great challenge for the 1990s is to harmonize these interests with a responsive and performance-oriented administration and to redesign organization culture and structure through a communication policy that creates internal and external confidence (EPA, 1991, p. 2).

PERSONNEL QUALIFICATION

The interests mentioned above include the civil servants' need to develop themselves professionally as well as their 'social competence'.

Training can be identified as the strategic factor of success which has to be oriented towards the federal 'business policy', and integrated into measures of personnel development. It requires professional support of organizational change processes and innovations. The scarcest resource is not the budget but working time and positions respectively. More time and capacity for both training experts and managers and subordinates are required. Long-term investment in additional positions (on-the-job training, job rotation) are assumed to pay off and contribute to a learning organization (EPA, 1991, p. 4).

IMPROVING ORGANIZATIONAL RESPONSIVENESS

This requirement concerns two areas: personnel service regulations and organization (structure and process). For the actual parliamentary term there is the demand for a total revision of the civil servants' law aiming at more autonomy in decision-making, the relief of too many detailed regulations, and the examination of the degree of employment that can be regulated by individual contracts.

Concerning the organization, the EPA feels that it should focus on the reduction of bureaucratic and hierarchical structures and the further development of flat hierarchies, decentralization and autonomy. As major instruments, project management, an open climate and flexible management of interorganizational tasks are proposed (EPA, 1991, p. 4).

STRENGTHENING OF LEADERSHIP AND LEARNING PROCESSES

Flatter hierarchies require better leadership: strategic and social competence, strong personalities and cooperation based on equality of rationality, emotion and intuition are increasingly in demand.

Major strategic instruments that have to be developed are management by objectives on all hierarchical levels, meaningful tasks and their critical evaluation, the creation of vision and a constructive working climate. In addition, so-called 'hard instruments' are required. Management by objectives must result in an integration of tasks, resources and results, and respective steering mechanisms enabling the organization to combine short- and long-term decisions as proposed in the concept of control (EPA, 1991, p. 6).

'Path as goal'

Based on the federal strategic model (decided in 1990) of promoting the focus on personnel and organization development and resulting from rather dissatisfactory implementation experiences, special attention is given to this issue. An expert group was installed to give active support to offices and to promote and coordinate the various endeavours: the path towards a new orientation of personnel and organization policy becomes a goal in itself for the legislative period 1991–1995 (EPA, 1991, p. 6).

Other reforms

REFORM OF CIVIL SERVANTS' LAW

The guiding philosophy of this reform component is deregulation and flexibility. The revision of this law was realized by the beginning of 1995. The focus is on top management employment with the possibility of dismissal, and on a new payment scheme including components of performance and a bonus system.

At the federal and also canton and community level it is planned to introduce the option of dismissing civil servants in order to increase flexibility of employment contracts. However, even now civil servants can be dismissed if there are good reasons.

At the end of their employment period civil servants are not entitled formally to be re-employed and can be dismissed. In practice, this does not occur frequently.

It is argued that the newly required attitudes and behaviours can develop only in a climate of security and confidence. There are fears that a too high degree of flexibility may lead to politicization and undesired dependence of civil servants (Müller, 1994, p. 33).

The new pay system is planned to include a 20 percent performance component, taking into account the task-specific and goal-oriented design of employment. In total, about 15 percent of all civil servants will be affected by the new pay and bonus system. It is interesting to note that bonuses which are not used expire at the end of the year and cannot be transferred to the next year. A performance evaluation system exists but is not institutionalized on an overall level. Management by objectives is one of the important training modules to foster the result-oriented philosophy.

TRAINING OFFENSIVE

In October 1993 the training committee decided on policy principles for the general federal administration. Training is integrated as an element of the personnel and organizational development concept contributing to three

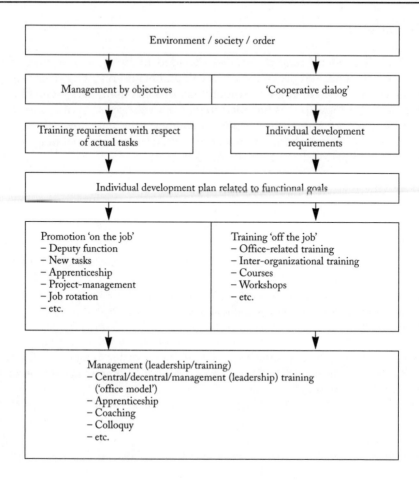

Figure 8.6. Training model. (Adapted from EPA, 1993a, p. 6.)

areas: personnel qualification, organizational responsiveness and improvement of leadership.

Training is perceived to be an integral management task: line managers are responsible for the development of their civil servants and take on training functions themselves. Training mainly takes place on the job and emphasizes best practice.

The major elements are the 'cooperative dialogue' between supervisor and subordinate and management by objectives. The model intends that based on these elements development and training requirements are defined and a personal development plan is designed in accordance with the respective functions of the job-holder (see Fig. 8.6).

In order to promote training according to the principle of 'equal shares for all', a management and training program is developed annually by the EPA

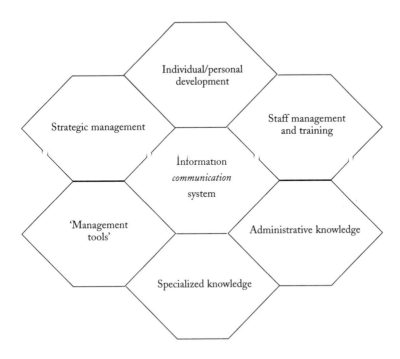

Figure 8.7. Areas of management training. (Adapted from EPA, 1993a, p. 7)

in agreement with overall goals and in close interaction with the organizational units concerned. The program consists of three central fields.[12]

Module seminars (basic, advanced and management seminars)
These are aimed at long-term development for managers and focus both on technical competencies and on social and strategic competencies like problem solving, teamwork and conflict management. Each module consists of three or four seminars of ten days each and include situation-oriented transfer work and support, and also foster peer learning. Seven main learning areas are covered (see Fig. 8.7).

Individual modules
These consist of short differentiated and independent learning units and cover mainly professional and technical contents which are not included in the module seminars. Topics are personality development, management methods, communication, presentation, bargaining and working techniques. This 'menu' provides individual and flexible demand-oriented learning.

'Office model'

This concept offers problem-oriented, tailor-made training within offices with reference to actual problems and projects. The main goal is to initiate and to support the development and change processes within the offices.

MANAGEMENT AND ORGANIZATIONAL CONSULTING

On-the-job orientation and office orientation of training indicate that training and consulting can no longer be clearly differentiated. Management and organizational consulting as a service of the EPA (EPA, 1993a) follows the strategic model of the Council of Ministers and is oriented towards the following:

- Planning and execution of specific programs.
- Consulting of offices upon request.
- Cooperation and support in projects and working groups.
- Contribution to training.
- Provision and coordination of external experts.
- Giving and drawing up of expert opinions on organizational and management issues at the federal level.
- Research and development in pertinent areas (EPA, 1993a, p. 20).

The EPA considers itself a consulting institution and acts like a private consulting firm, calculating internal prices for its services. However, the department is too small (eight experts) to answer all requirements of the offices, and therefore it cooperates closely with external firms and has developed manuals and guidelines for tenders and selection of firms.

In addition to the training concepts, there are several programs of personnel and organizational development in operation.

Program: enlarged discretion

The goal is to create differentiated rules and procedures and more autonomy for the management. It refers mainly to offices that are able to operate according to the principles of the private sector. They are supported in building up more competencies and autonomy in order to manage in efficient and effective ways. Market research, accrual accounting and management control are instruments that have to be implemented (EPA, 1993a, p. 12).

Program: strategic office management

The goal is to support the offices in undertaking task analyses, strategic scenarios, strategic plans and integrated tasks; resource planning and controlling and the concentration of resources on strategic important portfolios are also important.

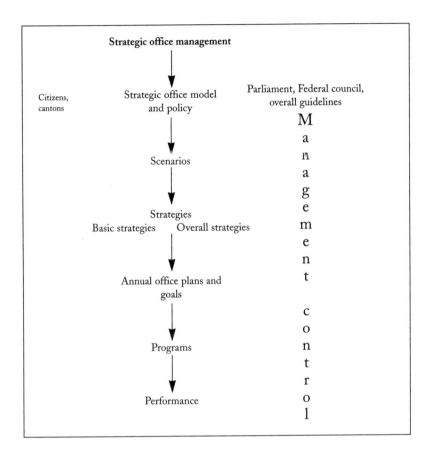

Figure 8.8. Strategic office management.

The idea is that organizational changes only make sense if there is a basic strategic orientation of the office's tasks and differentiation from other organizational units. Integrated office management is based on result and output orientation, and the development of a strategic model, and derives its own strategies from which annual program and performance plans are developed (EPA, 1993b, p. 13) (see Fig. 8.8).

Program: debureaucratization – better cooperation – attractive positions
The success of an office depends on the way in which the talents, knowledge and experience of specialists can be oriented towards common tasks and goals by an efficient organization.

The objective of this program is to increase the awareness that organizational structures can be adapted flexibly to the new situation, and single tasks can be integrated into meaningful (and more demanding) packages increasing the attractivity of positions. Unnecessary hierarchical layers can be eliminated, comprehensive organizational understanding can be created, principles of self-organization can be learned, mechanistic control procedures can be replaced by mutual trust and the development of responsibility and independence of civil servants (EPA, 1993b, p. 15).

Program: promotion of project management
Highly structured units are to be integrated according to specific tasks in a flexible and problem-oriented manner. Project management is applied primarily to interdisciplinary, interoffice and interdepartmental tasks. A precondition is that management engages itself actively and intensively with this approach and develops a high degree of commitment (EPA, 1993b, p. 16).

Case Study: Controlling in the Swiss Commodity Customs[13]

BACKGROUND

Commodity customs is a highly decentralized organization and includes about sixty offices. Six hundred of the approximately 4600 civil servants work in the general administration. Expenditures are Sfr 550 million per year, of which 390 million are personnel related. Revenues are about Sfr 7.2 billion and there are about 15 million operations per year.

The business sector demands a quick, simple and efficient service. The situation can be described by a very rapid traffic expansion, the change of traffic means (from rail to truck), and an increasing use of electronic data technology.

The freedom of action and possibilities of steering are rather small as far as goals and tasks are concerned; in the area of operations they are rather large.

For the innovative and willing management the starting point for the participation in the controlling project was the striving for efficiency and effectiveness. In addition, resource scarcity was to be expected and therefore the requirements for financial and personnel resources would be more difficult to argue. Commodity customs was chosen as a field of application of controlling; the main problem was steering the control activities of the customs. Before the project started some controlling elements already existed, but these were not interrelated. It was expected that controlling would be able to create these links.

PROJECT GOALS

- Reduction of control costs.
- Unified control approach.
- More efficient resource distribution.
- Improved control quality.

Approach

At the beginning of the project, problems of acceptance were high. The first steps could only be taken because of the full personal support of the chief executive, who perceived the project as 'his baby'.

The feasibility study was run on small scale with only a few civil servants who had no line functions. Only towards the end of the feasibility study was line management involved in the project; it was supposed that their resistance was very high because they were overloaded by day-to-day business. However, from this phase on the management strongly supported the project. Once they had been fully exposed to the concept of controlling it was seen and accepted as a necessary instrument to cope with the narrow capacity and resource margins in the centre and the offices.

Experiences

It proved to be difficult to define goals and objectives in concrete ways and to differentiate critical and non-critical operative tasks.

The data collection and analysis for the creation of relevant indicators and ratios as well as the definition of steering and feedback mechanisms were undertaken at great expense.

As usual in German-speaking countries, there was also confusion concerning the notions of control/audit and controlling. Civil servants without a business background had difficulties understanding the basic approach and elements of controlling.

From the point of view of the top management the following effects were reported:

- The approach resulted in a common language of all line managers in the customs offices.
- The transparency of processes and performance was improved.
- The responsiveness and flexibility concerning changing conditions in the customs' environment were increased.
- There are better foundations for personnel-related decisions leading to goal-oriented personnel capacity allocation.

Customs officers stopped controlling all commodities and began sampling, leading to decreased capacity loads and finally to law amendments.

The implementation of controlling modified roles and the distribution of the roles between the centre and the offices: the result was higher degrees of decentralization and higher autonomy for the operating offices on site, reflecting the local situational demands and peculiarities.

EFFECTS OF THE IMPLEMENTATION OF CONTROLLING

- On all levels learning processes concerning quality of work could be realized.
- There were some reductions of positions (30 out of 600).
- Civil servants in decentralized organizational units become more critical of the centre which increases pressure for better performance in the centre.

As an overall goal, a Switzerland-wide balance of resource allocation is aimed at. In addition, the application of the controlling philosophy should provide starting points for quality performance evaluation.

NOTES

1. Finanzhaushaltsgesetz (1989), Geschäftsverkehrsgesetz.
2. For details see *Eidgenössische Finanzverwaltung*, part 2, p. 11.
3. For details see *Eidgenössische Finanzverwaltung*, part 1, p. 14 and part 2, p. 79.
4. For details see the case study in this chapter.
5. In the discussion the Swiss term 'controlling' will be used as defined on p. 22.
6. See p. 224.
7. For details see Witschi (1993, p. 55).
8. For details see Witschi (1993, p. 55), Witschi (1994, p. 28 and figure annex 2) and Siegenthaler (1993a, p. 9).
9. See also Toriel (1992).
10. Bundesverfassung (Federal Constitution), Art. 85 Ziff. 1; VWOG, Art. 4.
11. For the following explanations see 'Leitbild des Bundesrates zur Personal- und Organisationsentwicklung in der allgemeinen Bundesverwaltung' (strategic model of personnel and organizational development for the legislature period of 1992–1995); 150,000 persons of the federal administration are affected by this model.
12. For details see EPA (1994).
13. The following description of discussion is based on Burgunder (1993, p. 18) and interviews with customs units.

REFERENCES

Berne, Leitbild des Bundesrates zur Personal- und Organisationsentwicklung in der allgemeinen Bundesverwaltung (1990) 6.
Botschaft zum Regierungs- und Verwaltungsorganisationsgesetz (RVOG) vom 20.10.1993 (ed.) *President und Bundeskanzler im Namen des Schweizerischen Bundesrates.*
Burgunder, C. (1993) Controlling in the Swiss commodity customs. In *Controlling in der öffentlichen Verwaltung*, Gemeinschaftsseminar mit der Eidgenössischen Finanzverwaltung, Bern.
Eidgenössische Finanzverwaltung (1989) *Finanzwesen des Bundes*, 11, parts 1 and 2.
EPA (= Eidgenössisches Personalamt: Personnel Management Unit) (1991) *Strategiepapier zur Personal- und Organisationspolitik der 90er Jahre*, 03/1991 (paper).

EPA (= Eidgenössisches Personalamt: Personnel Management Unit) (1993a) *Die Aus-bildung in der allgemeinen Bundesverwaltung Ausbildungspolitik und Ausbildungs-konzept*, 04/10/1993.

EPA (= Eidgenössisches Personalamt: Personnel Management Unit; Jenzer, R.) (1993b) *Führungs- und Organisationsberatung in der allgemeinen Bundesverwaltung – eine Dienstleistung des Eidgenössischen Personalamtes*, 09/1993 (paper), pp. 1–20.

EPA (= Eidgenössisches Personalamt: Personnel Management Unit) (1994) *Führungs-ausbildung* (training programs).

Horber-Papazian, K. and Thévoz, L. (1990) Switzerland: moving towards Evaluation. In Rist, R.C. (ed.), *Program Evaluation and the Management of Government: Patterns and Prospects across Eight Nations*, New York.

Mäder, H. and Schedler, K. (1994) Performance measurement in the Swiss public sector – ready for take-off! In Buschor, E. and Schedler, K. (eds), *Perspectives on Performance Measurement and Public Accounting*, Paul Haupt, Bern/Stuttgart/Vienna.

Mader, L. (1985) *L'évaluation législative. Pour une analyse empirique des effets de la législation*, Payot, Lausanne.

Müller, G. (1994) Keine Wahl von Beamten auf Amtsdauer mehr. Flexibilisierung oder Politisierung der Beamtenschaft. *Neue Zürcher Zeitung*, 11/06/1994, p. 33.

Neue Zürcher Zeitung (1993a) Effizienzsteigerung in der Bundesverwaltung. GPK kritisiert bundesrätliche Führungsschwäche, 268, 18/11/1993, p. 29.

Neue Zürcher Zeitung (1993b) Flexibilität als Organisationsmaxime. Regierungs- und Verwaltungsreform 1993, 249, 27/10/1993, p. 27.

Rist, R. (1990) *Programme Evaluation and the Management of Government*, Transaction Publishers, New Brunswick.

Siegenthaler, P. (1993a) Das Projekt 'Controlling in der Bundesverwaltung'. In *Con-trolling in der öffentlichen Verwaltung Gemeinschaftsseminar mit der Eidgenössischen Finanzverwaltung*, Bern.

Siegenthaler, P. (1993b) Marschroute für Controlling Projekte in der öffentlichen Verwaltung. In *Controlling in der öffentlichen Verwaltung Gemeinschaftsseminar mit der Eidgenössischen Finanzverwaltung*, Bern.

Toriel, E. (1992) *Le développement du controlling dans l'administration fédérale*. Séminaire sur le controlling dans les administrations publiques 5, Lausanne, p. 7 (unpub-lished paper).

Witschi, A. (1993) Controlling. Methodik und Projektablauf. In *Controlling in der öffentlichen Verwaltung Gemeinschaftsseminar mit der Eidgenössischen Finanzverwal-tung*, Bern.

Witschi, A. (1994) *Controlling in der Bundesverwaltung. Leitfaden Methodik*, Eidgenös-sische Finanzverwaltung (ed.) 1, Bern.

Conclusions

Changing Management Practices

Norman Flynn and Franz Strehl

While there is a great variety of management practice in the sample countries, we can identify some common themes in the ways in which management instruments are selected and applied. Of course, the degree to which these themes are relevant and/or implemented varies from country to country and can differ within the countries from department to department and between federal, state and community levels of administration.

The purpose of this conclusion is to review the general directions of change in the sample countries, paying particular attention to the following issues: decentralization, human resource management, financial management, 'controlling' and the process of reform management.

DECENTRALIZATION

A common theme is decentralization of responsibility and authority both from the centre to organizational units and subunits, and from federal or central government level to state or province and then from that level to municipalities. As we have seen, there are different reasons for devolving responsibilities to lower tiers of government: in the Netherlands it was part of a process of trying to keep expenditure under control. In Austria, Germany and Switzerland there are constitutional reasons for keeping some responsibilities at the lowest possible organizational level.

Decentralization of decision-making and control to units and subunits (with appropriate systems and instruments) is generally seen as an important way of improving the performance of the civil service. The focus is on increasing managerial autonomy in decision-making about resource use together with increased accountability for and transparency of activities and results.

The question is to what degree decentralization/centralization is appropriate and for which areas. Decentralization is not an end in itself and advantages and disadvantages of (de)centrally based activities and decision-making processes have to be compared. One important variable is the degree to which the government is concerned to maintain uniformity of service throughout the country: for example, the French education system, Austrian universities and the UK social security system all require uniformity of treatment of citizens. This desire for uniformity or equity of treatment places limits on managerial autonomy at local level. A most important question is: what needs to be controlled centrally in order to guarantee uniformity? If all the processes of service delivery are to be predetermined and controlled by a set of rules and procedures, there is little scope for managerial discretion. If managers are to be given a high degree of discretion, there needs to be a way of measuring and ensuring equity of treatment and uniformity of results. Hence, while aspects of management are devolved to delivery units, the basic services are centrally designed and controlled.

The degree to which performance can be measured and demonstrated is thus an important variable in deciding the degree of decentralization. Central government will only devolve authority if the units to which authority is devolved can demonstrate their performance. Hence, in Sweden and the United Kingdom the decentralization of responsibilities to agencies depends on an elaborate system of performance monitoring. In turn, such a system requires adequate information flows to enable the 'centre' to be confident in the performance of the devolved units.

The third condition is a process of negotiation on the matters which are to be devolved. This bargaining on resources and results is a complex matter involving not only the department and the managerial units but also central finance departments. Similar considerations apply to decentralization and delegation within organizational units. Managers of units need to be able to negotiate their ability to manage resources and their performance targets – both with their line management and with central functional units.

The fourth requirement for decentralization of control and responsibility is the existence of a common strategy for the organization as a whole. A shared understanding of the purposes, the direction of changes in priorities and service design is necessary for managers to be able to take decisions in their autonomous units.

A fifth question is whether policy-making can be clearly separated from service delivery or whether there is in practice a certain degree of interdependence which should be taken into account explicitly. In the United Kingdom, for example, most chief executives of agencies have both a policy and a service delivery role. In the Netherlands, the autonomous para-governmental organizations are represented in the policy process.

A related issue is the translation of policy goals into priorities for managers. Managerial reform is based on the assumption that the political and the administrative dimension have to be differentiated very clearly and that the policy requirements define the framework for the administration. We have seen that in Austria, for example, there is a formal system of translation of political goals into operational objectives for government departments.

We have seen that these conditions tend to be represented more strongly in subnational governments than central government, especially in Austria, Germany and Switzerland. In Sweden, the United Kingdom and the

Netherlands, central governments have managed a high degree of devolved management, while in France, decentralization appears to have run into problems partly because of a lack of the technical infrastructure and partly because of unwillingness of central departments to relinquish power. There are two separate issues: the constitutional autonomy of subnational governments and the devolution of responsibilities within ministries and departments.

While decentralization requires all these changes in management processes and attitudes, its advocates claim that it produces improvements in performance. Clarity of objectives and targets enables managers and workers to focus on those matters which are important. The benefits of management by objectives are also claimed for devolved management, that managers have a greater commitment to the achievement of objectives if they have participated in the process of defining them. Further, if responsibility is devolved within units as well as to them, services can be more responsive at the point of delivery, as staff can potentially have more flexibility in dealing with individual customer requirements.

ACCOUNTABILITY

There is a wide and controversial debate about the idea and practice of accountability and the interdependencies between the administrative and the political system. The issue is who is responsible to whom, for what and when.

The separation of policy-making from service delivery makes it essential to distinguish between the accountability for the success or failure of policy and the success or failure of management. For example, if the Netherlands government devolves services to municipalities but fails to provide sufficient funds, who is responsible for the deterioration of services? Or, if service delivery is delegated to an agency but policy is retained at ministry level, whom should the citizen blame for poor service? These ambiguities may be advantageous to governments which can claim that they are no longer responsible for those matters which have been delegated under contract to managers.

The concept of accountability is also closely related to the degrees of autonomy and freedom to manage decentralized units and the possibilities to really take decisions. It may be useful to refer to the basic meaning of the term 'accountability': to be able to account for, i.e. to dispose of the appropriate resources and managerial instruments to execute policy decisions within a given framework.

Concepts of accountability reflect the overall organization of and interfaces between the political and administrative systems and encompass three perspectives: accountability within the administrative system, accountability at the interface of the administrative and political system, accountability within the political system. Experience has shown that accountability within the administrative system is reasonably well developed and performance measurement and costing mechanisms are developing. More difficulty arises when the political level is taken into account. It is with some reluctance that politicians define their goals precisely enough for success or failure to be accurately reported.

Important to the accountability discussion is the dimension of ethical accountability reflecting primarily the general principles of right and wrong behaviour according to societal norms. This dimension goes beyond the legal requirements of right and wrong behaviour and reflects the overall culture of a public service. Competitive behaviour, the use of bonuses and performance-related pay, the tactics required to acquire contracts are all areas where 'traditional' values of impartiality and equity may fit poorly with business values of success.

It is generally agreed upon that under conditions of increasing decentralization and management focus administrators find themselves in an area of tension between probity, efficiency and effectiveness, and are confronted with an increasing pressure of ethical issues and the question to whom they are accountable when and for what.

HUMAN RESOURCE MANAGEMENT

The development of personnel-related management instruments is regarded as one of the most important contributions to and success factors of modernization and performance improvement. The instruments include increasingly complex personnel development and career development systems, performance evaluation approaches, leadership training, training for potential chief executives, interpersonal skills and functional training suited to defined target groups, and performance-based pay components.

However, traditionally, high priority was given to 'technical' management instruments like job and position descriptions, organizational measures, budgeting procedures, accounting systems, formal control and audit of rule compliance and expenditures, and formal individual appraisal (not of performance but of rule compliance). The changes are by no means complete and in many cases the traditional approaches coexist with the more modern ones.

Participation in decision-making procedures involves the instrument of delegation of decision-making power and responsibilities: in other words, behavioural changes are required as a result of the delegation of authority. The question is who holds legislative authority to make decisions; delegation does not relieve the superior of ultimate responsibility for results.

The concept of delegation has less a structural but more a behavioural and leadership dimension, but of course ultimately there are effects on the division of work and on organizational structures. In order to increase the degrees of delegation, leadership training and personnel development approaches play a major role. The traditional authoritarian (patriarchal) style of formal 'personnel administration' is intended to be changed towards modern 'leadership and motivational' ideas in order to take into account and activate the overall capacities of the most important asset – the human resources. It seems that these issues which have been part of management thought since the beginning of the century are being rediscovered also by public administration in recent years.

However, especially in the German-speaking countries, legal contingencies, personnel policy, existing formal pay structures and performance appraisal practice are not really promoting changes. The problem is that the personnel management methods which we have described as traditional are enshrined in law and legal norms. It is not as easy to incorporate ideas about leadership, motivation and performance into laws as it is to enact conformance.

FINANCIAL MANAGEMENT

Changing financial management is focused on the design of more effective and efficient budgeting procedures and on a higher degree of output (outcome) orientation. The traditional incremental input orientation did not ask what results were achieved by the use of the resources allocated. Pluri-annual budgeting cycles – especially for decentralized systems – and programme-oriented budgeting models are being developed. They provide a longer-term perspective of income and expenditure developments linked to expected results, but the problem is that these approaches do not fit given legal norms and formal structures. As with changes in human resource management, changes in financial management are constrained by the limits of legality. In addition, due to political dynamics and budget development uncertainties, the already fixed allocation of positions can be changed during the periods.

Cost information systems and especially accrual cost accounting approaches play an increasingly important role. Unified federal models like the Austrian integrated EDP-based accounting system provide a good starting point for the development of integrated cost information systems including cost type calculation, cost centre definition and unit cost and process cost calculations.

However, the overall impression is that cost transparency is not one of the preferred issues either in the political or the administrative system and there is large room for improvement and development.

Generally, an increasing emphasis is given to financial bargaining and agreements through such instruments as framework documents and business plans. These approaches are replacing more traditional processes of allocating funds and accounting for their expenditure.

Budget frames are defined by strategic decisions, and the authority to make operational decisions on spending items is devolved to the organizational units.

One major problem is to attain consistency between financial resources allocated to an organizational unit's goals/objectives and achieved results. Appropriate evaluation criteria and evaluation procedures have to be developed.

The performance criteria and the related management instruments usually are laid down in a document which is agreed upon by both the organizational unit concerned and the parent department. The agreements are based on general criteria of scope and areas to be defined, but in detail they are tailored to the needs and different situations of the units. This situation-oriented approach within a general strategic framework reflects the overall tendency to take into account to a high extent the specific requirements and contingencies under which devolved units delivery the services. (This holds especially for the United Kingdom.)

The transformation from an input-oriented administration (resource use, expenditure orientation) to an output-oriented administration (performance, results orientation) emphasizes the importance of mission statements, business plans, goals and objectives for the definition of tasks and performance criteria.

There are some common themes:

- Establishment of relationships of goals and objectives with results, budget and other resources.

- Development of criteria to measure performance against objectives.

- Transformation and interdependencies of political and administrative goals and their operationalization.

- There are areas in which it is difficult to define objectives for all services. It is important to note that it is neither possible nor fruitful to cover all activities by objectives and this may even be disadvantageous; the possible problem is that staff concentrate on tasks only which are explicitly related to objectives (and measurement) to prove performance.

The relationships between objectives, cost and performance is difficult to construct but progress is being made. A common problem is that there is no general clarity in which ways the results of performance measurement can and will be used.

Management of reform programmes

Problems

The reforms have been driven by a variety of pressures and have had different meanings for different parties: finance ministries emphasize expenditure savings; professionals are mainly concerned with service standards; politicians are seeking public support for their actions. Because of this managers are faced with competing demands, such as cost reduction with quality improvements or better targeting of services with spreading them thinly, or devolved management of services with occasional tight central financial control.

When these competing demands are combined with a multiplicity of initiatives, managers can be overloaded. Maintaining service levels can be difficult while also introducing a combination of performance management, costing systems and quality initiatives. Sometimes, the initiatives themselves can be inconsistent, such as the devolution of performance management with insufficient delegation of powers, or the introduction of performance contracts with inadequate performance measures.

Even when new systems have been introduced consistently, there has been a tendency towards information overload. Nervous central departments imagine that the production of a mass of retrospective statistics puts them in control. Middle managers are asked for information purely to satisfy people further up the hierarchy, rather than to help them manage better. In turn, this can lead to distortion in the information flows which produces an incorrect picture of the success of the changes.

For civil servants, the multitude of reforms causes confusion. Not only are traditional work methods challenged as people move from a requirement to conform to rules to a requirement to perform well, but the managerial instruments offered are diverse and in many cases new. There is frequently a suspicion that the overriding objective of the reform process is to save money by making people work harder. Middle managers and workers naturally resist these efforts, which in turn makes other aspects of the reform process more difficult to implement.

Not surprisingly, reforms are being undertaken at varying speeds and with many setbacks. However, there have also been many positive aspects.

Achievements

All the reforms have produced a shift of focus away from the mere administration of tasks towards management for results. The development of new management instruments forces both politicians and managers to set priorities and to set strategic and operational goals. This process forces the main stakeholders to define more precisely what they want public sector organizations to achieve. In turn this allows managers to know more precisely where they should put their efforts.

We have seen in the preceding chapters that the processes are not always as effective as their champions would like. However, there have been a series of positive results, affecting management and production processes, even if we cannot fully evaluate their final outcomes.

There is no doubt that responsibility has been devolved or is devolved in all the countries studied. In turn this has made managers, and especially chief executives of units, more aware of the resources which they control and makes for potential efficiency gains. This process has been supported by better accounting and a more transparent approach to resource allocation and control. For example, in every country there is a move towards accounting for costs rather than just expenditure.

Everywhere there are attempts to put more emphasis on the development of people. While there is not a single direction of change, all governments realize that it is important to motivate and develop staff, rather than manage through rigid bureaucratic procedures. As we have seen, this sometimes involves changes to pay systems which are of dubious value in motivation, either because they reward the wrong things or because the pay remains disconnected from the achievement of results. The Austrian efforts to reward performance became an exercise in job evaluation, for example. However, there are also positive examples of management systems which take account of the staff's real motivations, for example in Switzerland where the federal government recognizes that interesting jobs and personal development are important factors in motivating and retaining public employees

In all the countries there are attempts to make services more customer-oriented. We have seen that this involves more than the publication of service standards; it requires freeing up staff and management to respond to what customers say about what they prefer and how they judge services.

In some countries, especially Germany and the Netherlands, at the municipal level there is an increasingly holistic approach to public services as people advance beyond dealing with individual problems through separate programs. One of the dangers of decentralization is that the institutions delivering public services become focused on their own services and there is no one in a position to take a broad view of a community's needs. The 'new steering model', in which strategy is directed towards problem solving rather than fragmented service delivery, offers a solution to fragmentation.

The transformations which we are witnessing in public services are more than a collection of rhetoric, although they are all accompanied by their share of jargon. Not all of the language is that of business and management. The reforms in management practice are accompanied by ideas about the development of democracy, citizenship and public accountability. The 'new steering model' in Germany and attempts to improve public participation in decision-making in France are examples of management techniques taking account of the democratic context. Managing public services is very different from managing businesses and requires additional skills and techniques.

If further progress is to be made, there is a need for evaluation and for sharing knowledge about which strategies work best. As we have seen, practices are not uniform within countries, despite some common themes. What is clear is that there is no single set of measures which should be adopted everywhere: European cultural, political and economic diversity will continue to be reflected in differences in public sector management.

Index